Praise for Jodi Kantor's

The
OBAMAS

"A meticulous reporter, Ms. Kantor is attuned to the nuance of small gestures, the import of unspoken truths. She knows that every strong marriage, including the one now in the White House, has its complexities and its disappointments. Ms. Kantor also—and this is a key—has a high regard for women, which is why hers is the first book about the Obama presidency to give Michelle Obama her due. In the process we learn a great deal about the talented and introverted loner who married her, and how his wife has influenced him as a president.... Ms. Kantor retires wooden stereotypes of the political wife as a prop or a problem and instead explores what it means to be a modern first lady, one with her own opinions and an expectation that she will be heard."

—Connie Schultz, *New York Times*

"It takes a brilliant reporter to pierce the image and façade in which politicians are so invested and to give us the flesh and blood."

—Kati Marton

"Mrs. Obama's greatest influence on her husband's presidency will be through her influence on him, which is considerable."

—*The Economist*

"Jodi Kantor's *The Obamas* is among the very best books on this White House. It's a serious, thoughtful book on the modern presidency in general."

—Ezra Klein

"Sympathetic.... Deeply reported and nuanced."

—Ben Smith, *Politico*

"Jodi Kantor has done a first-rate job reporting on the Obamas in tandem. Her book gives you a better sense of their life inside the White House than any of the other insider accounts I've read."

—Jacob Weisberg, *Slate*

"The book seems to portray Michelle Obama as a complex yet human individual struggling with this unbelievable situation yet remaining the moral compass and center of an administration trying to find its footing."

—Jon Stewart, *The Daily Show*

"Energetically reported.... Kantor nails her story.... We political gluttons will lick the spoon clean."

—David Remnick, *The New Yorker*

"Much of the book is devoted to how the Obamas work to parent their children with an eye to both their safety and growing authority, and how the fame of politics makes that difficult."

—Farai Chideya

"How can being a couple in the White House with all the power that the president has be a marriage of equals?"

—Charlie Rose, *Charlie Rose*

"*The Obamas* is a portrait of a remarkable marriage.... Kantor's writing is insightful and evocative, rich with detail [and her] reporting rings true—and considering the administration's insistence on presenting a unified front, it is a considerable achievement."

—Kerry Luft, *Chicago Tribune*

"Jodi Kantor's thoughtful new book is fluidly written, with a canny sense for the way political marriages can be useful prisms to see into ambition, power, gender, and the contradictions of public life."

— Karen R. Long, *Cleveland Plain Dealer*

"Kantor really did, I think, pull the curtain back a little bit about how things work in the White House.... It is a fascinating insight into this White House."

— Bob Schieffer, *Face the Nation*

"The most talked-about book of the new year."

— *Hollywood Reporter*

"Kantor pours her insight into a compelling book, which is teeming with more than three hundred pages of intimate details and fascinating tidbits, all from her unique and novel perspective."

— Joshua R. Weaver, *The Root*

"Kantor seems to have gotten a fairly deep look into the administration's inner workings, but particularly into Michelle Obama's role in the whole show. There are plenty of juicy details...but mostly what emerges is a picture of a very smart woman struggling to adapt to her new life in the public eye—and mostly succeeding.... Rather than make her seem pushy or strident, the details of her fights to influence the White House just make her seem like exactly the kind of person you'd want in there—challenging the president as only a spouse can and fighting for what she believes is the right thing to do."

— Cassie Murdoch, *Jezebel*

"Perhaps the most penetrating look at Obamaworld to date."

— Jonathan Martin

"Keep your Bill and Hillary, this is the power duo that fascinates us."
— Tom Beer, *Newsday*

"A human-scale portrait that finds its true subject in Michelle.... The Michelle Obama who emerges from the pages is both Barack's greatest supporter and most crucial adviser — as well as a fierce idealist on her own terms."
— Megan O'Grady, Vogue.com

"A fascinating look at the intricate dynamics of an ordinary marriage, an unusual home, and an extraordinary presidency."
— *Publishers Weekly* (starred review)

"Jodi Kantor offers a glimpse into the tensions of a culture that expects our women to achieve as highly as our men but our first ladies to take a backseat to their presidents. The result is a sympathetic portrait of both Obamas that could help to humanize an administration criticized as being aloof and inaccessible." — Ilyse Hogue, *The Nation*

"Ms. Kantor provides good detail about the impossible logistics — and perks — of being a first family."
— Mackenzie Carpenter, *Pittsburgh Post-Gazette*

"Kantor's book details more personal aspects of the Obama White House, serving up glimpses of the first couple's marriage, parenting, sometimes tense handling of staff issues, and even the president's sly sense of humor."

— Michael Gartland, *New York Post*

The

OBAMAS

The
OBAMAS

Jodi Kantor

BACK BAY BOOKS
Little, Brown and Company
New York   Boston   London

Back Bay Books / Little, Brown and Company
Hachette Book Group
1290 Avenue of the Americas, New York, NY 10104
littlebrown.com

Originally published in hardcover by Little, Brown and Company
January 2012
First Back Bay paperback edition, August 2012
Updated Back Bay paperback edition, January 2017

Back Bay Books is an imprint of Little, Brown and Company,
a division of Hachette Book Group, Inc. The Back Bay Books name
and logo are trademarks of Hachette Book Group, Inc.

The publisher is not responsible for websites (or their content) that are
not owned by the publisher.

The Hachette Speakers Bureau provides a wide range of
authors for speaking events. To find out more, go to
hachettespeakersbureau.com or call (866) 376-6591.

Maps by George Ward

ISBN 978-0-316-09875-5 (hc) / 978-0-316-09876-2 (pb)
LCCN 2011940240

10   9   8   7   6   5   4   3   2   1

LSC-C

Printed in the United States of America

For Hana Kantor,
my grandmother and a survivor among survivors

And for Ron Lieber, my husband

Contents

PART THREE: CHANGE

1. Dining Room. *Where the Obamas ate nearly every night at 6:30. The president was unwilling to miss dinner with his family more than twice a week.*

2. Elevator. *Whisked the Obamas upstairs. Quentin Roosevelt, Theodore's son, once brought his horse inside.*

3. Grand Staircase. *The ceremonial staircase down to the public rooms on the state floor below. For dramatic entrances.*

4. Stairs to the Third Floor. *To guest rooms, the exercise room where the Obamas worked out every morning, and the pool table where the president sometimes played late at night with a friend. Marian Robinson, the first lady's mother, lived on the third floor.*

No

Kitchen

1.
Dining
Room

West
Bedroom

2.
Elevator

West Hall

Center Hall

5.
Dressing
Room

6.
President
and
First Lady's
Bedroom

Sitting
Room

Yellow O

Trun

5. Dressing Room. *Laura Bush showed Michelle Obama a window that would allow her to watch over the Oval Office and Rose Garden without being detected.*

6. President and First Lady's Bedroom.
The actual bedroom of Obama's role model, Abraham Lincoln. Until the Ford era, presidential couples slept separately.

7. Yellow Oval Room. *The formal room used for entertaining foreign leaders and site of Obama's spontaneous late-night health-care-overhaul victory party.*

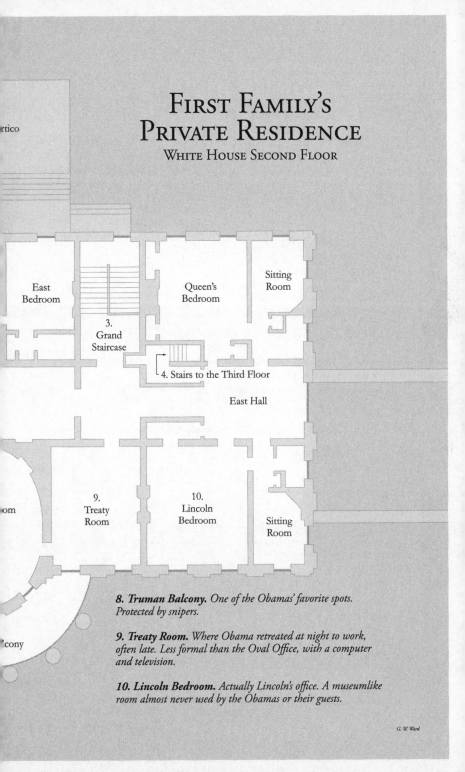

First Family's Private Residence

White House Second Floor

tico

East Bedroom

3. Grand Staircase

Queen's Bedroom

Sitting Room

↳ 4. Stairs to the Third Floor

East Hall

9. Treaty Room

10. Lincoln Bedroom

Sitting Room

om

cony

8. Truman Balcony. *One of the Obamas' favorite spots. Protected by snipers.*

9. Treaty Room. *Where Obama retreated at night to work, often late. Less formal than the Oval Office, with a computer and television.*

10. Lincoln Bedroom. *Actually Lincoln's office. A museumlike room almost never used by the Obamas or their guests.*

G. W. Ward

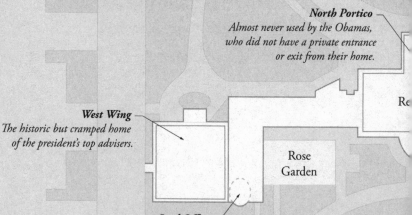

Eisenhower Executive Office Building
For executive branch staff.

North Portico
Almost never used by the Obamas, who did not have a private entrance or exit from their home.

No

Re

West Wing
The historic but cramped home of the president's top advisers.

Rose Garden

Oval Office
The room that symbolizes American and presidential power. Obama redecorated it to make it less imposing and more comfortable.

Swimming Pool
Before the Obama daughters used it, they had to check that they would not run into public events on the way.

Sou

Basketball / Tennis Court
A tennis court that the Obamas converted so it could be used for either sport.

Michelle Obama's Vegetable Garden

G. W. Ward

East Room
*Site of many White House concerts
and parties, including Obama's private
late-night inauguration celebration and
a splashy 2009 Halloween party that
made White House officials nervous.*

East Wing
*The first lady's domain,
initially referred to as
"Guam" by one of Michelle
Obama's advisers: pleasant
but powerless.*

**Treasury
Department**

Kennedy Garden
*Though it was called the first lady's garden,
Michelle Obama rarely visited because of
tours and public events.*

Back Entrance
*The first family came home through the Diplomatic
Reception Room and then passed behind everyday-looking
brown screens to avoid being spotted by tour groups.*

WHITE HOUSE
GROUNDS
USED BY THE OBAMA FAMILY,
STAFF, VISITORS, AND TOUR GROUPS

PREFACE

A decade ago, Michelle Obama was dining with an old friend and for-mer aide, Kevin Thompson, when she posed what was then a rhetori-cal question about her husband: "If he runs in 2008 and serves two terms, he'd only be fifty-five afterwards," she said. "What would we do then?"

Back then you could still reach Barack Obama at the email address senobama@aol.com. He had never really run anything larger than his Senate campaign. The four Obamas had not lived full-time under the same roof. They had only just moved on from the narrow apartment with worn fixtures where they had spent most of their years as a fam-ily. Michelle Obama's mother was still a secretary who often started her mornings at a Chicago McDonald's before heading upstairs to her office building.

That was then.

The Obamas chronicles how Barack and Michelle arrived at the White House and transformed themselves into president and first lady. This did not happen in an instant on inauguration day, but far from public view, the two of them working apart and in concert, writ-ing the story of the first African American presidency. I wrote here about how their history of heated debate shaped their approaches to their new roles; the unseen figures, such as their closest friends, who helped steady them; and the near-impossible demands that the presidency imposes on any leader and family entering the White House.

This book, reported through more than two hundred interviews, is less about the most private aspects of the Obama union — marriages are hard to know, sometimes even for the people in them — than their political partnership. The Obamas have opponents who smear and lie about them and, partly in response, a phalanx of protectors who try to make them look flawless. My goal was to provide information and nuance so that the Obamas can be seen, back in the White House and now into the future, with perspective and depth.

Since this book was first published, many readers have described it as Michelle Obama's story: the behind-the-scenes narrative of how she mastered a world in which she initially struggled, infusing with meaning a job often regarded as a throwback. As you will read here, her success as first lady was far more hard-won than is generally known. The point is not that she struggled, because almost all first ladies do; it's that her initial trials are essential to understanding her performance as first lady.

The president's story, meanwhile, looks different after the election of a man who appears to be his opposite in every way. Did Barack Obama's distaste for politics — an unusual quality in a president — weaken the Democrats? Did he know that pushing his health care legislation would essentially mean losing Democratic control of the House of Representatives, and the ability to pass legislation, perhaps for a very long time? If Donald Trump repeals even part of that law, what will historians say about that tradeoff? Trump rose to power in part by lying about Barack Obama's birthplace. Did Obama, who felt the destructive power of fake news earlier and more personally than the rest of us, dismiss Trump — or take him seriously before almost anyone else?

Once they left Chicago for the White House, the Obamas had to reinvent their lives. Now they have to do it again. Not much is left of the day-to-day texture of their Chicago world, and as Michelle Obama surmised all those years ago, their post-presidential careers could be many decades long. Last year, Barack Obama told a group of school-children that he wanted to go back to community organizing in some form. "Help young people get educations, and help people get jobs, and try to bring businesses into neighborhoods that don't have enough businesses," he said. "That's the kind of work that I really love to do."

That was before he realized his legacy would be under assault. He and Michelle, two of the only unifying figures in a fractured Democratic party, will face enormous pressure to help the Democrats oppose and rebuild. They will need to decide how ambitious they want to be—and whether that means trying to heal the nation's divides or pushing a progressive agenda.

Democrats dream of Michelle Obama running for president in 2020, but her distaste for politics is hard to overstate. I'm watching for a different change, one that those who have known her for a long time have awaited. When she became first lady, old friends saw her hide some of her sharpest qualities—incisive social criticism, an ability to argue with lawyerly force—to take on an innocuous mom-in-chief role. Now she must decide if she is ready to share a fuller version of herself, the one who asks tough questions even of those she loves best, whose jokes are so witty that I often had to beg, to no avail, to put them on the record.

The Obama marriage has included a decades-long debate about whether politics can be an effective avenue for social change. Barack Obama saw the possibilities in politics, while Michelle Obama saw the flaws. He believed that running for office could lead to profound progress. She was skeptical: the system was flawed or even corrupt; idealism was punished; good policy ideas went nowhere, she believed. I have a question for the Obamas that I will probably never get to ask: Where did two terms in the White House leave this debate, especially with an election-night upset that could erode so much of what they worked for? Were Michelle Obama's original concerns prescient? The ultimate answers to their private debates have long mattered for rest of us, and now they do more than ever.

Jodi Kantor

November 2016

The
OBAMAS

INTRODUCTION

One late September afternoon in 2009, Barack and Michelle Obama were sitting together in the gold-and-ivory splendor of the Oval Office, discussing the most personal of matters in the most official of settings. I was interviewing them for an article in the *New York Times Magazine* about their marriage, and as they sat in matching striped chairs, Gilbert Stuart's portrait of George Washington watching over them, they spoke about their partnership.

The president was analytical that day, the first lady funny and expressive. But it was clear that the perfect-seeming couple that had glided across the dance floor at the inaugural balls nine months earlier were still privately grappling with the very fact of being president and first lady. Michelle Obama said she still asked her husband, whenever she found him seated behind John F. Kennedy's desk, a few feet away, "What are *you* doing there? Get up from there!" When I asked how it was possible to have an equal marriage when one person was president, the first lady let out a sharp "hmmmpfh," as if she were relieved someone had finally asked, then let her husband suffer through the answer. It took him three stop-and-start tries. "My staff worries a lot more about what the first lady thinks than they worry about what I think," he finally said, before she rescued him with an answer about how their private decisions were made on an equal basis.

A few moments later, the president made the implausible case that his wife should be somehow walled off from political culture—"the silliness of Washington," he called it. Yet when she insisted that she was wholly uninterested in politics or policy, he eyed her with a bemused expression and gently contradicted her, saying he relied on her feel for public opinion on every domestic policy issue.

After the article was published, I couldn't stop thinking about the subtle tension I had felt in that room. Some of it was between the Obamas themselves. But the real mismatch was between the first couple and the world into which they had catapulted themselves. For all of their ease together in public and the stunning ambition they had shown in pursuing the presidency, the Obamas were not entirely comfortable with the bargains they had made.

How could they be? At the start of the presidential race in 2007, the candidate everyone still called Barack was just two years out of the Illinois State Senate, while his still-unknown wife bought her size-ten shoes on the Nordstrom sale rack, knew her way around a McDonald's drive-thru menu, and expressed little desire to live in Washington. Back then, they seemed like the rare political couple who were residents of our world, not a universe of green rooms, briefing books, and sycophantic handlers. They told us they were different from others in political life; they vowed to remain normal in the White House and to change the nation's capital without letting it change them.

Now, after a career criticizing the establishment, Barack Obama was the establishment. He had little Washington, managerial, economic, or national security experience, and yet his agenda was vast, the country's crises severe, his glow already dimming that autumn. He was a solitary figure in a job where emotional engagement, not just policy accomplishments, was essential to success. The Obamas had disappeared deep into the White House; their friends had become their staff, their children celebrities, their new dog the recipient of letters requesting his official portrait. By 2012, would they still be the couple we met in the 2008 race? How would they cope with the difficulties and failures that were just starting to come into view that fall? Had the Obamas' freshness to political life really been an asset in the first place?

There was something else, too. The Obamas had spent their marriage debating how much change was possible within the political system and whether public life could be made livable. The first lady was the worrier, with little trust that government could create lasting change and fear that political life was inherently corrosive. "I didn't come to politics with a lot of faith in the process," she had said years earlier. "I didn't believe that politics was structured in a way that could solve real problems for people." The president didn't disagree, exactly; his critique of the powerful was nearly as unsparing. But he had an astonishing faith in his own abilities: he believed that he *could* solve those real problems; that together they could protect themselves from the toxic forces Michelle feared. He told the country, but also his own wife, that he could reconcile the seemingly irreconcilable: red and blue America, the legislative process and lofty goals, a political life and a private one.

The White House was already testing those promises severely. "The strengths and challenges of our marriage don't change because we move to a different address," the first lady said in the interview. It was my first clue that the Obamas' private debate hadn't ended on election night 2008—that it continued in the White House, with greater force, scope, and complexity than ever.

Exploring the impact of the presidency on the Obamas' relationship was not nearly enough, I realized. The question was too small. The more difficult question was the reverse one: the impact of their partnership—their debates and differences, shared ideas about themselves, and deep hesitation about politics—on the presidency, the job of first lady, and the nation. In public, they smiled and waved, but how were the Obamas *really* reacting to the White House, and how was it affecting the rest of us?

I reported and wrote this book to answer those questions. I discovered an untold story of Michelle Obama's deep initial difficulty in the White House—her disorientation in a strange, confined new world, tense relationships with many of her husband's advisers, struggle for internal influence, and eventual turnaround. I also found that reporting on her was a way to better understand her elusive, introverted husband. She is his sparring partner, early-warning system, refuge, and guardian—tougher, by his own admission, than he is. Hers are the ultimate standards he tries to live up to, with consequences we will be debating for a long time to come. Knowing her real experiences in the White House helps us understand not just one of the most influential women of our time but fresh and essential truths about her husband's tenure.

ONE OF THE STRANGEST THINGS about the presidency is how unsparingly intimate it is. The White House is an office, home, and museum all at once, those three functions constantly colliding. The president and first lady often hide just inches from public view. Their jobs are performed the same way, with little separation between public and private, political and personal. Instincts, aversions, blind spots, and vanities that would not matter much in ordinary workplaces have huge significance. Again and again, working on this book, I saw how the Obamas' personal dynamic had consequences for the rest of us: a shared mistrust of politics so strong it sometimes hurt the presidency; the president's sometimes unrealistic assessments of what he could accomplish and the first lady's worry about them; the way the president's career repeatedly required the first lady to take a backseat to him, and the various ways she has reasserted her power; their frequent desire for escape and relief from the life they worked so hard to attain; and the way Michelle Obama rescues Barack Obama, again and again, personally and politically. With many Americans frustrated with Obama's stewardship of the economy, his reelection in 2012 increasingly rests on attractive images and charming stories of him and his family, even though the true story of the Obamas in the White House is far more complex.

Two years after the Oval Office interview, with a great deal more reporting behind me, the idea of discussing marriage in that setting no longer seems strange to me but exactly right. Barack and Michelle Obama have been married to each other since 1992, but for at least another year and possibly longer, they are married to us, too.

PART ONE

ARRIVAL

Chapter One

THE DEBATERS

FALL 2008

Michelle Obama was wearing dark sunglasses and a baseball hat, trying to escape notice.

In early November 2008, just a few days after her husband had won the presidential election, she slipped out of the armed fortress formerly known as her Chicago home with her seven-year-old daughter, Sasha. Their destination was Sasha's tennis lesson at a public court behind an elementary school a few blocks away. The leaves had already turned but the weather was still warm, and boys were playing baseball next to the tennis court.

The notion that her husband was truly going to be the president of the United States was just sinking in. It had only started to seem real on election night, when she stood on stage for his victory speech in front of celebrants in Chicago and far beyond. ("You actually pulled this off?" she murmured to him.) But things were happening fast: he was sketching out what his senior staff and cabinet would look like, and people were already standing for him when he walked into the room. A new Chicago transition office was being prepared, the Secret

Service laying thick sheets of bulletproof plastic over the windows. Laura Bush called to invite Michelle to come see the White House. A nationwide guessing game was already erupting over where her daughters would attend school in Washington and even what breed of puppy they would get. Dazed by it all, almost as if reluctant to face the enormity of what had happened and what she would need to do, the president-elect's wife was clinging stubbornly to familiar routines: hence the tennis lesson.

At the park, they ran into Susan McKeever and her daughter, Alana Sahara. They were part of the close-knit group that had seen the Obamas through their rapid rise, watching the girls, keeping the candidate and his wife company in hotel suites in strange cities. They were real friends, from the neighborhood, not political acquaintances. Michelle and Susan were on the board of the same African dance troupe, and just a few years before they had been planning fund-raisers together, including one that filled the Obamas' brick home with loud, rhythmic drumming.

As the two women caught up, McKeever discreetly inquired about an issue the Obamas had quietly been discussing.

"What's the plan? Have you figured things out yet?" she asked.

The first-lady-to-be shook her head. "I still don't know what we're doing," Michelle said, looking worried.

Only a handful of friends and aides knew what Michelle was considering: staying behind in Chicago with her daughters for the rest of the school year while the new president moved to Washington alone. They would all attend the inauguration, of course, but Michelle wasn't sure the rest of the family had to relocate so soon. Perhaps they could take the rest of the year to research school options, slowly move homes. She could commute back and forth, and her mother, Marian Robinson, could stay with the girls in Chicago on the days Washington duties called. That was how the Obamas had lived during the presidential campaign and for a long time before. Why not continue for six more months?

Barack Obama hated the idea. At forty-seven years old, he had never lived full-time under the same roof as his daughters. He started commuting to Springfield, the Illinois capital, as a state senator in 1997, before they were born, and in 2005, when he became a U.S. senator in Washington, he had initially wanted his family to move with him, before conceding they would be better off in their familiar Chicago world. The 2008 presidential campaign had made him a near-stranger to his own bed. In an unusual bit of logic, the prospect of finally living with his wife and daughters had helped him get excited about running for president in the first place: it was a reward for all of the years of separation. He argued that even when the Obamas moved to Washington, they would hold on to their old lives, return to Chicago frequently.

Outsiders would have found his wife's hesitation shocking: wouldn't living in the White House be a matchless experience, filled with moments and opportunities of which most people could only dream? First families always moved in on inauguration day, part of the pageantry that accompanied every new administration, and the idea of a commuter first lady was hard to conceive. Any presidential victory was thrilling, but Barack Obama's came with extra superlatives: the fastest rise in memory; the fall of the ultimate racial barrier. Michelle had worked her heart out to help drive him to victory, and untold numbers of strangers looked forward to the Obama family moving into the house of Jefferson, Roosevelt, and Kennedy.

If people all over the world were celebrating the prospect of the Obamas arriving at the White House, why was she hesitating?

MICHELLE OBAMA COULD BE A hard figure to understand: both more charming and more cutting than her husband, his most ardent supporter on the outside and his most devastating critic in private, more idealistic but also more cautious than he was, far less sophisticated politically but also quicker to sense problems.

The idea of lingering in Chicago was impractical, an indication of her innocence about how the presidency or politics really worked. She was a contrarian by nature, often skeptical of what others wanted or expected her to do; just because others assumed she would be excited about something didn't mean she would be. She was anxious about relocating her children to a new city in the middle of the school year, as the president's children no less. And both Obamas were still attached to the idea that they could make private, independent choices about how to live, instead of surrendering to public opinion. Even though staying behind in Chicago could set off criticism, the Obamas barely consulted their political advisers on the question of when Michelle and the girls would move, and the public never found out what they had been considering.

Their discussions about the move were only the latest in the long series of private debates that stretched back to the beginning of their relationship. Some political couples ran hand in hand together toward power, fame, and glory, hoping that one day they might have a shot at living in the nation's most famous residence. The Obamas were not like that. Behind every one of Barack Obama's decisions about his political career, behind all the speeches and announcements and races, lay a series of heartfelt, sometimes contentious debates with his wife about the nature of politics. He believed that he could use politics to achieve true, lasting change, that he could surmount the obstacles that limited others, that his career would not cost his family a normal life, that his wife would find a comfortable place for herself within his universe. She wanted to believe all of that, and sometimes she did. But over the years, she had also found considerable reason for doubt.

*　　*　　*

THE FIRST TIME THE OBAMAS laid eyes on each other was in the summer of 1989, at the Chicago law firm Sidley Austin. He was a student working there for the summer after his first year at Harvard Law; she was the recent graduate assigned to mentor him. Early on, he would watch her while she worked in the law library. When he walked into her office, she appeared disinterested, but as soon as he left, she would turn to her office mate with her mouth open and eyebrows up. *Wow.*

Soon each was gushing to friends about how smart the other was. Barack was worldlier and more mature than many other law students, with a beguiling willingness to ignore barriers and dream big. He was not yet thirty, but he had already lived in Indonesia and Hawaii, where he was raised, and organized public-housing residents in Chicago. When he became the first black president of the *Harvard Law Review,* the nation's most prestigious legal journal, other students cried, newspapers across the country wrote about him, and his new girlfriend back in Chicago had her first concrete evidence of what he might achieve.

If Barack opened Michelle's horizons, she offered him something he never had: the prospect of a stable family life. His upbringing was exotic but lonely. His father, a Kenyan graduate student, returned to Africa when Barack was two, barely kept in touch, drank too much, and died in a car crash. His mother was a wanderer, a white anthropologist who sent her son to live in Hawaii with his grandparents while she worked in Indonesia. As a result, he was unusually solitary and self-reliant; law school classmates remembered him as too serious, too much of a loner, to attend first-year parties with everyone else.

Michelle had never kept boyfriends for long before. She was statuesque, impassioned, and loyal, with a wicked comedic glint. But she was as tough as she was warm, with expectations others sometimes found unrealistically high, and few compunctions about calling people out when she felt they had failed. Those standards appealed to Barack. He wanted to live up to his potential, to hedge against the bitterness and disappointment of his father's life. He sought a partner who would "help him remember what he was there to do and who he was," said his sister, Maya Soetoro.

The bedrock of the budding Obama relationship was their shared passion for social change. Each had spent time on Ivy League campuses and in the poorest Chicago neighborhoods, and had seen the way certain advantages—education, employment, health—fostered others, while one disadvantage led to a cascade of others. The two young lawyers believed that the gaps between the two places lay less in talent or hard work than in opportunity, power, access, and wealth.

Behind the backs of Sidley partners, Barack chided fellow summer associates for pursuing private-sector careers. Over after-work beers, he grilled them on what they wanted to do. Banking or litigation, most said. "What do you want to do with that?" he would prod. To advance, to provide for our families—he dismissed those answers. He didn't care about money and didn't always relate to people who did. "It's got to be about what you can give back," he would say, a former fellow associate, Thomas Reed, recalled.

Obama envisioned himself as a writer, among other things, and he was awarded a contract to write a book about race relations after winning the law review presidency. But he threw himself into the project without much planning, changed the book to a memoir, ran a voter registration project as he wrote, and blew his deadline. After the Obamas were married, in 1992, he spent weeks alone in Bali with the manuscript, and in Chicago, he slipped off for long hours to write, leaving Michelle behind. "Barack Obama does not belong to you," Yvonne Davila, a friend, used to tell her. She meant that there were big things in store for him, bigger than family; people were always making that kind of portentous prediction about Barack. But that raised a question for Michelle: where did her husband's ambitions, not to mention his solitude and tendency to overestimate what he could handle, leave her?

EARLY IN THEIR MARRIAGE, the Obamas made two discoveries: the world of politics and government was not the right place for Michelle, and, as Barack admitted, it was in many ways an uncomfortable fit for him, too.

In 1991, Michelle left Sidley to work as an aide to Chicago's mayor, Richard M. Daley, the new and still unproven heir to his father's machine. She and Barack were nervous about the job. Daley senior had opposed the desegregation of schools and presided over an ethically challenged political operation, and the new mayor's first run for the job had ended in ugly racial divisions. "Having grown up in a proud African American family, she wasn't sure if there was a conflict between her values and his," said Valerie Jarrett, the mayoral aide who recruited Michelle and became a mentor to both Obamas. Jarrett, young, elegant, and educated at top schools, was an example of how the younger Daley intended to be different. She was from one of the best-established African American families in Hyde Park, a generally anti-Daley neighborhood, but she believed in gaining power to change things from above.

Some of Michelle's work was straightforward, like helping downtown businesses during a massive flood, but when she served as a liaison to agencies that provided for the city's most vulnerable—seniors, the disabled, and children—she was distressed by how heavily the projects were influenced by connections and favors. It was "the ugly underbelly in city government on how decisions are made—or not made," Kevin Thompson, who worked with her, said. Underlying issues of poverty and education had little chance of being addressed. She questioned how closely Daley held power, surrounding himself with three or four people who seemed to let few outsiders in—a concern she would echo years later with her own husband. At work, Michelle always seemed crisp and professional, but she could be critical of the mayor's administration behind closed doors.

According to former colleagues, she protested the way power in Illinois was locked up generation after generation by a small group of families, many of them Irish Catholic—the Daleys in Chicago, the Hyneses and Madigans statewide. "Someone doesn't have the right to be elected because of whose womb they came out of," she would say a few years later to Dan Shomon, her husband's political adviser. "You shouldn't have a better chance if you're a Kennedy than if you're an Obama. Why is it that they have the right to this?"

She stayed only two years before moving on to a job leading a program that spoke volumes about her conclusions. It was called Public Allies, and its aim was to train a new generation of urban leaders from more diverse backgrounds—an alternative to the established power structure. Two years later, in 1995, Valerie Jarrett was unceremoniously dumped from her post: she was standing in the way of powerful developers, who convinced the mayor to let her go, and even though Jarrett and the mayor were close, he never spoke to her about the decision. The Obamas were horrified, their worst suspicions about that world confirmed.

Barack saw the same problems with politics as Michelle did. But for him, those weren't reasons to stay out; they were reasons to get in. He believed in his own talent and singularity; he felt sure that the usual rules would not apply. That summer, a state senate seat representing Hyde Park was opening up, and Barack, who had been teaching law and working at a civil rights firm, told Michelle he wanted to run. "I married you because you're cute and you're smart, but this is the dumbest thing you could have ever asked me to do," she told him.

As a state senator, he insisted, he would do nothing less than redefine the job and restore ethics to politics. "What if a politician were to see his job as that of an organizer," he said in an interview, "as part teacher and part advocate, one who does not sell voters short but who educates them about the real choices before them?" He would have to raise funds from wealthy donors in the short term, he conceded, but would be able to do without them once he was better known.

Those sorts of statements worried Michelle: how was a person like that going to fare in a notoriously corrupt state capital? Later, others would wonder whether her husband was too earnest, too conflict-averse, but Michelle had seen and said all of it long before. "I think he's too much of a good guy for the kind of brutality, the skepticism," she worried to an interviewer at the time. The former law review editor was going to become part of a system she deplored—and at the same time, they were talking about starting the close-knit family they both craved. He told her it would work out; she was dubious.

Still, Michelle made a decision she would repeat over the years: she dedicated herself to his victory and success. If he was going to run, she was not going to let him lose. She tried to elevate the campaign with a nice office and a classy fund-raiser at the local black history museum—none of the usual tackiness or tawdriness of state politics. She became the arbiter of who on the campaign was performing and who was not. If a volunteer promised to gather three hundred petition signatures, "two hundred ninety-nine did not work because three hundred was the goal," said Carol Anne Harwell, the campaign manager. If you underperformed, "you met the wrath of Michelle." And for the first time in his political career but not the last, she helped connect him with other people. Some voters were quizzical about Obama's unusual name, even rude—he clearly wasn't from the South Side. But when Michelle knocked on doors on his behalf, neighbors instinctively understood that she, and therefore he, was one of them.

* * *

IN DECEMBER OF 2003, Barack and Michelle gathered with family and friends at a lush nature preserve in Oahu to celebrate Maya Soetoro's marriage to Konrad Ng, a Canadian Chinese doctoral student. The Obamas had two small daughters by then, Malia and Sasha, dressed in identical red-and-white sundresses that day. The bride and groom had asked Barack to start off the ceremony. He rose to speak to the assembled guests against a spectacular backdrop: green lawns, rocky cliffs, the sparkling Pacific Ocean, the occasional peacock wandering past.

His remarks were not particularly idyllic or romantic in tone; he spoke about the challenges of marriage. The odds were stacked against enduring happiness, he told the small crowd. "Our society has not necessarily equipped us to sustain relationships," Ng recalled him saying. Careers, not to mention children, drove partners in opposite directions, he warned.

Only a few guests knew that the Obamas were just emerging from the lowest point in their relationship. Barack had won the state senate seat, but his time in Springfield had been frustrating for both Obamas. As soon as he arrived, he complained it was not serious enough: legislation he drafted was not even heard and some new colleagues—Democrats!—even poked fun at his name. "He would call me and say, 'This person is an idiot. They get an F,'" Harwell recalled. Michelle reached her limit when, in 2000, her husband rushed into a poorly planned challenge to Representative Bobby Rush, a former Black Panther and well-connected South Side operator. Rush swatted Obama away easily, labeling him a pretentious interloper whose lofty ideas about reform did nothing for people who didn't have *jobs*. Michelle felt her husband was self-absorbed and unrealistic: he was trying to run for Congress, serve in Springfield, teach law on the side, and be a father and husband. Their disagreements had grown so deep that the Obamas needed two or three years to recover, the president said later.

While Michelle wished he had chosen a more stable career, not to mention a more lucrative one, she also felt he wasn't achieving as much as he could. If he was going to be a politician, she believed, his accomplishments were going to have to be weighty enough to justify the sacrifices. Michelle always reminded him "about his own potential and power to effect change," as Soetoro put it later. Smarting from his loss to Rush, Obama had publicly questioned whether seeking elective office was the best way for him to improve people's lives.

Now, at the Hawaii wedding, he alluded to his wife's faith in him. The key to a lasting union, he told the gathering, was to choose the right partner— "somebody who sees you as you deserve to be seen," he said; someone who recognizes your potential *and* your vulnerabilities.

At an open microphone a few hours later, Michelle told the newlyweds to expect to labor over their union— "part of the contract," as she put it. Marriage could be worth it, she promised: not easy, but ultimately worth the struggle.

As the terraced hills and Pacific views faded into darkness, five-year-old Malia paired off with a little boy on the dance floor. Barack was such an eloquent speaker that he should run for president, guests clucked. Unbeknownst to them, he was running for U.S. Senate. He had made a deal with his wife: it would be his last run, and if he lost, he would leave politics forever.

THAT WAS WHEN THE STORY turned in a way that neither Obama could have dreamed. First, Barack won the Democratic primary for the U.S. Senate seat in March 2004, with surprising support from many white voters in rural areas. Over the summer, his new communications director from Washington, Robert Gibbs, helped convince staffers for Senator John Kerry, about to become the Democratic presidential nominee, to give Obama the keynote slot at the party convention. In an electrifying speech, he created an instant reputation as a counter to the sitting U.S. president. Unlike George W. Bush, Barack Obama was self-made, introspective, intellectual, and gifted with words.

It wasn't just a speech; it was a statement of the Obama worldview. He emphasized his unique story, his ability to overcome odds and do what others could not. He conjured up an appealing image of American unity, arguing that the divisions between red and blue America did not even exist. He was rising in politics by arguing against politics, casting himself as a new kind of leader who would look past ossified labels, unify the country, and tackle long-standing issues.

It was as if a river that Barack Obama had been swimming upstream spontaneously reversed course to send him surging ahead. State politics had punished his erudition and earnestness; now those qualities were rewarded. Instead of making fun of his name, many people admired his life story. His campaign staff had used boxes of *Dreams from My Father,* his long-dormant memoir, as doorstops; now the book became a best seller.

Michelle found a way of finally accepting that her husband was a politician: by refusing to admit he was one. "Barack is not a politician first and foremost," she told a reporter around that time. "He's a community activist exploring the viability of politics to make change." Together they were like tailors who called themselves "garment reconstruction engineers," loath to fully acknowledge the business they were really in.

Over the years, many Chicagoans thought Michelle showed just as much promise as her husband did, maybe more. "If someone said to me, one of them is going to grow up to be president, I may have bet on her," said Ann Marie Lipinski, former editor of the *Chicago Tribune,* as she recalled meeting the Obamas for the first time. But his success in 2004 put them on different planes: he was the instant celebrity, she the still-unknown spouse, an administrator at the University of Chicago Medical Center. At some events, he was so thronged by fans that he would escape into the men's room to speak with his wife on the phone. Sometimes Michelle flipped on the radio or television and heard her husband's voice talking at her. "Look, I'm in the picture, too," Michelle told a friend at the supermarket checkout line, showing her a glossy celebrity magazine with Barack's picture in it. "That's my elbow!"

Michelle could be funny about it: At Malia and Sasha's school, the Obamas were upgraded from the planning committee for the annual fund-raiser to honorary chairs. When they were introduced at the event, Barack reached for the microphone but Michelle snatched it out of his hands. "I know you came here to listen to Barack," she announced, "but tonight he's just arm candy." The crowd roared, and Barack smiled a Cheshire cat smile, looking amused to play number two.

But she felt left out in other ways, too. She worried that her husband was not home enough, that campaign staff weren't sharing daily talking points with her or helping her get to a campaign event and then home again to feed her kids, and she spoke to them bluntly about it. "Her very direct way is very direct and it can rub some people the wrong way at times," said Thompson, who served as Barack's personal aide on the race. Sometimes as he and Barack drove back from an event in some remote Illinois county, Michelle would call to ask him to bring home eggs and milk. Some staff members were dubious. As later generations of aides would continue to wonder: her husband had been slogging around all day; couldn't she go easy on him?

In her few campaign appearances during the Senate race, she was just as direct; in front of a fifty-person crowd in Edwardsville, she ripped into then President Bush. Her father suffered from multiple sclerosis but managed to send two children to Princeton, she said. So to hear a "rich, spoiled president" lecture about family values was insulting, she told the audience.

At moments when she was expected to say standard political-wife things—to tell anyone who would listen that Barack Obama was simply the best—she delighted in playing against type. "If he loses, it might not be so bad," she told a reporter during the final stretch of the Senate race in September 2004, rubbing her hands together with mock glee. She was willing to speak up for herself, too: "What I notice about men, all men, is that their order is me, my family, God is in there somewhere, but me is first. And for women, me is fourth, and that's not healthy," she added. "I've had to come to the point of figuring out how to carve out what kind of life I want for myself beyond who Barack is and what he wants." Her long-standing debate with her husband was now spilling into the pages of the *Chicago Tribune*.

Michelle may have felt overlooked by her husband's staff, but they saw the gap between Barack's soaring career and Michelle's desire for stability, and they were always trying to smooth things. As Barack sailed to victory in the Senate race, the Obamas had dinner with Rahm Emanuel, then a U.S. congressman from Illinois, and his wife, Amy Rule. Though Barack wanted his family in Washington, Emanuel and Rule urged the Obamas to do as they had: keep the family in Chicago and endure the commute. Otherwise Michelle and the girls could end up with the worst of both worlds, living in a strange town with no support network and a busy Barack. Rule was pointed: she had been to Washington to see her husband sworn in and she had not been back. Emanuel and Rule's message had been planned out with David Axelrod, a top campaign consultant who was now advising Obama.

Soon after Barack won the U.S. Senate seat, in November 2004, with 70 percent of the vote—the bid by his Republican opponent, Jack Ryan, melted away in a marital scandal—the public and private calls for him to run for president began. Michelle tried to calm every-one down. He was a man, not a prophet, she told anyone who would listen, and he had barely done anything on the national stage yet. For many others, his boundless enthusiasm inspired hope; but it caused her worry, because she sensed expectations were getting out of hand. But the satisfaction of watching others see her husband as she saw him eroded some of Michelle's resistance. "It really clicked with her that this may be the destiny everyone was always talking about," Thompson said.

"If he runs in 2008 and serves two terms, he'd only be fifty-five afterwards," she said over dinner with Thompson. "What would we do then?"

But Barack sometimes had trouble discussing the prospect of running for president with his wife. He had asked so much of her already, and never anything nearly as great as this before. He could be in physical danger. She was new to the public stage, in uncharted ter-ritory. Forget a black first lady—at that time, the country barely had any famous black professional women to begin with, only entertain-ment and sports celebrities.

In September of 2006, Obama accepted an invitation to attend Sen-ator Tom Harkin's annual steak fry in the early-voting state of Iowa—the strongest hint yet that he was considering running. Michelle found out from a news alert on the *Chicago Tribune* website. When Obama, back in Washington, admitted to Robert Gibbs that he had not told his wife, Gibbs was alarmed. "Are you *crazy?*" Gibbs asked.

IN OCTOBER 2006, BARACK PUBLISHED a new book, *The Audacity of Hope,* a virtual White House audition memo. On a rainy night in Chicago that month, the members of greater Obamaworld gathered for a book party under a tent in the backyard of Valerie Jarrett's par-ents. As Barack took to the center of the tent to address the crowd, the guests all had the same question on their mind, one to which even Axelrod and the other advisers present didn't know the answer: would he run?

Initially, Barack had tuned out the presidential talk, too. But he was just as disappointed with the U.S. Senate as he had been with the state senate — he had gone to Washington to do big things, but he was a junior member of a slow, rule-bound, Republican-controlled body. "Shoot. Me. Now," he wrote to an aide, in the middle of a particularly long-winded oration. (The speaker was Senator Joe Biden.) The appeal of a 2008 run was hard to resist. Top Democrats were telling him he could skip the grind of Capitol Hill — where he was so new he still got lost in the hallways — and go directly after the presidency. "This country is ready for a transformative politics of the sort that John F. Kennedy, Ronald Reagan and Franklin Roosevelt represented," he told Joe Klein, of *Time* magazine, that same month, a bold self-comparison. Most of the country still had no idea who he was.

Audacity was a typical political-manifesto book, with one exception: Barack had devoted an entire chapter to what his career had cost Michelle and the girls. Standing under the tent at the launch party for the book, he said it again: "I just want to talk about my family and how hard this journey has been on them," his toast started. And there it stopped: he stood alone at the front of the tent, overcome with tears.

Though the public didn't know it, Michelle was really the one everyone was waiting on. Barack had given her veto power over the run and she was inclined to use it. With a few more years of Washington experience, she told her husband, wouldn't he have a better chance of success?

And a presidential race was potentially a curse upon her children, she knew. That's what people in Washington quietly said, too: to run for president was to sacrifice the next generation. Children of candidates grew up watching their parents attacked on a daily basis, and sometimes they themselves were taunted. But she believed in what her husband wanted to do as president. The responsibility of the choice weighed on her, said Susan Sher, then her boss at the hospital. Was she really going to be the one who stopped him?

As Barack stood silent before the crowd at the party, Michelle made her way from the back of the tent and wrapped her arms around him. He had been making an offering, the grateful husband prostrating himself before his wife for all to see. The Obamas did that sometimes—they said things in front of other people that were mostly meant for each other. The guests broke into hoots and claps: most of them knew what the Obamas had been through together. And maybe this was a sign, a hint Michelle would agree to the run.

A few weeks later, she told her brother, Craig Robinson, "I guess we're going to do this thing." Her husband's advisers, shocked she had said yes, joked that she was only allowing her husband to run so that he would lose and purge his presidential ambitions. In truth, she had decided that her family could handle the stress, that her husband actually might win, and that he might "be able to break through the partisanship, the gridlock that had existed for the last twenty years" to accomplish big things, her husband said later. Michelle extracted one promise in return, something she had wanted from the beginning of her marriage: Barack had to quit smoking.

For all of his bravado about transforming the country's politics, Barack could sound surprisingly hesitant about the run, too. He was standing on the diving board, preparing to jump, realizing the water below might be very cold. "Life is good," the candidate-to-be told friends. I'm not like Bill Clinton, he said. He meant that he was not intrinsically a politician, did not crave the contact high of strangers. "I don't need this," he continued. "I don't need anything." He announced his candidacy a few weeks later.

*   *   *

AS OFTEN HAPPENS OVER YEARS of marriage, Barack and Michelle Obama's positions were no longer quite as contrary as they once had been. She had cause to see the world in an us-against-them way, friends said, but that no longer made as much sense. White voters in Iowa were clutching dog-eared copies of *Dreams*, and even the Kennedys seemed invested in her husband's success. In June 2007, the candidate stood with Dan Shomon at a Chicago fund-raiser, both watching slack-jawed as Michelle delivered an upbeat pitch to donors. "Can you believe it?" a thrilled Obama asked Shomon.

Barack had begun fatherhood a near stranger to the rituals of family life, and initially she had to teach him basic things such as calling home every day from a trip. (Barack, so rational, didn't see the point of phoning if you had nothing to say.) Now her concerns had more fully become his as well. "I've missed all this," he told their friend Allison Davis, tears in his eyes as he watched Malia practice dance moves.

Earlier in his career, he had shown up to tiny events, shaken every hand. Now fame and demand drew him deeper within himself. When he signed copies of *Dreams* for friends in 1994, he had written long, heartfelt inscriptions; when *Audacity* was published eight years later, the same friends got a couple of words. His time and patience were shrinking, his desire for self-protection and privacy increasing. Some staffers had a word to describe the moments when he seemed unable or unwilling to connect: Barackward, a combination of "Barack" and "awkward." The problem was psychological, he said during the first spring of the campaign in 2007, when he was having trouble answering debate questions with concision. "I'm still wrapping my head around doing this in a way that I think the other candidates just aren't," he said.

Sometimes Michelle, of all people, was the one to yank him back into it, focusing him in a campaign meeting with a sharp "We're talking about *you* right now." Meaning: shut up, pay attention. "Barack, feel — don't *think!*" she once interjected on a debate preparation call, when he was wallowing in policy detail. He hated posing for pictures with strangers, but she did not let him off the hook. "Do your job," she would say. The instruction carried a whiff of revenge: this is what you wanted. *Smile!*

The presidential campaign supported Michelle's highest hopes about politics but also validated some of her worst fears. The question of where she fit in her husband's operation became more confusing than ever. She learned that the advisers who were supposed to protect her sometimes could or would not do so, that the public could decide to believe the worst with chilling speed.

To introduce her to the public, the original plan was, as everyone put it, to "let Michelle be Michelle." She had no national campaign experience, but she was a hit — warm and confiding in Iowa and New Hampshire living rooms, instantly familiar to the African American voters who delivered her husband's crucial South Carolina victory. Her frankness buttressed her husband's image as refreshingly honest, and her toughness became the subject of affectionate jokes: "Everyone in our family is afraid of her," Craig Robinson said in an early interview. Asked how his brother-in-law planned to fulfill his promise to quit smoking, Robinson chortled, "Michelle Obama, that's one hell of a patch right there!"

This time around, the frictions between her and some of her husband's advisers grew more intense. David Plouffe, the campaign manager, was frugal, a quality that ultimately earned him wide praise, and she was only campaigning two days a week. But she had no speechwriter and only two staff members, and, as during the Senate campaign, she had trouble getting the daily talking points. And, in her lawyerly way, she would ask the advisers challenging questions, sometimes via email, sometimes in person. (Friends affectionately called her "The Taskmaster.") Why weren't they doing more to recruit women and minority voters? What if Plouffe's electoral strategy failed; what was the backup? The thrust was always that her husband and his team were too improvisatory and insular, with the same tiny group making all decisions.

In the mornings she exercised while watching *Morning Joe,* the political chat show on MSNBC, and emailed advisers queries: Do we have a person on this problem? What's our argument in the face of this? The missives were a "nightmare," one adviser said, the last thing the exhausted team wanted.

The advisers were learning a key difference between the Obamas: Barack was unusually tolerant of staff failures, and Michelle was not. After the campaign fumbled its strategy for the Texas and Ohio primaries in March 2008, prolonging the contest between Obama and Hillary Clinton, the candidate was diplomatic with his team. "After blowing through twenty million dollars in two weeks, I could yell at you," he told them. "But I'm not." Michelle was so angry she would barely speak to the advisers or her husband, "giving them only uninterested, monosyllabic responses" as they attempted to cheer her up, Plouffe wrote later.

It was a classic campaign standoff, a candidate's concerned spouse versus advisers who felt criticized, and it resulted in a very visible casualty: Michelle Obama's public image. Her belief in her husband's specialness, the same faith and vision Barack had praised in Hawaii, could make her sound judgmental: "Barack will never allow you to go back to your lives as usual—uninvolved, uninformed," she said in one speech. In another, she made the remark that would be played and replayed: "For the first time in my adult lifetime, I am really proud of my country," she said, talking about the hope that her husband's campaign had created.

No one inside the campaign told her her words might be misconstrued. They were avoiding her, one adviser said. When she learned that, Michelle was furious but guilty. "She could not live with that idea: what if he doesn't become president because of something I said or did?" one adviser said. As the general election began in June 2008, she refused to campaign until her image problems were under control. "I'm not going to go out there if the consensus is that it's a net negative," she said. She had never done this before, she told aides; they just needed to tell her what to do.

That was the beginning of the new Michelle, carefully edited for public consumption. The campaign scrapped a frank documentary it had commissioned about Michelle to "put it all out there," as an aide put it. Instead she appeared on morning shows where she talked about bacon (which she liked) and pantyhose (which she didn't). "We went into a little fluff," another adviser admitted, "a much more traditional woman's role," showing that Michelle was "like the mom on *The Cosby Show*." There were so few public images of warm, accomplished black mothers that the campaign had to turn to a two-decades-old fictional one. The era of the Obamas openly debating each other about politics was over, too; from now on, their discussions would remain private.

For Barack, the autumn of the 2008 race was marked by the dawning realization that he really was going to win, and the strangeness of passing from one world into the next. His elderly grandmother died in Hawaii, but he barely had a moment to mourn. The economy slid from crisis into paralysis, and Obama threw himself into the problem, supporting Bush's unpopular emergency efforts to bail out financial firms and absorbing obscure details of the subprime mortgage problem. He wanted to learn as much as possible as soon as possible, he told aides, and no wonder. He had run to lead one country, and he was about to take over a far more troubled one.

In the days after the election, he was not in the mood to entertain doubts or dissent; he needed to move fast. In his first major decision, he asked Emanuel to be his chief of staff. Emanuel had the Washington experience Obama did not, and, unlike the president-elect, he was combative, unafraid to push or even insult.

Emanuel stood for the idea that Democrats, stereotyped in the past as ineffectual do-gooders who were weak on national security issues, could stand tough and get things done. (His father had fought with a militant Zionist group before Israel's founding, and the idea that Jews, contrary to stereotype, could fight and win wasn't far from his idea that Democrats could do the same.) He was a Clintonian who absorbed the lessons of that White House—avoid symbolic issues and ideological battles—and put them to work as an Illinois congressman and House leader. He was restless, sly, casually abusive, and almost always willing to cut a deal. He could yell at you and eat a brownie off your plate at the same time, and a phone call from him might involve thirty seconds of profanity followed by a cooed "love you" and a suddenly dead line.

Not everyone in Obamaland was happy about the choice: the pensive, reformist new president would have a White House run by an impatient dealmaker? Michelle had doubts about Emanuel, according to advisers. But the nature of her debates with her husband was about to change. Her husband was about to deal with issues from appointments to the Federal Reserve to the Israeli-Palestinian conflict. She was a hospital executive who had never held office; what did she really know about those? And she was already confronting the essential dilemma of first ladyhood: was it better to be frank with her husband about potential mistakes or to keep criticism to herself? The consequences of a presidential misstep were enormous, but so was the need for unwavering support from their wives for men who were constantly picked apart by everyone else.

Besides, others who protested Obama's choice paid the price. The day after the election, when word of Emanuel's appointment began to circulate, Obama's old friend Christopher Edley, the dean of UC Berkeley School of Law, sent him a note about it. During the campaign, Obama had tolerated, even welcomed, Edley's critiques and that summer Edley had warned Obama away from Emanuel, calling him "a tactician unencumbered by value commitments." Now, Edley did not directly criticize Emanuel but suggested how to organize the White House to reinforce what he saw as Emanuel's strengths and compensate for his weaknesses. Soon after he sent the note, the phone rang. It was Jarrett, warning Edley of a very angry phone call to come.

"Why would you do this today, of all days?" Obama demanded of Edley. He wanted to savor his moment of victory free of any criticism, Edley concluded; he did not have much tolerance for seeing his judgment doubted.

The old friends never spoke again.

THE WEEK AFTER THE ELECTION, the Obamas flew to Washington to meet with the Bushes in the White House. While the men talked about economic stimulus, Laura Bush showed her successor her soon-to-be home. They lingered in a sitting room on the southwest side used by first ladies as a dressing area and private retreat. One window looked across the Rose Garden and over the exterior of the Oval Office. During her husband's critical meetings and long days at work, Laura Bush would stare out the window of her hideaway and feel somehow more connected to him. This is what Hillary Clinton showed me, she said, according to Anita McBride, her former chief of staff. Before that, Barbara Bush had shown it to Clinton, and when Michelle Obama left the White House, Laura Bush said, she should show it to the new first lady, too.

It was hard to think of a better symbol of the true duties of first ladyhood than that window: Keep a close eye on your husband. Do it quietly. There will be things about the presidency that only you will be able to see. Don't expect to be at the heart of the action.

The Bushes invited Michelle to return with her daughters, who immediately slid down the banisters of their future home. The girls visited and liked Sidwell Friends, the prestigious Quaker school that Chelsea Clinton had attended; it reminded them of their school in Chicago. Relocating to Washington immediately had begun to make more sense to Michelle: drawing out the move now looked like "six more months of stuff we couldn't control," an aide said. And like her husband, Michelle wanted her family to be together. Over the next weeks, the notion of lingering in Chicago receded until it was just a blip in the Obama story, a road not taken.

Besides, hadn't Barack finally won their larger debate about whether change could be accomplished through politics, about whether political life could be livable? They had made it: through the lower ranks of politics and childbearing, the challenges of sudden success and the presidential campaign, and the years of living apart. Obama had addressed his wife's objections about the failings of politics in the most dramatic way possible, by getting himself elected leader of the free world. Systemic change was what they had always dreamed of, from the beginning of their relationship, and now the new president would have his chance. Their running debate was part of what had driven him so far forward, and now he had won it for good.

Michelle wasn't exactly overjoyed to move to the White House, an aide said, but she was determined. This was what they had decided to do, and failure was not an option.

Chapter Two

THIS IS NOT MY BEAUTIFUL HOUSE

JANUARY–FEBRUARY 2009

On the afternoon of Barack Obama's inauguration as the forty-fourth president of the United States, as over a million celebrants streamed through the streets of Washington and the Obamas pumped hands at a congressional luncheon, a stray aide quietly made his way through the inner sanctum of the presidency, the two-story suite inside the White House where every president had resided since 1801. He wanted to check out the place where the new first family would actually live. Their brief peeks with the Bushes aside, the Obamas did not know the place themselves.

The Bush moving vans had already departed, and for the moment, the place seemed to belong to no one, a series of rooms with high ceilings and polished floors that had the frozen-in-time quality of a museum and the blankness of a high-end hotel lobby. Since the Obamas had not arrived yet, anyone with a White House pass could walk right in.

In private, Laura Bush's staffers raised eyebrows at the adjustment that the Obamas would face. When George and Laura Bush moved into the White House, it was a familiar place from his father's terms as vice president and then president. They had spent the Fourth of July at the White House many times and bonded with the staff. Nearly every other modern president had lived in some sort of state residence, either a governor's home or the vice president's house, before moving into 1600 Pennsylvania Avenue. Until four years before the presidency, the Obamas still lived in the apartment they bought after they were first married, a narrow condo with aging fixtures and a dark master bedroom with an improbably tiny closet for Michelle. Only after the 2004 Senate victory, and an ensuing book deal that made them instantly wealthy, did they move to the kind of house Michelle had wanted for years: a $1.65 million historic brick mansion.

But if the Obamas' first two homes represented the speed of their rise, nothing quite matched the White House for symbolic weight. With 132 rooms, 6 levels, 35 bathrooms, 412 doors, and 3 elevators, it was an executive mansion for a man who had never been an executive and a fortresslike setting for a first lady who had always prided herself on leaving elite settings—Princeton, Harvard, Sidley Austin—to return to the South Side. The marble- and chandelier-bedecked house, its Disneyland perfection, also underscored the contrast between the splendor of the Obamas' new lives and the mounting economic dread experienced by the rest of the country. The house was at once the nation's museum, the president's office, the commander in chief's secure compound, and the first family's home. With the White House, as with the presidency, it wasn't always clear where professional life ended and personal life began, whether the Obamas' lives would now belong to them or the nation.

In the hours before the Obamas moved in, cleaners were scouring the place top to bottom because Malia had allergies and her parents did not want her sneezing from the recently departed Bush pets. As they did so, Michael Smith, the Obamas' new decorator, was moving furniture around, and the residence staff were opening boxes, arranging mattresses and sheets, making sure the bathrooms had soap. According to tradition, the new president and first lady were supposed to arrive in the late afternoon and find all of their things unpacked and in order.

In phone calls to prospective interior designers a few weeks before, asking them to audition for the job of redecorating the residence, the first lady's staff had stressed that the Obamas wanted to make the high-ceilinged, imposing rooms feel like a family home. They would bring their African art collection along, and they might decorate with the same hunter green color they had used in their Chicago home. The kids' rooms would be the most urgent task. Designers would have to find a way to make Malia and Sasha's posters of teen pop idols the Jonas Brothers work in bedrooms with towering ceilings and layers of intricate molding.

No matter what could be done superficially, the presidential residence hardly resembled an American home, even a lavish one. It did not have a private entrance or exit, meaning there was no way for the first family to come and go without detection. Coming in from the outside world, they generally entered through the ornate gold-and-blue Diplomatic Room at the back of the White House. From there they proceeded into the wide central hallway of the ground floor, where they ducked behind some dull brown screens—the kind you might see dividing a church social hall—in order to hide from staff and tourists. (White House regulars could usually tell when the president was behind the screen, because of all the feet—belonging to Secret Service agents and aides—that shuffled around his.) From there the president and his family could either stride up a private stairway or slip into a small wood-and-mirror-paneled elevator. Its doors slid closed, and when they opened a few seconds later, a different world materialized: the quiet of the presidential residence, maybe a housekeeper finishing the daily vacuuming, the Lincoln Bedroom just feet away. In other words, the home part of the White House was not a house at all. It was a box within a larger box, the world's most prestigious executive apartment.

Some of the rooms looked like historical exhibits. Laura Bush had redone the Lincoln Bedroom with strict fidelity to the 1860s, with elaborately carved wood and shiny gold fabric. A six-foot-tall head-board, swagged in purple cloth, loomed over the bed, topped with a gilded, crown-shaped canopy. Across the hall, the Queens' Bedroom had a similarly rococo look, in bubble-gum pink, with rose-and-green prints running riot over the bed canopy, drapes, and wing chairs. The living spaces were imposing, too: the West Sitting Hall, with a spectacular Tiffany window through which the afternoon sun streamed, and the Yellow Oval Room, with Louis XVI–style furnishings, open shelves of decorative porcelain, and gilt edges everywhere.

It was a house for people with a fleet of help, with a small kitchen for finishing meals that had been prepared in the main kitchen downstairs, a station for linen inventory, and a beauty salon where the first lady could have her hair and makeup done. The household staff were often so deeply dispersed through the nooks of the house that on September 11, 2001, well after the White House had been officially evacuated, butlers were still emerging, according to Walter Scheib, a former chef there. The residence was such a world of its own they had no idea what had transpired.

The third floor was not as grand as the one below, with lower ceilings, an exercise room and pool table, and slightly less formal bedrooms, including one that would belong to Marian Robinson. The Obamas planned to decorate her room immediately, because she was moving with great reluctance from the little Chicago bungalow where she had lived for decades, and they wanted her to feel at home. In a family of unlikely White House residents, seventy-three-year-old Marian Robinson was the least likely of all.

She never told her life story publicly; during the campaign, she did not give a single speech and hardly ever spoke to the press. Her difficult, modest life stood in quiet contrast to the splendor of the home in which she would live. The daughter of a factory worker turned house painter who had moved to Chicago from the South looking for work, Marian Shields met Fraser Robinson at a city swimming pool, where he was working as a lifeguard. Around the time they married, he dropped out of college because he could not afford the tuition and was afraid to borrow it, according to his brother, Nomenee Robinson. He was diagnosed with multiple sclerosis four years later.

The Robinsons kept his illness a secret from their children until they were teenagers, and he still went to his job at the city pump station every day. They lived in a small apartment inside a house, where the Robinsons gave their children the sole bedroom and slept in the living room. Marian was a determined mother, volunteering at her children's school so she could keep an eye on their educations. Fraser was stubborn, dignified, and persistent. Later, he used to drive all the way from Chicago to Princeton to see Craig play basketball, despite his disability. Once he stared in quiet dismay at the arena parking lot: it was gravel, meaning he could not traverse it in his wheelchair. Even when he could not walk unassisted, he insisted on fixing drinks for guests himself.

Marian returned to secretarial work when Michelle left for college, in part to pay her ailing husband's medical expenses. (The Robinsons had paid for their share of Craig and Michelle's Princeton tuition with credit cards, leaving them with high-interest debts for years.) In his final years, things got very bad. One day he fell in the snow and lay there for hours before anyone found him, his brother said. Later Michelle said that her father's condition explained why she was a meticulous planner: when you were trying to maneuver around Chicago with a disabled father, avoiding embarrassment or emergency, you left nothing to chance. When he died in 1991 after mysteriously collapsing, Marian and her children had to make the decision to take him off life support. Barack was still just Michelle's boyfriend then, and he was far away in Cambridge, but he flew in to be by the family's side.

During her son-in-law's climb, Marian remained an outsider to political life, pining like a schoolgirl to meet Hillary Clinton, her heroine, during the 2004 U.S. Senate campaign. At the start of the presidential campaign, she still woke up every morning in the same house where she had lived with her husband, stopped into a McDonald's downtown for coffee, and then took her seat as an executive assistant at a downtown bank. She had the same blunt but proper quality as her daughter, and she taught her granddaughters to call adults "Mr." and "Mrs." and to thank everyone politely. But when campaign staffers first tried to film her for commercials, they had to scrap the footage because she was too outspoken.

In a rare interview early in the race, a reporter from *O*, Oprah Winfrey's magazine, asked Robinson if she would move to the White House if her son-in-law won.

"That I can do without," Robinson said. "When you move in, you just hear a little bit too much."

The reporter pointed out that the White House was big. "It's never big enough for that," Robinson shot back.

As Barack Obama watched election returns declaring him a winner, he clutched his mother-in-law's hand, as if he were hanging on to the most solid thing in the hotel suite. A few hours later, at the celebrations in Grant Park, friends remember Marian trying to get out from behind the security rope. The expression on her face said: I'm seventy-three years old, I've seen a thing or two in my day, and do I really have to stay behind this thing? The Secret Service agents let her out.

The bond between the first lady and her mother was private and deep. Marian could "communicate with her daughter with just a look between them," said Susan Sher, Michelle's former boss at the hospital, who took a job as a White House lawyer. Aides noticed that Michelle craved her mother's presence the way adult daughters seldom did, and that the two women seemed to allow few of the usual resentments to pile up between them. In interviews, the first lady talked about how her mother sustained her, gave her strength and courage and a measure of separation from the political clamor. "I've never seen her react to a story" in the media, Valerie Jarrett said of Marian. "If she reacted, that would be pressure on the first lady."

She agreed to only a three-month trial in the White House. She would help everyone get settled, make sure her granddaughters were fine. Perhaps she would even travel abroad with the president and first lady on a diplomatic trip or two, flying along with them on Air Force One, descending the famous staircase for arrival ceremonies. It would be nice to finally see some of the world. She had never been outside the United States.

WHEN THE NEW PRESIDENT and the first lady finally reached the White House on inauguration day, it was late — the parade had taken longer than expected — and they had been outside for hours. But they had no time to pause or look around: ten inaugural balls were waiting, and they had less time to prepare, one aide pointed out, than most teenagers did for their proms. Malia and Sasha saw more of their new home that evening than their parents did: the staff planned a scavenger hunt for them amid the house's historical treasures, and when they walked into the East Room, the actual Jonas Brothers were standing there, ready to give them and their friends a private concert.

In real life, the balls were rushed and exhausting for the Obamas to attend. They danced ten times to the same song, "At Last" by Etta James, hearing the same lyrics over and over. But the version shown on television was stunning, one of those rare moments when presidential symbolism, personal history, and the nation's emotions met and fused. The Obamas were so young, Michelle like a bride in her long white dress, and what they had accomplished was so monumental. They had arrived, African Americans had arrived, the country had arrived. The pop star Beyoncé Knowles serenaded them, looking a little choked up. "Life is like a song," she crooned. "Here we are in heaven."

At 1:00 a.m., the Obamas returned to the White House for the real celebration, a private party for their family and closest friends and allies—downstairs, in the entertaining spaces, not upstairs in the home they still had not really seen that day. Celebrities including Oprah Winfrey and Gayle King mingled with new cabinet officials, the first lady's relatives from the South Side, and the president's best friends from Chicago, Marty Nesbitt and Eric Whitaker and their wives, as Wynton Marsalis played. A major topic of discussion was what to call the man who had just been sworn in that morning. Strangers and West Wing colleagues would call him Mr. President, of course, and Vernon Jordan, the former Clinton adviser and a relative of Valerie Jarrett's, told them to address him that way as well. "You have to have that reverence for the office," he had told Whitaker earlier that day.

But the new president had given Nesbitt and Whitaker a special charge: they were the ones who were supposed to keep him normal while in office. They were black men in a sea of white advisers, a midwestern businessman and a doctor among Washington regulars, friends who affectionately razzed Obama and had shared too many basketball games with him to count, so close to the president they earned inauguration seats right near Jill Biden, the vice president's wife. While they were staying put in Chicago, they had arranged to spend each one of the first few weekends of the administration in the White House with the Obamas. It wasn't the first time they had served a protective function: during the painful fracas over provocative statements made by their pastor, the Reverend Jeremiah Wright Jr., during the campaign, they had rotated, along with Valerie Jarrett, traveling with the candidate, so he would never be without a friend close by. Now their friend told him to keep calling him Barack.

The first lady could not stay awake. It was too late, she had done too much, and she went upstairs to fall asleep for the first time in the presidential bedroom alone. The new president was in no mood to let the day end. The scene that day on the mall, with citizens of every color and class, had been everything he hoped for, he said later, visual proof of his conviction that the country really could move past its old divides. He had felt a little disembodied from the celebrations, though, because he could not experience the Metro trains crowded with revelers, the festive air in the streets. Now he could let the day's solemnity slip away. He chatted and beamed, more relaxed than friends had seen him in a while.

"Tomorrow morning you're going to wake up in the White House," Rachel Goslins, a friend, commented to Obama as the hour grew very late. The remark didn't really register. After two years of campaigning on the road, he could pretty much sleep anywhere, he replied.

Listening to the remark, Julius Genachowski, Goslins's husband, realized how programmed his friend's life had become. The prior few days had been a series of moments for Obama to master, lines to say, and he hadn't had time to think about what it would be like to wake up in the morning, stare at the same bedroom ceiling that Nixon and Reagan had, and realize that he was president of the United States.

"Yeah, but you only have your first morning in the White House once," Goslins countered. Obama paused, the thought sinking in. "You know, you're right," he said, smiling.

He turned to head upstairs. But there was one problem: he had no idea where he was going.

That was the Obamas' situation as they moved into the White House: they were supposedly in charge, but they had surprisingly little control over the world around them. Through the decades, the residence staff, Secret Service, and military attachés had formulated the rules that ran presidential life: how many sharpshooters on the White House roof provided cover for the figures relaxing below on the Truman Balcony; how many Secret Service agents had to accompany each family member when they left the White House grounds. They determined when the first lady could taste a cookie baked for her by a first grader and how many staff were wholly devoted to the president's practical needs (at least two valets to dress, groom, and pack for him, a navy steward to serve him meals, a maître d' and six butlers for the residence, and two personal aides for everything else). Certain staff members could watch over the moment-to-moment locations of first family members on little screens that noted their Secret Service code names ("Renegade" for the president, "Renaissance" for the first lady) and their whereabouts inside or outside the White House. In historical terms, it was ironic: part of the very idea of the United States was that its leader should be a regular citizen; George Washington, who supervised the plans for the White House, wanted it to look like a house, not a European palace. Yet twenty-three decades later, European monarchies had mostly faded away, while the Obamas stepped into new lives that seemed in many ways to belong to nineteenth-century regents, with a circle of staff whose size and degree of specialization seemed to rival that of a royal court.

Starting that first week, Barack and Michelle found themselves drawn into two separate worlds. Advisers planned the president's first days as a tableau of action and progress, to show him quickly making good on his campaign promises. His first calls to foreign leaders went to Mahmoud Abbas, of the Palestinian Authority, Israeli prime minister Ehud Olmert, and Jordan's King Abdullah, to tell them he was committed to achieving Israeli-Palestinian peace in his first term. He met with the Joint Chiefs of Staff and the national security team to discuss ending the war in Iraq and signed directives tightening rules on lobbyists working in government.

Obama knew he would have no time to settle into presidential decision making. Over three million jobs had vanished in the prior year, and the pace of the losses was still increasing. Over three million households had received foreclosure notices. In the worst-hit cities, entire neighborhoods looked hollowed-out, the driveways empty. Food banks were reporting bare shelves. "That was the worst economics briefing of a president-elect since 1932," Austan Goolsbee, an economic adviser from the University of Chicago, told Obama after a particularly grim meeting a few weeks prior to the inauguration.

"That's not even my worst briefing this week," Obama replied.

He was talking about the national security situation. Eight years after the September 11 attacks and the launch of the U.S. war in Afghanistan, the country was still home to al-Qaeda forces, an unstable government, rampant corruption, a resurgent Taliban, and possibly Osama bin Laden. Pakistan, its neighbor, was an expensive and slippery American ally with uncertain loyalties and nuclear material that did not seem entirely secure. Years of U.S. military action in Muslim countries had roused the resentments of a new generation of fighters who were planning attacks on American soil. The military brass wanted tens of thousands more troops to prevent the war in Afghanistan from being lost, but that meant sacrificing more American lives, not to mention funds, to what might be a hopeless cause.

Obama believed that shuttering the Guantánamo detention camp, a symbol of Bush's post-9/11 wars and American abuses of power, would help restore the U.S. reputation abroad and calm tensions with the Muslim world. Two days after his inauguration, he signed orders saying that the facility would be closed within a year. During the signing ceremony, Obama's lids were heavy, his face puffy with exhaustion, and he tripped a little over his lines. America would not "continue with a false choice between our safety and our ideals," he said, repeating his campaign promise. "The message we are sending around the world is that the United States intends to prosecute the ongoing struggle against violence and terrorism . . . and we are going to do so in a manner that is consistent with our values and our ideals." An audience applauded and news cameras clicked away.

The following day, American drone aircraft launched missiles at two houses in the remote Pakistani mountain region near the Afghanistan border. It was Obama's first strike on terrorist suspects; he had signed those papers without an audience or the media present. Some of his supporters had predicted he would scale back drone attacks, which spared U.S. troops but frequently killed civilians, and spurred Muslim anger that the United States was conducting a callous, remote-control war. The supporters were wrong. Fifteen people died in those first two strikes, at least four of them suspected al-Qaeda recruits. Three of the other dead were children.

The new first lady, meanwhile, was figuring out how Malia and Sasha could have playdates with their new school friends. Hosting friends was fine, but if her daughters were invited elsewhere, how much did she need to know about the other parents and whether they could be trusted? Other pressing questions were how the girls should move around the greater White House and who should and should not be allowed in their presence. Thousands of tourists tramped through the White House each year — a fact that, according to Laura

Bush, inevitably horrified visiting foreign leaders, whose homes were not open for public viewing. The Obamas were committed to expanding the tour program, but would that mean confining Malia and Sasha to the two floors of the private quarters? To shield them from view would mean restricting their movements; to let them run freely might mean strangers snapping cell phone pictures. All Michelle wanted was for her girls to be able to run and play and not worry, said Susan Sher.

Those were just two of the puzzles of White House life she confronted. The house was grand but antiquated and eccentric. The landline in the residence rang in only one room, and if she happened to be in another room she missed the call. (After that happened multiple times, the first lady set up phone dates ahead of time with her brother, Craig Robinson.) The White House florist, chef, and curator needed to confer regularly with the first lady, but a decade after most Americans had work email addresses, they still did not. The Internet connections throughout the White House were old and balky. Living there was also expensive. The first family did not pay rent, official entertaining was covered with government funds, and the Democratic National Committee sponsored political events. But presidents and first ladies paid for their own food and personal entertaining, and because of the huge residence staff, the prices were at Ritz-Carlton levels.

One long-standing precept of the Obama household was that Barack was not a big shot at home—he was another member of the family, with the same responsibilities. As Michelle said countless times during the campaign, he was not excused from picking up his dirty socks. "When Barack's home he's going to be part of this life," she said. "He doesn't come home as the grand poobah."

But things did not work that way in the White House, where the president received a different level of service than everyone else, including members of his own family. The military valets looked after his wardrobe, laundered his clothes, packed for trips, and arrayed his closet with surgical precision: every t-shirt folded with origamilike perfection, each pair of trousers hanging the same distance from the next. But the valets did not touch the first lady's or the girls' things. (Jill Biden, wife of Vice President Joe Biden, had it worse: she lived with him in the Naval Observatory, their official residence, but often took her laundry home to Delaware.)

The residence staff were like a religious order, devoted to the first family and cloistered from the world. Presidents and first ladies came and went, but the household staff almost never changed. Many employees worked at the White House for thirty or forty years at a stretch, and jobs were often passed from parents to children. The staff performed their work with total seriousness; when it was time to order a swing set for the Obama girls, Rear Admiral Stephen Rochon, the chief usher, traveled to the factory in South Dakota where it was being made to inspect it. They were also discreet. Speaking to television shows or writing tell-alls, as some aides to Princess Diana had done in Britain, was unthinkable. William Allman, the White House curator in charge of historic furniture and artwork, liked to tell the story of an elderly staff member who returned to the White House Christmas party after his retirement. He was a bit unsteady on his feet and his former colleagues urged him to take a seat. "In forty years, I never sat in a chair here, and I'm not going to begin now," he replied.

At first, when the residence staff entered their private quarters, the Obamas tended to fall silent; could they discuss their business while people worked around them? The staff were supposed to be invisible, but the Obamas and their guests couldn't bring themselves to treat them that way. Many were middle-aged and older African

Americans—strangers to the president and first lady but also instantly familiar to them.

"The people who work in the White House remind me of my parents and grandparents, and I talk to them and respect them in that way," Marty Nesbitt said later. "My mother worked parties for people to help pay for my education," he said, and he and the Obamas felt they owed a debt to the older generation. "This is what all of our parents did in some way or another to make this possible for us. Those folks are our heroes, you know what I mean?" Indeed, Marian Robinson's father, Purnell Shields, had worked as a handyman in Chicago. When Michelle attended Princeton with the children of bankers and CEOs, one of her own aunts was a maid in town.

Now the Obamas and their guests were the ones whose sheets were being ironed and whose dishes were being cleared. "I'd be happy to take my plate back into the kitchen," Nesbitt tried to tell the staff during the first days of the administration, to no avail. "I'd be happy to get this for myself."

Marian Robinson refused to let the White House staff do her laundry. When Oprah wanted to interview her, she declined, because she liked to browse the discount racks at the Filene's Basement just up Connecticut Avenue, where no one recognized her. "They think I'm just another person who works at the mansion," she told an aide.

The president and first lady never publicly discussed the racial history of the White House, but it was baked into its very bricks, many of which had been fired and molded by slaves. During construction, slave pens stood across Lafayette Square, and several presidents brought their slaves with them while in office. Even the building's name had to do with race. After Theodore Roosevelt invited Booker T. Washington to dinner in 1901, the public outcry was so great that Roosevelt officially changed the building's name from the Executive Mansion to the White House, the multiple meanings clear. Until the Kennedy years, there were no black Secret Service agents. Even by 2009, only five of the four hundred and fifty or so artworks in the White House collection were by African American artists, and there were only a few nonwhite faces among the portraits and busts. It was a visual reminder that for over two centuries, the United States had been an ethnically, racially, and religiously diverse nation ruled by forty-two white Protestants and one white Catholic.

The Obamas' initial relationship with the staff, warm but awkward, was a clue. Behind the closed doors of the North Portico, there was going to be another, more private experience of being the first African American president and first lady, one that was less about the historical dimensions of the role than the simple, day-to-day experience of going where no one like you had ever gone before.

THE OBAMAS' RESPONSE TO THE strangeness and newness of the White House can be summed up in two words: they left. On February 13, only twenty-four days after the inauguration, the Obamas turned around and went back to Chicago. They had brought as much of their old world as possible with them to Washington: Marian Robinson; the Whitakers, and the Nesbitts on weekends; also their personal trainer and their personal chef. Still, the family was eager to return home as frequently as possible—every four to six weeks, the president predicted, they would slip back into their old lives for a weekend at a time.

The trip fell in the middle of an almost absurdly momentous seven days. Two days before, the administration had announced a $2.5 trillion bank bailout to stabilize the financial markets and prevent any more large institutions from going under. The day the Obamas flew westward, Congress passed the president's $787 billion stimulus package, a massive infusion of government spending intended to boost the economy. The following week, Obama would announce that he was sending 17,000 additional troops to Afghanistan. In a quieter presidency, any of the three decisions might have been enough to define an entire term.

Walking back into their old, familiar, comfortable house was strange. "When they moved to the White House, they really picked up and moved," one aide said. They had moved the girls' knickknacks and photos to the White House, to make it feel more familiar, but now their absence made everything look changed.

Back when the Obamas bought the house in 2005, it stood at the center of a busy patchwork of urban life. A main artery, Hyde Park Boulevard, was half a block away, another side of the house faced a synagogue, and a bus stop stood right out front. All day long, their home was surrounded by daily sidewalk dramas. But over the following few years, tourists arrived to gawk, and then the Secret Service set up surveillance. The day after the senator accepted his party's nomination for president, ugly concrete barricades went up at either end of the block. Three bus stops were permanently moved. Police officers and agents kept vigil and prevented passersby from strolling through. Neighbors had to give the Secret Service lists of visitors.

Now the Obamas came home to find massive black curtains dropped down two of the exterior sides of the house. This way, no one—nosy neighbors, photographers with long lenses, more menacing characters—would be able to target members of the first family. They were cut off even from familiar patches of trees or sky.

Secret Service agents later told neighbors and synagogue members by way of apology for the inconveniences that they were just improvising. Presidents and ex-presidents usually lived on estates or in large suburban homes, easy to protect because they were surrounded by generous margins of empty land. George and Laura Bush could escape to their ranch house in Crawford, Texas; after the presidency, they hadn't just bought a large house in spread-out Dallas but the one next door, too. The Secret Service had little experience with protecting a president who lived in a busy, dense environment, the agents confessed.

Staff had been confused about food for the weekend. Were the Obamas supposed to go back to making their own dinners? They couldn't just dispatch someone to pick up groceries and takeout, because the Secret Service was supposed to vet the purchase and preparation of everything the president ate. No option was easy; every option was costly. In the end, navy mess stewards came home with them to prepare their meals, which was a little bit strange; their house was not set up for a fleet of workers. Part of the point of coming home had been to regain some privacy, to slip back into their old lives for a day or two.

Valentine's Day fell on the second evening of their trip, and the first couple left their home for dinner at Table 52, a high-end downtown restaurant that served southern food. Like every modern president, Obama was constantly trailed by a handful of reporters and photographers on rotating "pool" duty, meaning that they shared whatever photos and information they got with fellow members of the media. The theory was that news could happen at any time, even when the president attended a birthday party or parent-teacher conference. The reality was that the system bred mutual resentment: presidents hated being unable to move around without a media team or change plans at the last moment, and pool reporters usually sat in vans outside wherever the president was visiting, often getting no more than a quick glimpse. That night the Obamas departed for dinner without the pool group, which caught up almost an hour later—a breach of standard practice on the first couple's part, and a sign of their newness to their suddenly confined lives.

As the weekend drew to a close, the Obamas came to the depressing realization that the simple act of going home had now become, as one staff member put it, "an ordeal." The place they thought would be a refuge was not easily accessible to them. A weekend trip back to Chicago would require weeks of preparations by staff members, another set of staff on the ground, a virtual blockade of the neighborhood, and considerable outlays of personal and federal funds. They had tied up traffic at rush hour, the president observed with dismay, looking down from the helicopter at a long line of stopped cars on Lake Shore Drive. They weren't trying to invade Normandy; they just wanted to go back to their house and neighborhood. "If you really want to just rest, it's easier to go to Camp David," Susan Sher said later.

As Air Force One brought them back east, Marian Robinson said something about going home — to Washington. Everyone's ears pricked up: *home?* The White House was still foreign, a museum, but Chicago was not the refuge they had imagined. When the Obamas arrived, aides asked them how the weekend had gone. They noticed that the president and first lady seemed subdued.

"We live in the White House now," Michelle Obama told them.

Chapter Three

LADIES AND GENTLEMEN, THE PRESIDENT OF THE UNITED STATES

FEBRUARY–MARCH 2009

The approach of the forty-third Super Bowl, with the Pittsburgh Steelers playing the Arizona Cardinals, raised a question in the White House: where would the forty-fourth president watch the game?

He would want to see it with friends, Valerie Jarrett, still one of his closest advisers, knew, and she asked aides to pull together a small party with Nesbitt, Whitaker, and a few others. But when the aides sat down to plan, they found themselves questioning just what they were putting together. This was one of the first times the president and the first lady would entertain in the White House, so perhaps their Super Bowl party should include a wider circle and send a welcoming message. They decided to include a few cabinet and congressional officials, including Republicans, from Pennsylvania and Arizona, and a few wounded veterans from the Iraq and Afghanistan wars, too.

Before the event, the first lady looked over the guest list, noticing unfamiliar name after unfamiliar name. Who is this person? Why are we inviting him? she asked aides. Explanations were summoned and provided. But she had made her point: the White House was her home, too, and she wanted some say over who was coming in. "There is nothing passive or unquestioning about her," one aide who worked on the party said, "and she is going to want to be consulted on even the small details." Those who had drawn up the guest list cringed at their mistake.

The party was held in the red-and-gilt White House theater, with movies and Nintendo Wii set up in the hallway outside for children. Waiters served pizza, hot dogs, and chicken sandwiches, and someone had managed to procure a batch of the gold-and-black Terrible Towels that Steelers fans waved around at games. Wounded veterans who had come straight from Walter Reed Army Medical Center, some with severe burn scars on their faces or with limbs missing, stood together in a cluster with a military aide.

The host greeted everyone and shook hands, but as soon as the game started he settled into his seat: a big velvet chair in front, marked off by a little name card. Nesbitt and Whitaker slid in next to him. The president had done his welcoming duties, and he was serious about following the action on-screen. "He was sitting up front, he was watching the game, and he didn't move," said Mike Doyle, a Democratic congressman from Pennsylvania. "He is not someone who is going to hold a Super Bowl party and spend the time talking, greeting, delivering messages, working," an aide observed. Obama just wasn't a classic political personality like Lyndon Johnson or his own vice president, Joe Biden; he didn't relish contact the way they did. Sometimes at social events, Michelle gave him his cues: sit here, be sure to say good-bye to so-and-so.

His high-minded views about principles and pandering extended even to which football teams he rooted for. Obama considered himself a true sports fan, and he had long-standing allegiances. He disdained the fact that some politicians rooted for whichever team was convenient or feigned neutrality for fear of offending rival fans. When it came to football, he rooted for the Chicago Bears, of course. He loved another team, too. Because Hawaii, where he'd grown up, had no football franchise, he became devoted to the Steelers, whose string of victories in the early 1970s rallied a city suffering from the collapse of the steel industry. When Dan Rooney, the team owner and a lifelong Republican, campaigned for him during the difficult days of the April 2008 Pennsylvania primary, the bond deepened. At a rally before the general election, Obama spotted Franco Harris, a star player from the glory days. He was so excited he called him out of the crowd and later campaigned with him, said Pennsylvania senator Bob Casey.

At the party, just two people cheered with abandon: Doyle, a rabid Steelers fan, and the president, who rooted equally hard for the team. (Several other guests said they were inhibited by the setting: could you really let loose in the White House, in front of the president?) Just before halftime, when a linebacker for the Steelers sprinted 100 yards for a touchdown, the president jumped out of his chair with excitement. "What do you think of that, Doyle?" he yelled. When another of the Steelers scored, a White House photographer captured the scene inside the theater: the president with his arms hoisted in a "touchdown" gesture. Everyone else had their hands by their sides.

After the Steelers had won and everyone went home, at least one of the party planners wondered if they should have kept the gathering entirely private — Barack Obama had only so much patience for official entertaining, people would expect a similar Super Bowl party the next year and the year after, and, once an event migrated from a private event to a political one, it was hard to take it back.

* * *

EVEN AMID THE CONFOUNDING CRISES of his first months in office, Barack Obama took satisfaction in a simple, glorious new truth: he was the president of the United States.

One day he walked out of a meeting in his chief of staff's office and began to flip through a stack of magazines on the desk of a young assistant to Emanuel. "Whose are these?" he asked the assistant. Well, they just get sent here, addressed to the chief of staff, she replied. Then she paused and rethought her answer. "But everything in the White House is yours...so technically they're yours," she said. The president shot her a satisfied look.

The following day, he passed her desk and the magazines again. "*Whose* magazines are these?" he asked. She had the answer ready this time. "They're *your* magazines, Mr. President," she said. Obama grinned and continued on his way.

He savored the perks of the presidency, like gliding over the Washington Monument in Marine One and holding swear-ins in the Oval Office for old friends like Julius Genachowski, who became his Federal Communications Commissioner. But his excitement at arriving ran much deeper than that. He had spent the entirety of his earlier career frustrated by the limits of what he could accomplish: he tried and rejected community organizing, and then the law, the Illinois state senate, and finally the U.S. Senate. They were all too slow for him, too ineffectual, and so he was always trying to climb higher, leveraging everything he had to get to the next level. (In the U.S. Senate, he did not pass any major legislation of his own.) Now that he was finally in the highest office in the land, he wanted to pass sweeping bills that would tackle long-term, fundamental problems, which would create more stability for the country. He had to clean up the financial crisis first, but then he would be able to move on to his real agenda, which included dealing with a rapidly warming earth and fixing a health care system so expensive it might eventually bankrupt the country. "If you can't do it as a president of the United States it likely can't be done," was the way Whitaker put it.

Those early months of the presidency took on a strange quality in retrospect. Obama had stepped into the job with such apparent ease. Even with the harrowing task of stabilizing the country's financial system, even with a terrifying ratio between his level of experience and the tasks he faced, he almost never allowed himself to look ruffled or skittish in public, and advisers said he remained confident and deliberate in meetings. He was relying on the lessons of his campaign, an aide said later—ignore the naysayers, don't change course. But mistakes and problems from that period—with management, isolation, and relationships with Republicans—would haunt him later. It wasn't clear if Obama was oblivious at the time, too new to the presidency to see the trouble, or just too stubborn to acknowledge it.

His first task was to pass a massive government stimulus program to kick-start the economy, and he was eager, hopeful, in the mood to brainstorm about it. He wanted a dramatic, innovative centerpiece for the stimulus: a moon shot–type project to demonstrate that Americans could still pull off ambitious public works. His favorite idea was to build an advanced smart grid to transport new forms of power across long distances—say, from wind farms in the Dakotas to the people of Chicago. Legally, though, the project was a nightmare: the government had no eminent domain power for electricity lines, so building such a grid would mean negotiating with every tiny municipality along the way.

I'm the president. Can't I get this done? he asked his advisers.

Actually, no, they told him. The smart grid idea was scrapped.

The president thought he would be able to win at least some Republican support for the stimulus. The two parties had a history of coming together at times of crisis, economists across the spectrum agreed it was necessary, and he rejected some advisers' calls for a $1.2 trillion package in favor of an $800 billion package he thought would be more politically palatable—a compromise before he came to the table. That package, his economists were telling him, would hold the unemployment level, then at 7.6 percent, below 8 percent.

Being the Democrat who could work with Republicans was part of his political identity, and it was true to his conciliatory nature and the way he had grown up, mediating and translating between disparate groups. He had won the *Harvard Law Review* presidency by signaling, shortly before the election, that he was no knee-jerk liberal—though he was black and supported affirmative action, he sympathized with conservative objections to it. In the Illinois state senate, he had been closer to some Republicans than Democrats; in the presidential campaign, he argued that Hillary Clinton was too partisan to unify a badly fractured country and succeeded in winning the votes of some prominent Republicans.

Not this time. The stimulus passed without a single Republican vote in the House and only three in the Senate, a worrying sign for the Obama promise of bipartisanship.

The Republican strategy was led by Mitch McConnell, the Senate majority leader, a Kentuckian with large, calm eyes, and as natural a foil to the president as any novelist could have conjured up. Obama's political career could be seen as a quest to be accepted; McConnell relished being vilified, hanging unflattering editorial cartoons on the walls of his Senate office. Where Obama was subtle and intellectual, McConnell was a tough, canny tactician who believed in brute repetition of anxiety-inducing messages about the mounting federal deficit, bailouts, and terrorist attacks. Facing Democratic control of Capitol Hill and the White House, not to mention a party that seemed adrift, McConnell told Republicans that the key to remaining relevant was voting together to oppose Obama's agenda. Together they could deny him the bipartisan label he craved and make his agenda look one-sided, even extreme.

The most effective political attacks are often psychological, aimed not just at convincing the public but stunning the target. Like the swiftboating campaign against Senator John Kerry during the 2004 presidential race, they attempted to take away the accomplishment the victim most prided himself on—in Kerry's case, his distinguished record of combat in Vietnam, which opponents called fake. McConnell's attacks on Obama were cunning in their assault on his own self-image; it was as if he had been in the Obamas' apartment all of those years, listening in on the president's hesitation about politics, his desire to be a postpartisan collector of the best ideas. Without Republican votes, he could not fulfill the very premise of his candidacy, and he looked more like the thing he never wanted to be: a typical Democrat.

Obama responded to the stimulus votes with disappointment and incredulity. "He really couldn't believe it," one former adviser said. "He seemed stumped, truly stumped."

The dire economic circumstances, coupled with the enormous agenda he had promised to deliver, cut his patience with politics even further. He privately complained that even tasks that seemed outwardly serious were often filled with what he called empty Washington symbolism. Obama felt the federal budget he and his team had to prepare in February played "into every annoying thing about Washington," as Peter Orszag, the former budget director, put it. The economic projections required to make a budget could not responsibly be made years in advance, and besides, the president's budget was never passed as is; he would propose one and then Congress would take his recommendation and pass its own. So the administration document, requiring massive effort to produce, was really just a target for attacks, more ritual than substance, the new president felt. "It's all a Kabuki thing," he said with exasperation, and he did not want to participate any more than necessary. "Let's not get in a holy war over things that don't actually have any meaning," he counseled his staff — words that took on special irony years later, when budget battles resulted in the gravest defeat of his presidency.

That first budget ended up being "an awkward mix of idealism and ignoring reality," an official who worked on it later said. Despite rapidly mounting concern about federal spending, including the bank bailout and stimulus, Obama included everything he wanted to do in his first year, including massive, costly health care and energy bills. The economic crisis made those measures *more* necessary, not less, he argued: the crisis had resulted from the neglect of long-festering problems, and American stability would ultimately depend on having affordable health care, less dependence on fossil fuels, a stronger education system and more renewable energy resources. In addition to retooling the health care system by Memorial Day and energy policy shortly thereafter, he also wanted to overhaul immigration laws, revamp the financial regulatory system, and tackle a host of other matters. That was just the domestic to-do list; foreign affairs were a whole different, equally daunting matter. Nearly everyone told him his plans were too ambitious, including his vice president and chief of staff, who opposed taking on the health care initiative immediately. Obama brushed them aside. "I wish I had the luxury of just dealing with a modest recession or just dealing with health care or just dealing with energy or just dealing with Iraq or just dealing with Afghanistan," Obama told *New York Times* reporters in March. "We've got to use this moment to solve some big problems once and for all so that the next generation is not saddled with even worse problems than we have now."

In fact, an entire movement was burgeoning across the country to tell the president his plans were too ambitious — that government spending was out of control. In late February, after the administration announced a plan to refinance home owner mortgages, a former trader named Rick Santelli took to the cable airwaves to say that Obama's plans rewarded bad behavior; that they subsidized irresponsible home owners. "This is America! How many of you people want to pay for your neighbor's mortgage [for a house] that has an extra bathroom [when that family] can't pay their bills?" he asked. He suggested holding a tea party in Chicago, a modern equivalent of the revolutionary protests about unfair government burdens. In his daily briefing with reporters, Robert Gibbs said Santelli had misinterpreted the president's plan but also lashed back at him in unusually personal terms: "I'd be happy to buy him a cup of coffee — decaf," the press secretary said. Gibbs, a former goalie, was highly protective of the president; at his best, he could speak with eloquence, force, and precision. But he also tended to be sarcastic and dismissive at the podium, and that day in February, he did not seem to recognize that many viewers had found Santelli's speech galvanizing; it reflected their own anxieties about the state of the country. Santelli's video became an Internet sensation, and fans planned rallies for the following week across the country: the first wave of protests by the Tea Party, which would eventually halt the Obama agenda.

The irony was that in those early days, Obama countered his disappointment with Washington with his faith in the country and citizens beyond it. The presidential campaign had left him feeling extremely optimistic about voters: at the end of the day, they were serious-minded, and even if Washingtonians didn't always understand him, people beyond its borders would, he believed. "If you just play it straight with them, if you explain to them, here's our challenge, here's how we've gotten here and here's where I think we need to go, then I have enormous confidence that the American people will rise up to the challenge," he said in another early interview.

He said it again in a late February press conference. "I am the eternal optimist," he told reporters. "I think that over time people respond to civility and rational argument."

THE HIGH DRAMA OF THOSE early months initially imposed unity on Obama's team, a sense of working for an extraordinary president at an extraordinary time. "Everyone was in the foxhole together," recalled Orszag, making emergency decisions on rescuing banks and modifying mortgages. When the first lady encountered economic advisers in the hallways or at events, she greeted them with a little cheerleading: pats on the back, great job, thank you for what you are doing to help him.

The new president had never run anything larger than his presidential campaign (which was actually run by David Plouffe, his campaign manager). He was autonomous by habit, with a suspicion of traditional organizational structures and a penchant for direct control, and he set up his team in an unusual way that seemed intended both to compensate for his lack of Washington experience and protect him from Washington.

He stacked his White House with heavyweight experts who were strong in areas where he was weak: Joe Biden, an expert retail politician with warm relationships on Capitol Hill and years of foreign policy experience, and Robert Gates, George W. Bush's secretary of defense, who continued in the same role for Obama. He not only convinced Hillary Clinton, his former rival, to be his secretary of state, but backed her up with separate envoys for the Middle East, Pakistan, Afghanistan, and Iran, and in addition to a full array of cabinet officials, he added high-level subject-matter specialists to his staff, like Carol Browner, in charge of energy policy. Some of his appointees held clashing philosophies — for example, Timothy Geithner, his Treasury secretary, was concerned with deficit reduction, while Lawrence

Summers, his chief economic adviser, favored aggressive stimulus spending—but Obama said he wanted rich debates, and that he would be able to mediate disagreements and make the final calls.

But for his closest advisers, he chose personal intimates who had been crucial in his rise. David Axelrod took charge of the presidential message even though his experience was in campaigns, not government. Pete Rouse was Obama's chief of staff in the U.S. Senate and one of the few Washingtonians to whom the president was close. Robert Gibbs, who had devoted the past five years of his life to the president but did not seem to care much for reporters, became press secretary. Technically, everyone reported to Emanuel, who reported to the president, but that was just on paper. Obama had his own relationships, and there was little hierarchy to the group.

His most unusual and revealing appointment was Jarrett, serene, watchful, and ever-present in the Obamas' lives since Michelle's city hall days. An African American woman raised in Iran, where her father could get a better job than he could in the United States, she kept a list of "life lessons" on her computer, including: "Take time to be kind to everyone" and "Effective leadership depends on your ability to connect and motivate people, not on your title, position or power." She was only five years older than the president, but her relationship with the Obamas was so nurturing and vigilant it was almost maternal. (When Michelle Obama spoke about her, she alternated between mother and sibling analogies.) Since leaving city hall to become a real estate executive, she had absorbed the Obamas into her professional and social network, helping to cultivate the elite African American donors who helped propel Obama to the U.S. Senate and then the presidency. That network was "The Family," as Brian Mathis, a financier, put it, and Jarrett was "the mother of all of our ambition." During the 2008 campaign, Obama told friends he couldn't look at Jarrett during speeches lest he become too emotional and start to cry.

Obama lived on the road in 2007 and 2008, and Jarrett did many things he couldn't, keeping an eye on headquarters, serving as emissary to outsiders, dealing with tricky matters of race. She was deliberative, diplomatic, and precise, but Jarrett's relationship with other advisers could be awkward: she wasn't fluent in national politics, and her very presence sometimes seemed like an implicit critique of them. "I have no agenda" other than the president's success, she liked to say, which suggested her colleagues had others. Her closeness with Michelle Obama, so often critical of her husband's team, only underscored the impression, and other aides thought they were in cahoots. Jarrett represented, second only to Michelle Obama, a way of thinking that some Washingtonians, including Rahm Emanuel, had little patience for: that Barack Obama was different from other politicians.

Because Jarrett was petite and soft-spoken, it was easy to miss how much protection she gave the Obamas, how she had watched over them as they entered one foreign world and then another. Sometime between 2004 and 2008, their lives had become too much for two people to handle. Jarrett, who knew them better than almost anyone else, became the third person to make the leap with them, the way you would add extra memory to a computer to handle a massive task. She was ready to do anything for them, from vetting potential secretaries of state to calling a restaurant to say that the Obamas were coming in for dinner and expected no gossip items. She served another, hidden function too, two people close to the Obamas said: as marital guardian and glue, mediating between the president and first lady when they were at odds. In the White House, she was the only person integrated into every aspect of their lives: she was a senior adviser in the West Wing, in charge of outreach to government officials and community groups; she was the first lady's closest counselor; and she, Nesbitt, and Whitaker had become tight friends. She even vacationed with the Obamas.

Emanuel had not wanted Jarrett to come, even speaking to former Illinois governor Rod Blagojevich about appointing her to Obama's old Senate seat (and inadvertently stepping into the middle of a federal investigation of the governor). Hometown friends often fared poorly in the West Wing, Jarrett didn't have a clear place in the organization, and she couldn't be both friend and staff at once—the roles were inherently in conflict. For instance, would Jarrett repeat everything she heard to the Obamas, or would she maintain solidarity with other senior staff?

Obama dismissed concerns about not just Jarrett and Emanuel but other crucial members of his team. The job he gave Summers, a top economist and former Treasury secretary, required furthering the views of others, and Summers was not exactly the collaborative type: he had been forced to resign as president of Harvard University because of his poor relationship with the faculty. But during the campaign, Obama had come to depend on his lucid explanations of the economic crisis, and he was confident he could extract the best from Summers and compensate for his weaknesses.

Obama had always had a high estimation of his ability to cast and run his operation. When David Plouffe, his campaign manager, first interviewed for a job with him in 2006, the senator gave him a warning. "I think I could probably do every job on the campaign better than the people I'll hire to do it," he said. "It's hard to give up control when that's all I've known." Obama said nearly the same thing to Patrick Gaspard, whom he hired to be the campaign's political director. "I think that I'm a better speechwriter than my speechwriters," Obama told him. "I know more about policies on any particular issue than my policy directors. And I'll tell you right now that I'm gonna think I'm a better political director than my political director."

Shortly before inauguration, when a Democrat with years of White House experience questioned Obama about who was going to manage his administration, Obama repeated pretty much the same thing he had said to Plouffe and Gaspard. Summers had the wrong personality to head the National Economic Council, the outside adviser said, and Emanuel was a fighter by nature. Who was going to make sure the whole structure worked, to hold everyone together in tough moments to arrive at the best decisions, the way a White House chief of staff inevitably needed to? "*I* will," Obama said, leaving the more experienced man concerned. Did he have any idea how busy, how under assault, a president of the United States could be?

ON MARCH 5, THE SAME DAY he spoke at a kickoff event for his health care overhaul efforts, the president met with Brad Pitt. The movie star was an architecture aficionado and he wanted to speak with the president about government funding for low-cost, environmentally friendly homes in New Orleans's Ninth Ward, devastated by Hurricane Katrina.

Waiting outside the Oval Office, Pitt was friendly and chatty with his escorts, but after he walked in, the encounter turned awkward. The actor, so assured on-screen, barely said a thing, and he seemed overcome by meeting the president. (He was in a state of "respectful awe," Pitt said later.) The president gently chastised Jarrett afterward for doing all of the talking. She was just trying to help Pitt relax, she said.

By that time, the president and Jarrett had seen similar reactions many times: Walking into the Oval Office sometimes did strange things to people. Visitors entered through a narrow, dark hallway, a plain wooden door swung open, and there stood one of the most famous and powerful people in the world, in a room that seems designed to amplify his authority. Visitors' own voices often sounded unfamiliar to them, said Bill Burton, a former deputy press secretary, because the curved walls made sound bounce in unexpected patterns.

Some grew silent like Pitt, others babbled, and a few burst into tears. The effect was particularly strong for older African Americans, laying eyes on a fellow black man at the president's desk.

Even the president's advisers were not entirely immune from the Brad Pitt syndrome. Earlier in his career, they had been mentors: in the 2004 U.S. Senate race, Axelrod had been a guru, an authority Obama was lucky to work with. When Obama gave a lackluster performance in a radio debate—he had barely prepared, flipping through a binder a few minutes beforehand—Axelrod chewed him out over the phone. You should have blown the other candidates out of the *water,* a staffer remembers Axelrod saying.

But in the presidential campaign, Obama took Axelrod and other advisers on the ride of their lives, making them famous, securing places for them in history. They were dazzled by what he had accomplished, and the White House, with its "Hail to the Chief" rituals, formalized the change. Jarrett gave an interview to writer and *New Yorker* editor David Remnick in which she said that Obama was "just too talented to do what ordinary people do." When Axelrod, Gibbs, and others walked out of the Oval Office, they tended to relive their conversations with the president, other aides noticed, going over the best parts out loud.

ONLY FIVE YEARS BEFORE he became president, Obama was advertising his email address (senobama@aol.com) in the *Hyde Park Herald,* and during the presidential campaign, he had kept in touch via Black-Berry with hundreds, maybe thousands of people—former law professors, basketball buddies, donors, relatives. Now the network he had spent his life building was no longer accessible by email; because of legal and security concerns, he could only correspond with his top advisers and a few friends. Every one of his meetings was a big deal, with a fixed agenda and carefully chosen representatives. The stiffness of it all, the loss of natural, spontaneous conversation, left Obama impatient, exasperated, and hungry for information. Unable to email with more than a few confidants like Nesbitt and Whitaker, he scanned nytimes.com headlines on his clunky BlackBerry, not the real thing but an expensive, hack-proof military facsimile. It was a staggering shift for the politician who had, more than any other, embraced the wired world in his campaign. "What's in the news, Burton?" he continually asked, even though Burton was reading the same stories as the president. He requested that his staff share with him ten letters per day, out of thousands he received, so he could gain a more direct sense of what Americans were thinking. Compared with real, everyday contact with the outside world, ten letters seemed like nothing. But in the White House, it was something, and the president referenced them constantly.

Of all the concentric rings that surrounded Obama—staff, security, and the like—the hardest to escape was his own body. He had always been able to step outside himself, to play the writer and observer, but how could he watch everyone when everyone was watching him? One day Obama told Jarrett he had something important to discuss with her, but first he had a question. "Can I talk to you just as Barack Obama your friend, not Barack Obama the president?" he asked.

At least one person still treated Barack Obama normally: his wife.

Michelle Obama had never been easy to impress, and she had a way of "puncturing"—his word—the pomp around him. She poked fun at his long motorcade, saying "it's like the stagecoach, the caboose, the helicopter, the ambulance...the dogsled." And when he briefly introduced Stevie Wonder at a small concert in the East Room in late February, she wondered out loud why he needed to speak from a little podium with a presidential seal. Couldn't he just grab a microphone? If they were taping a video message together and he flubbed a line, she teased him and he teased her back.

Only she and the girls walked into the Oval Office unannounced. On a snowy day in early March, the president and his advisers were conferring when high-pitched peals of laughter drifted in from the Rose Garden. Obama and aides gathered at the window to see the president's wife and daughters chasing each other across the snow-covered lawn. A few minutes later, the president's family, dusted in white and laughing, tumbled into the Oval Office to tell him about their adventures.

Occasionally the president greeted his wife in a terse *I'm-working* tone. But typically he seemed thrilled, after all the years of separation, to see her in the middle of the day. He had a new nickname for her: FLOTUS, short for "First Lady of the United States" and a spin on POTUS, the acronym for his job. "So how's FLOTUS today?" he liked to ask her. *Floe-tuss* — it was a silly-sounding word, a government acronym for the woman who slept beside him and gave birth to his children, but coming from his lips, it had the ring of told-you-so triumph. For so long, she had questioned his promises and reassurances, and now Michelle Obama was — what do you know? — successor to Martha Washington and Eleanor Roosevelt.

One day during that first March in the White House, the Obamas found each other in the Red Room just before entering a reception for an African American publishing group. In addition to his usual briefings, the president had spent the day addressing state legislators about the stimulus and speaking with New York mayor Michael Bloomberg, California governor Arnold Schwarzenegger, and Pennsylvania governor Ed Rendell about decaying transportation infrastructure. The sessions weren't meetings in the conventional sense of people sitting around a table talking; they were highly choreographed, with prepared remarks by the president in the first meeting and a visit from reporters during the second.

For a few moments before the event in the Red Room, he paused and relaxed. "Hey, you look good," he said to the first lady, eyeing her gray top and long strand of pearls. He slipped both arms around her waist and grinned; she gave him a small, satisfied smile. Staff members wondered if they should give the first couple a moment to themselves, but the audience on the other side of the door was waiting.

BY SIX THIRTY OR SO, the Obamas were usually reunited for the evening. The president's journey from the Oval Office upstairs took just a few minutes, and Malia and Sasha often ran to greet him. They still were not used to him being around, and they sometimes tackled him as if he might escape again.

Obama had an unusual rule for a president: he refused to miss dinner with his family more than two nights a week. Barring special circumstances, that was the most he was willing to tolerate being away from his family. Quick trips downstairs for receptions were fine, but anything that caused him to miss the family meal—cross-country trips, dinner parties, gala invitations, fund-raising or working dinners, and so on—were limited to twice a week.

Obama enforced the rule avidly. "You, you, and you, stay here," he would sometimes say at the end of a meeting with advisers, pointing to a few of those assembled, and after everyone else left, he would bring up a particular event on the schedule. "I'm really unhappy about it," he would say. "We have an agreement I'm only supposed to be out twice a week."

He set up his schedule that way intentionally, for Michelle's sake. "Because he had been on the road for two years before that, he wanted to make sure he was home for dinner and spending time with his family," Jarrett said. In the White House, he wanted to finally give his wife what they had never had: a family life like the one she had grown up in, with everyone sitting down together every night. But the decision came with a price, reinforcing the already severe isolation of the presidency.

Though Obama was relatively new to Washington, he wasn't going to spend his evenings getting to know people there; the White House turned down virtually every dinner party or gala invitation the president got, and many excursions were never even proposed in the first place; staff knew his limitations. And because Obama was so intent on making up the time with his family, "there just weren't that many hours in the day left for reaching out and just picking up the phone" to outsiders, Jarrett said. Obama delegated that task to his staff, she said.

So nearly every evening, the family sat at their round dining room table and ate a meal prepared not by the White House chef but by Sam Kass, who had cooked for them in Chicago. Outsiders rarely joined them. The Bushes had frequently hosted dinners upstairs, Laura Bush let television crews in to document the décor, and President Clinton invited officials over for chats, sometimes asking them to wait a few minutes on the Truman Balcony while he helped Chelsea with math problems. Once, after a late-night interview, Clinton invited the historian Taylor Branch to stay over, and the next morning over breakfast, Branch found himself staring at the president's pale, hairy legs resting on the polished floor. The Obamas did not let others, especially not outsiders, see them like that. They never hosted political events at home, and only a few of the president's aides had ever seen the place. Often, even Marian Robinson did not join them for dinner, preferring to give them time as a foursome. "I'm going home," she would say as she went up the steps to the third floor.

Sometimes the Obamas slipped into formal wear afterward and headed back downstairs for a reception. (In those early months, Wednesday nights meant congressional charm offensives, receptions downstairs for elected officials from both sides of the aisle.) But aides dreaded calling the president back down to the Oval Office to deal with emergencies, because he so clearly wanted to be upstairs. Crises at 8:30 or 9:00 p.m. were a little less uncomfortable than those at 6:30

or 7:00 p.m., they said, because at least they didn't have to pull him away from dinner with the girls.

Once Malia and Sasha were asleep, the first couple was finally alone. For the two years of the campaign, they had spoken mostly by phone, checking in once or more a day, sometimes speaking in generalities if others were around. Now they could confer at the end of the day in private.

In public, the first lady said little of substance about her husband's work. But she was tracking things keenly. Beyond Jarrett, she had only a few sources in the West Wing, and she barely knew many of her husband's cabinet members and aides. She viewed the events of the presidency more as an outsider, her aides said, reading the daily press clippings distributed throughout the White House, following the public conversation online and on television. (Of course, she had the best source of all: her husband, following long presidential habit, sometimes told her about top-secret matters; after the fact, when the information became public, she would sometimes admit to aides what she had known beforehand.) There were also entire swaths of the presidential portfolio in which she had little knowledge or interest: nuclear disarmament, for example, or trade negotiations with China.

But Michelle Obama knew and cared a great deal about what was going on in the United States, and she also cared tremendously about the internal workings of the White House — how her husband was holding up, how things were working inside, how the administration was communicating with the public. On those fronts, she was worried from very early on, and she challenged her husband in a way that few others dared.

She knew he wanted home to be a refuge, and she did not want to hound him after a long day, but she was genuinely troubled by problems, sometimes more troubled than he was, and she could not stand by. She was a planner, a long-term thinker, and she did not see the president's work governed by a cohesive enough strategy. His agenda was ambitious, and yet things still felt far too improvisational to her. "She's detail-oriented," said an aide. "She's a hard worker herself so she requires perfection. That was true on the campaign and it's true now." The message and communications operation also worried her. It seemed too reactive, like the administration was issuing day-to-day responses instead of telling its own compelling story about the president's actions.

Throughout his political career, Michelle had been the person who helped link her cerebral, self-contained husband to other people. Now she told him for the umpteenth time to let go of the policy details and communicate more simply and directly. "You know what? People don't care about that," she would say upon hearing him describe the details of some initiative, according to an aide. "This is what people care about," she would declare, describing a more basic, more immediately comprehensible need.

She also saw the demands that others placed on her husband and the demands that he was placing on himself. Whatever the problem was, the White House seemed to view some sort of speech or statement by the president as a solution. He would go on a trip, come home for just a few hours of sleep, and launch into another presidential workday, exhausting himself, and she did not understand why the vice president and cabinet officials were not sharing more of the load. By March his hair was already a more silvery shade than it had been at inauguration. "He was aging before her eyes," as one former aide put it. Washingtonians often saw Obama as too controlling—someone who didn't like others, even cabinet members, to speak for him or even write his speeches. It was a problem that he had admitted to himself in the past, acknowledging that it was hard for him to surrender control. But the first lady cast the problem in slightly different terms: he wasn't getting enough support from his direct advisers, she told others. The fact that he was now president only seemed to reinforce her exacting standards. This wasn't a campaign—it was the *White House*. They couldn't afford mistakes.

Unlike during the campaign, however, Michelle rarely confronted her husband's advisers directly; she did not want to be, or be seen as, the kind of first lady who interfered in West Wing business. Her relationships with Emanuel, Axelrod, Gibbs, and others took on an indirect quality, with tension communicated through a quiet word from Jarrett or, sometimes, in the West Wing, through rumors of her dissatisfaction. Michelle still sent emails when she saw a news item that concerned her, but now she sent them to Jarrett, who passed them on to others with the first lady's name taken off. "I didn't see this myself," Jarrett would write to an aide, "but can you track it down?" Everyone knew that the messages had originated with Michelle.

However, it wasn't clear how seriously Obama took his wife's opinions about strategy or message. He was charmed by her concern, advisers said, but she wasn't fluent in those matters; she tended to overworry about what she saw on television. Once Susan Sher watched as the first lady brought up a personnel problem, her argument building and building to a crescendo. "She was like, you should do this, *dah dah dah dah* and *dah dah dah*," Sher said. The president just grinned at his wife, she smiled in recognition of how forceful she had been, and they both started to laugh. Sher's point was the intensity of Michelle's feelings, and the president's ability to diffuse them; but the question remained: was he listening to what she was saying?

The first lady liked to slip into bed by 9:30 or 10:00, but the president often spent several more hours in his upstairs office, formally called the Treaty Room. Unlike the Oval Office, which could seem more like a stage set than an actual place to work, this was a real office, with a computer and a printer, a television for keeping an eye on basketball games, and books and papers scattered over the huge desk.

Obama spent hours every night studying material, to the surprise of some of his advisers. As a candidate, his self-confidence often made him lazy, and he left even consequential tasks—such as writing and practicing his convention speech—until the last minute. But as president, he inhaled information, studying so hard in the evenings that he waved PowerPoint presentations away the next day. (He has a photographic memory, according to Jarrett.) As the hours ticked by, he went over memos from advisers line by line and returned them the next day with notes in his distinctive, bold handwriting. He went to the upstairs office on weekend evenings, too. After dinner he would say to his wife and the Whitakers or Nesbitts: you guys stay, have fun, I need to go work for a while.

Obama almost never made decisions downstairs, around other people. Faced with a big choice, he would absorb information and then talk things out with advisers, soliciting dissenting points of view, buttonholing meeting participants individually afterward to hear more. The conversation would usually end with: thanks, I'm going to sleep on this, with his aides often having no idea which way he was leaning. As a result, many of the most important moments of Barack Obama's presidency had no witnesses at all: they took place upstairs, the president silent and alone in his office.

Chapter Four

THE LADY WHO DID
NOT LUNCH

APRIL 2009

President Barack Obama spent the morning of Thursday, April 2, meeting with fellow world leaders about the slumping global economy. First lady Michelle Obama spent those hours clapping and nodding her way through a series of activities set up for the leaders' spouses.

The two were in London for their first official trip abroad. The day before, the Obamas had been received at Buckingham Palace by Queen Elizabeth: the world's most enduring personification of inherited privilege hosting two people who stood for the power of social mobility. Everyone smiled politely and posed for pictures.

The next day, as the leaders discussed stimulus levels, their wives sat together in the Royal Opera House, taking in snippets of classical music and ballet performances, nibbling at a luncheon. Not all in attendance spoke English, which made conversation awkward; they tried to communicate through translators or just improvised. The food was elaborate, as it always was at these sorts of events: the cuisine of one country trying to impress those of nineteen others. Dessert was "mocha mousse cup with honey crunch; white chocolate beignets with sour raspberry dip; and biscotti bruschetta topped with semifreddo and vin santo blueberries," along with cheese and biscuits. When Hillary Clinton was first lady, she found the meals on diplomatic trips so excessive that the White House chef taught her to cut the portion size by dumping salt over half her plate to render that part inedible.

Amid the burgundy carpets and gilded surfaces at the opera house, Michelle stood out like a tall, brightly plumed bird. Everyone else wore demure outfits in somber or creamy colors. She wore a sweeping turquoise skirt and a glittery cardigan with an asymmetric burgundy-and-turquoise pattern.

Shortly after lunch, she slipped away from the group. She had dutifully participated in the program organized by Sarah Brown, wife of Britain's prime minister, but this was her maiden trip abroad, and she was making one independent stop, something truer to her own inclinations.

TO ANYONE READING THE NEWS or watching television, Michelle Obama's first months as first lady looked triumphant. She invited Washington schoolchildren to dig into the cold ground of the White House lawn to plant a vegetable garden and brought prominent women like Alicia Keys, the musician, and Mae Jemison, the first female African American astronaut, to visit local schools and mentor young women. ("I want to do what *you're* doing," the president told his wife that day.) She posed for her official portrait in a sleeveless black sheath, showing off her now famously toned arms. The new first lady seemed spirited, enthusiastic, and active, and more youthful and hip than most of her predecessors had been in their day. A year after critics accused her of being aggrieved and anti-white, her approval ratings climbed so high they became a running internal joke. "Not as high as

Michelle's," the president would say with a grin when aides reported his still-solid numbers and her superior ones.

The truth, however, was that the first lady was initially having a difficult time in her new role, several advisers said. Many of her fears had come true. She was far from the city where she had almost always lived and she had given up a life she'd spent a long time building. Some of her friendships had fallen apart: she was sensitive to any hint of exploitation, and some old friends had crossed the line, she felt, using her name to try to get jobs. And she was especially dissatisfied with her part in the administration. She wanted her husband to rely on the vice president and cabinet officials more, but she also wanted him to rely on *her*, she told her own aides—not in setting policy but in communicating the kind of clear overall message about the administration she so wanted the public to see. "She was very frustrated that so much of the strategy was president-driven," one aide said. "There was no consideration of how she fit in the broader Obama narrative."

They were finally in the White House, this was their chance to pursue the change they had sought for so long, she saw how exhausted her husband was, and no one had a longer history of explaining Barack Obama to other people than she—so why wasn't the West Wing using her? She was a strong asset, she felt; she wanted to help, and the male advisers at the other end of the building just didn't see it. "She wanted to be part of the strategy, she wanted to make sure everything was coordinated," said Anita Dunn, the White House communications director at the time and one of the few advisers close to both the president and the first lady. Later, there would be specific goals of her husband's—one in particular—that she wanted to champion; but in the first few months of the administration, she just wanted to participate, to help with the urgent tasks at hand.

Her frustrations were largely the same as during the presidential race: once again, she felt ignored by her husband's advisers and under-supplied with resources. (Then again, some West Wing aides quietly pointed out, she said she wanted to work only two days a week.) During the campaign, she was consistently able to escape back into her own job and world. Now, as far as she could tell, she was stuck in a position with little definition and no clear goals. Whatever little struc-ture the role carried was dictated by a series of mandatory events. Laura Bush's staff had left her team with several large binders of instructions: how to order Christmas cards, pack for a foreign trip, organize the holiday tree lighting, and all the rest. But in her own career, Michelle Obama just didn't do ceremonial events; she wanted strategy, impact, results.

The new first lady did not identify much with those who had filled the role before her, and she showed limited interest in studying their examples. Outsiders sometimes compared her to Jackie Kennedy for their shared interest in beautiful clothing, or to Hillary Clinton, a fel-low Ivy League–trained lawyer. But being compared to a socialite reared in boarding school seemed a bit absurd to the daughter of the South Side, and unlike Clinton, she had no desire to wield power in the West Wing or hold elective office. "She's so her own person," Susan Sher said. When Michelle heard the media questioning whether she was more like Hillary Clinton or Laura Bush, she just shrugged, Sher said: she didn't consider herself terribly similar to either woman.

Everyone knew what the West Wing was, from the television show and from history books. The first lady's counterpart, the East Wing, did not have nearly the same status: aside from entertaining, it came with no urgent tasks, and because things in the West Wing were so frenetic, their counterparts on the other side of the building were often left feeling uninformed and left out.

Michelle and Rahm Emanuel had almost no bond; their relation-ship was distant and awkward from the beginning. She had been skeptical of him when he was selected, and now he returned the favor; he was uneasy about first ladies in general, several aides close to him said, based on clashes with Hillary Clinton in the 1990s that became so severe that she had tried to fire him from her husband's administration.

Now Emanuel was the chief of staff, a position that almost never included an easy relationship with the first lady. They were the president's two spouses, in a sense, one public and official and one private and informal. One was charged with executing the president's agenda, and the other would have to live with him and his decisions into old age.

Valerie Jarrett and Emanuel were West Wing foils, and often opponents on internal matters, but the contrast between Rahm and Michelle was far more fundamental: they were an almost perfect mismatch. She was a meticulous planner who believed that how you played was nearly as important as winning; he operated day to day, and when he was negotiating, almost nothing was sacred. ("He would promise Malia and Sasha's hands in marriage" for votes, aides joked.) Michelle was the chief standard-bearer for the idea that her husband was exceptional, transformational—that he was above politics. Emanuel was skeptical of the idea that the president floated on an exalted plane. ("The rules apply to everybody," as one former adviser put it, and complaining about how Washington worked "is like crying over the rain.") She had a tentative command over the language and rules of politics; he was fluent.

Initially Michelle tried to break through to him. One former aide summed up the first lady's initial attitude toward Emanuel as: I'm not Hillary Clinton, this is a clean slate, give me a shot. But Rahm seemed to avoid her at all costs, figuring Jarrett would take care of the relationship between the East and West wings.

Not knowing much about Washington, the incoming first lady

had hired as her own chief of staff Jackie Norris, a former teacher and Iowa campaign hand who had worked as a scheduler for Al Gore when he was vice president. Norris was cheerful and capable, but she wasn't a skilled infighter, and she didn't have the status to go up against the president's advisers. Dealing with the West Wing, Norris "just got steamrolled," another member of the group said. She wanted to attend Emanuel's crucial 7:30 a.m. planning meeting, but the president's chief of staff did not include her. As in the presidential campaign, the first lady initially did not have a speechwriter, even though she was giving remarks several times a week: Camille Johnston, her communications director, wrote many of her early speeches. Another member of the first lady's team began referring to the East Wing as "Guam" — pleasant but powerless. When the Obamas paid a visit to a local school, a little girl told Michelle she wanted to grow up to be first lady. "Doesn't pay much," she shot back. She was joking, but the message was clear.

Before the inauguration, she had pinpointed three issues she wanted to work on as first lady: more support for military families, promoting general volunteerism and community service, and helping Americans achieve better balance between work and home. For all of her hesitation about being in the spotlight, she was eager to instruct and prod, to make personal examples out of herself and even her children when it came to exercise, parenting, education, and even marriage. If she was going to move to Washington, she decided after the election, she would make her move a demonstration of "how people can get engaged in their communities," said Jocelyn Frye, her policy director. But she had few specific plans beyond symbolic gestures like visiting soup kitchens across the city, and topics like volunteerism and work/life balance were vague. The president, meanwhile, had little interest in telling her what to do as first lady, said several aides: he just wanted his wife, so often unhappy in the political arena, to be satisfied. He did not want her spreading the administration's message for protective reasons: he wanted to keep her out of the line of fire.

In the meantime, the office was just trying to cope with the massive flood of invitations that arrived each day. The first lady laid out a few principles for her staff to keep in mind as they sifted through the requests. She did not want to do a little of this and that, a heart disease awareness event on Monday, an education project on Tuesday, and so on, lest she get lost in a fog of mandatory but unmemorable events. "She only wanted to do a few things and do them well," Susan Sher said. Anything too policy-driven or partisan was tossed out, and so were events that seemed stuffy or overly traditional. She wanted everything to be strategic, to accomplish a concrete goal, and she was especially vigilant about the use of her time: if she was going to an event, it had to be good enough to justify hours away from her family.

In a way Michelle's unhappiness put her very much in the company of her predecessors. The recent history of first ladyhood was filled with public fortitude and moments of true national impact, as when Barbara Bush hugged an AIDS patient to demonstrate that the disease was not transmissible by touch; but it was also laced with private struggle. Jacqueline Kennedy had an anxious time in the White House from the beginning, pouring out her worries in long secret phone calls to a young doctor in Virginia. Her outfits and parties were perfect but her fingernails were bitten to the quick. Lady Bird Johnson, naturally ebullient, sank under the weight of the disastrous war her husband was commanding in Vietnam. Betty Ford captured the country's affection yet numbed herself with alcohol and painkillers. Hillary Clinton suffered the collapse of the health care initiative she led, the suicide of Vincent Foster, one of her closest friends from Arkansas, and the humiliation of the Lewinsky scandal before vaulting herself to a new life as a U.S. senator. Even self-contained Laura Bush admitted to melancholy and frustration, writing in her memoir of lonely afternoons spent reading in the empty grandeur of the residence and feeling underestimated and misunderstood.

The role was just extremely difficult. To be first lady meant enduring scrutiny and confinement; watching your husband make excruciating decisions and then be attacked for them; and advising in secret, rarely acknowledging your real influence. Openly influential first ladies like Nancy Reagan and Hillary Clinton were deemed meddlers, unelected figures who held unearned power. That was the contradiction of the job: presidents made it to the White House in no small part because of their hardworking, canny wives, but once they arrived, the women were exiled to the East Wing and recast solely as helpmeets.

To make matters worse, instead of feeling that she was contributing to the presidency, Michelle found herself at the center of an awkward, anxious internal debate over how she and her family should look, live, and entertain. During the campaign, political advisers had little dominion over how she decorated, what parties she threw, or what she did on vacation. But in the White House her home and life were not entirely her own. Almost everything about the way she and her family lived was up for external and therefore internal debate: social events, redecoration, vacations, even as small a question as whether or not she should bring a makeup artist and hairdresser on foreign trips. On these matters, she did get attention from the West Wing, but it wasn't the kind of attention she wanted.

The debate stemmed from a fundamental difference in worldviews between the first lady and her husband's political advisers, particularly Robert Gibbs. She envisioned a White House that was inclusive, diverse, attractive, and chic, showcasing the best of American culture and style. She found Washington stodgy, and she "wanted to push the envelope," one former aide said, making everything as sophisticated as possible. She had operated the same way since her husband's first campaign: when advisers wanted to plan a beer-in-a-bar fund-raiser, she organized a more dignified evening at an African American history museum with good music and wine. It was another of her attempts to get away from what she disliked about politics.

She was also acutely aware that she and her family were the country's, and the world's, most important African American role models. Changing stereotypes was part of why the Obamas had run in the first place, part of why she wanted everything to look as beautiful and refined as possible. She knew how persistent negative stereotypes of African Americans were—the way she was misrepresented during the campaign only proved it—and she saw her tenure as a rare, valuable chance to correct them.

When it came to race, Michelle Obama had always known exactly who she was: a proud African American daughter of the South Side. But class was a more confusing subject for her; she had traveled an enormous financial distance fast, and she veered back and forth between two roles: the down-to-earth mom who pushed a cart through Target and the glamorous figure who strode through formal White House events in custom-made gowns.

In his own appearances, her husband did not like to exploit the visual power of the presidency, and he avoided doing events with the kinds of dramatic backgrounds that predecessors like Ronald Reagan and George W. Bush had used and had at times been criticized for. But Michelle Obama cared deeply about how things looked. She hired a wardrobe assistant; when she traveled abroad, she wanted to bring her own hair and makeup assistants; and to redecorate the private quarters of the White House, she passed over little-known designers in favor of Michael Smith, who had done houses for Steven Spielberg and Rupert Murdoch.

The first lady's position was "this is what I need to be successful," said one aide, and she did not welcome criticism of her choices. In discussions, her opinions were often backed by Desirée Rogers, the new social secretary. Rogers had no Washington or government experience either, but she did have a Harvard MBA, a brilliant sense of style, and a bone-deep understanding of being a high-profile African American woman. The two had not been close friends in Chicago — they knew each other mostly through Valerie Jarrett — and where Michelle Obama was precise and pragmatic, Rogers could be airy. But in the early months of the administration, the first lady and Rogers mostly stood together.

Their emphasis on style gave the president's political advisers, Gibbs in particular, the willies. They were consumed with responding not just to joblessness but bailouts and banker bonuses, and they knew the public mood was resentful and sour. Besides, wasn't the original idea that the Obamas came from humble roots; that Barack Obama had a more normal wife and family than many politicians? The advisers preferred to keep things tasteful but moderately priced, in the spirit of the two- and three-figure off-the-rack dresses that had won Michelle Obama applause on the campaign trail. One aide said he even worried about the *In Performance at the White House* concerts that were broadcast on PBS, featuring musicians like John Legend and Sheryl Crow singing in the East Room, because anything that said "the president and first lady enjoy privileges that you don't" was a problem. With critics chanting more and more loudly about Obama's excessive spending, anything that looked lavish, even if it was paid for with private funds, could send the wrong message.

Of all the president's advisers, Gibbs took the hardest line, and he was one of the few people in the White House unafraid to confront Michelle Obama, even though it was often through aides. He was acutely aware that a single misstep could brand a public figure forever, especially if it included a purchase that most people couldn't afford.

"We all have watched what happens when people get caricatured," he explained. Before John Edwards, the former presidential contender, was tarred by marital scandal, "the biggest thing that impacted his political brand was a four-hundred-dollar haircut," Gibbs said. "You can't put that back in a box. Once that's out, there's no way to correct that." The list of similar mistakes was long: Bill Clinton's own expensive haircut, Sarah Palin's shopping spree during the campaign, John McCain's pricey shoes. After all the effort they were putting into communicating the president's policies, after all the work they had put into Michelle Obama's image, he did not want her to be remembered as materialistic or self-absorbed.

And after failing to warn their boss's wife about potential missteps during the 2008 race, Gibbs and other advisers swung in the other direction. During the campaign, "we were probably guilty of not making sure that she felt completely protected," Gibbs said. "That always animated my actions in the White House." Besides, Gibbs added, he wasn't actually making decisions on how the first lady dressed, decorated, or entertained. "My MO on this whole thing is to protect," he said, to give "my best advice on how I think things can get portrayed and can be reacted to."

So Gibbs began to play an unenviable role: the internal enforcer of the rules of the political world, issuing a steady stream of warnings and nos. Barack Obama, who felt guilty about the sacrifices his wife was making, was unwilling to tell her what she could not do, other aides said, so Gibbs took on the task. No, the Obamas should not add a private vacation onto a state trip: they might look like they were hitching a free ride on a government plane to their getaway. "You're going to make me go and defend that in public?" aides remember him saying about one or another East Wing proposal. "I don't want to have to explain it to Fox News." Gibbs almost never discussed the concerns with the first lady directly: instead, he communicated through Jarrett or her own staff, who were in the awkward position of telling Michelle that the West Wing had reservations about something she wanted to do. When the first lady heard the cautions, she often felt criticized and underappreciated, they said. All she wanted was to be an asset to the administration, and instead she was being treated as a potential liability.

The longest-running headache was over redecoration. A few days after the inauguration, news broke that Michael Smith, the decorator the Obamas had just chosen, had redone the executive suite of John Thain, the ousted chief executive of Merrill Lynch, at a budget of $1.2 million. Under Thain's watch the company had lost $15 billion in the fourth quarter of 2008; now taxpayers were keeping it afloat with $20 billion in rescue funds. Thain eventually reimbursed the company, but his $87,000 rug, along with a $1,200 trash can, became instant symbols of everything Americans hated about Wall Street.

Smith's work for Thain was news to everyone in the White House, the social secretary and first lady included. But political advisers marveled that the two women had managed to pick, out of all the designers in the United States, the one guy whose work was at the center of a blowup over Wall Street decadence. Redecoration was a classic trouble area: nearly every first lady, from Nancy Reagan to Hillary Clinton, who had tried to change the look of the White House had been torn apart for her efforts, which was why the public rooms looked largely the same as they had in the Kennedy era. The same thing could happen to Michelle Obama, with the Smith-Thain connection providing the final flourish: "If you didn't like the president, and you wanted to score some cheap political points, there you go: the president redecorated the White House!" Gibbs said.

But jettisoning Smith wasn't an option; that would only attract more attention. The first lady protested that she was just trying to make the White House a comfortable place for her family; to establish a new home for her girls. (The Bush-era carpets had stains from their pets.) And while touching the public rooms tended to set off criticism, she was only trying to decorate the private quarters, which had always been the prerogative of the first family. Smith wasn't taking a fee — by tradition, decorators donated their time — and the Obamas, concerned about the costs of their new lives, were planning on redecorating as inexpensively as possible. With each new administration, Congress even set aside $100,000 for the task, and because the Bushes had used their own funds instead, $200,000 was sitting in the account, waiting to be spent.

The negotiations dragged on, well into the spring. The president thought his advisers were right: the risk of an uproar over redecoration was high. They would go ahead, but they would not touch taxpayer money, and some of the redecoration would wait. Smith repurposed old presidential furniture wherever possible, using new fabric to reupholster pieces from a warehouse of White House leftovers, and adding items from chain stores like Anthropologie and Walmart. The president grew surprisingly involved in the redecoration project. "He is very thoughtful about what he wants and how he wants to live, and very particular," Desirée Rogers said that spring. With every new piece that arrived, he double-checked "to make certain it looks exactly like what the pictures were." The Obamas replaced the white wicker furniture the Bushes had on the Truman Balcony with a darker, more contemporary set, and the first lady ordered a rocking chair so the president could sit outside and read.

Some of the first lady's own advisers had doubts about the importance she placed on style. A few weeks before she traveled to London, her image had appeared on the cover of the American edition of *Vogue*. The appearance had been the subject of some of the most uncomfortable exchanges her advisers could remember.

In general, her clothes made a lot of aides nervous. Just a few years before, she had dressed like everyone else in Hyde Park, in cardigans and slacks from chain stores. She had always loved pretty things—for example, diamond stud earrings, which her husband eventually gave her, said Cindy Moelis, a friend from Chicago—but for a long time, the Obamas could not afford such luxuries. In *The Audacity of Hope*, published in 2005, Barack Obama described his wife's looks as the "lived-in beauty of the mother and busy professional rather than the touched-up image we see on the cover of glossy magazines."

As her husband became more successful, that changed fast. Clothing became a compensatory pleasure for having to participate in his political life. "If I have to go, I'm getting a new dress out of it," she would tell neighbors before flying off to Washington to accompany him to an event. Once she saw how she looked with top-flight clothes and styling, one friend said, there was no going back. By the inauguration, her husband's three-year-old description no longer fit: her hair was perfect; her eyebrows were more subtly arched; her makeup was always flawless; she looked at home in top designer labels and some even created fashions just for her. Questioning the way she attired herself was not advisable; one former member of the first lady's staff said she learned in her first day on the job "to not go near her clothes."

Looking fabulous gave her confidence, Michelle told others. It was her armor against ubiquitous cameras, yet another way she sought protection from public life. "All you need is one photo of you when you're not looking perfect," Susan Sher noted. With clothes, Michelle could say things she never would out loud: women did not have to be blonde or skinny to be attractive, and by the way, she was not the stuffy, frumpy, or self-abnegating kind of political wife. Besides, she felt "the pressure on her to always be perfect and look perfect was so much more intense than on any first lady because everyone was waiting for a black woman to make a mistake," a former adviser said.

Even the president made uncomfortable jokes about why his wife needed so many new things. Behind the scenes, aides said, the Obamas were concerned about money: the president's books could only sell so many copies, and it would be years until he could write more and the first lady could write her own. From vacation rental homes big enough to accommodate the Secret Service to all the personal entertaining they did at the White House, their lifestyle had grown fearsomely expensive.

The invitation to pose for the cover of *Vogue* had come during the transition, and her advisers' reactions were mixed. The first lady dismissed their concerns in an email. If you guys can't figure out how to manage this so that it's not a negative, then I obviously have the wrong team, one former aide recalled the message as saying. A conference call was arranged to discuss the matter further, with Michelle Obama, Valerie Jarrett, Anita Dunn, Desirée Rogers, and Jackie Norris all dialing in.

Within the first few minutes of the call, it became clear that the women were largely divided across racial lines. Dunn and Norris, both white, were concerned because *Vogue* was a pure fashion magazine, featuring ten-thousand-dollar handbags and with a newsstand price of five dollars. Michelle Obama was a person of substance who had devoted her career to community work; did she really want to be known as America's number-one fashionista? Desirée Rogers, Valerie Jarrett, and the first-lady-to-be were in favor, in part because so few black women appeared on the covers of the major fashion magazines.

The first lady heard everyone out but reiterated her decision: she was accepting the invitation. "I don't have to be on the cover of *Vogue* wearing something that costs twenty thousand dollars," she said. In posing for other magazines, she had always chosen her own clothes, and she would do it again this time. "There are young black women across this country and I want them to see a black woman on the cover of *Vogue*," she told the group. They would try to inject a theme of female empowerment into the piece to counteract the glitz.

In the end there was little criticism of Michelle Obama's appearance in the magazine. She posed in clothes by J. Crew and Jason Wu, a young designer whose dresses usually retailed in the low four figures. In an innocuous interview, she discussed her desire to bring a "spirit of warmth, openness and stability" to the White House and to continue being a regular mom, bringing her daughters to school each day. The cover showed her in a Wu dress and a shy smile, next to the words "The First Lady the World's Been Waiting For."

The first lady's desire for African American girls to see her on the cover of *Vogue* was telling. If there was one thing she knew how to do, it was relate to young people, especially those who were outsiders in one sense or another. In the early months of the administration, as she waded through invitations for speaking engagements, the ones that appealed to her were from groups that were new or upcoming or somehow represented underdogs, the kind that had never been visited by a first lady before. She had little interest in lending her presence to the powerful, in speaking at Ivy League university graduations. Among the events she did in her initial months as first lady, the mentoring event that had brought prominent women to Washington-area schools and then back to the White House was her favorite; surrounded by a diverse group of high-achieving women and high school girls, she was in her element. "Every event we do is with an eye towards opening a door for someone," Melissa Winter, her deputy chief of staff, said. Rather than just give speeches from behind a podium, she and her colleagues looked for opportunities for a first lady to form some sort of emotional bond with the audience. "If Michelle Obama is not going to go out and connect, then we are wasting her," Winter continued. "What is special is that she's not aloof, untouchable, unreadable."

Of all of the jobs Michelle Obama had held over the years, the one she took after leaving the mayor's office, directing the Chicago chapter of Public Allies, the leadership program for twentysomethings, had been the most formative. The project was based on an idea called "asset-based community development"—the belief that people in struggling neighborhoods, instead of being written off, should be treated like valuable assets, capable of lifting their communities up without government support. Each year, she recruited a new crop of participants, ranging from graduates of the University of Chicago to high school dropouts with an arrest or two on their records, placed them in internships with public service organizations, and trained them in how to become community leaders.

The university graduates in the group admired Michelle, but the public-housing residents and teenage mothers were transfixed by her. She told them that they were just as talented as those who had gone to college, and she worked with them to master the things they did not know or feared, even tasks as basic as navigating the Chicago bus system. If participants did not arrive on time in the morning, even an El breakdown was no excuse: "If you know that you are responsible to get here on time, you have to have a plan A, B, and C," Public Allies participant Paris Brewer remembers her saying.

She was intent on dismantling stereotypes: young black men as superpredators, black women as welfare queens, as well as the stereotypes the participants had about others. When the *Chicago Tribune* called Malik Nevels, one of the Allies, "a former gang leader"—he was nothing of the sort—Michelle rolled her eyes. "Welcome to the world of the media," she told him, and instructed him to write a letter to the paper. Brewer, a young African American woman, said she entered the program with a general mistrust of white people, but Michelle "would just call me on my BS," Brewer recalled. "She would always tell me, before I make a statement, make sure I have facts to support it." At one session Brewer stormed away from her peers and out of the room. Michelle followed her. "Don't ever let anyone see you thrown off your square like that," Michelle instructed her.

"She's not going to cry with you, that's not the kind of woman Michelle is," Brewer said later. Other Allies came to the program scared of gay people. When Krsna Golden, who actually was a former gang member, complained that he was given a gay roommate on a retreat, Michelle sat him down. "She helped me see where there might have been fault," he said. "At the end of my retreat, I felt like a bigger, stronger, smarter person."

At some level, some of the Allies said years later, it was the very presence of Michelle Obama, more than anything she said to them, that made the strongest impression on them. She had not come from a privileged background; she was just like them. And though she had made it to Princeton and Harvard Law School and could have worked anywhere, she was choosing to spend her time and energy on them, casting her lot with them and the idea that they were capable of great things.

THE PEOPLE MICHELLE WAS GOING TO see that afternoon in London had no idea she was coming. For two hours on that April day, students at the Elizabeth Garrett Anderson School had been waiting in an auditorium decorated with a modest arrangement of sunflowers, waiting to perform for a mystery guest. All of the school's students were female, few were white, and two-thirds spoke English as a second language. Twenty percent were the children of refugees or asylum seekers. They sat and waited in neat gray uniforms, some of the girls wearing headscarves, watching the film *Mamma Mia!* to pass the time.

When they realized who their guest was, they greeted her with a deafening wall of schoolgirl screams. The White House was quiet; events there tended to be muted affairs. Buckingham Palace and the G-20 events had been quiet, too. This was loud.

Earlier, at the opera, the first lady had sat still next to her peers. Now, as the girls danced and belted out ballads, she raised her hands high to clap, whispered conspiratorially to the headmistress beside her, and high-fived students as they walked offstage. When the performances were finished, she rose to speak.

"Although the circumstances of our lives may seem very distant, with me standing here as the first lady of the United States of America and you just getting through school, I want you to know that we have very much in common," she said. She was starting to well up, and her staff did as well. "Nothing in my life's path would have predicted that I would be standing here as the first African American first lady of the United States of America. There was nothing in my story that would land me here. I wasn't raised with wealth or resources or any social standing to speak of."

Foreign trips were exhausting, a blur of flights, ceremonies, and costume changes, and with all the logistical details and schedules, the first lady and her aides had not fully realized the potential significance of the school visit. She looked at the girls looking at her and saw herself through their eyes, noticing how they hung on her every word. "She knew they could see more possibilities for themselves by seeing themselves in her," said Katie McCormick Lelyveld, her press secretary at the time. She saw the responsibility, the impact, the potential, of her role. Her time in the White House had been isolating, yet now across the Atlantic she felt so connected. Standing on the modest stage, aides said later, Michelle Obama's new position began to make sense to her for the first time.

"History proves that it doesn't matter whether you come from a council estate" — meaning a housing project — "or a country estate," she continued, her voice heartfelt. "We are counting on every single one of you to be the very best that you can be, because the world is big, and it's full of challenges, and we need strong, smart, confident young women to stand up and take the reins."

She finished her speech but did not leave. Instead she turned to the members of the student choir standing behind her. "I do hugs," she told the girls, and one by one they approached. When she finished with them, she still wasn't done. She moved to the front of the stage, dropped to her knees, and spread her arms. Secret Service agents were lunging forward protectively, but she was still reaching out for more girls to embrace.

FOR THE REST OF SPRING 2009, however, Michelle continued to struggle. Her relationship with her chief of staff was falling apart, in part because she felt Norris was not a forceful enough advocate for her with the West Wing. There was still no central project to her first ladyhood, no major goal into which she could pour her natural intensity, years of professional experience, and desire to contribute. Until she found that project, aides agreed, she wasn't going to find much satisfaction in her role. And in the meantime, she was still frustrated with some of the timeless ceremonial duties of first ladyhood.

Washington had a long-standing tradition of polite spousal diplomacy, of wives of Capitol Hill and other high-ranking officials coming together a few times a year to mingle and bond over their common experiences. Many of the events had a retro feel; they harkened back to a time when the wives of senators and congressmen didn't work, when they were adjuncts to their husbands. But such gatherings were part of the city's social glue, and they provided an opportunity for Republicans and Democrats to get to know each other and to form social bonds that transcended party labels.

Before her husband assumed the presidency, Michelle had never attended these events, and she had even laughed at them a little from afar. After her husband was elected to the U.S. Senate, an invitation had arrived for her to attend a luncheon in Washington honoring Laura Bush. Michelle had been amused and dismissive, a friend said: she had a *job,* and she was not flying to Washington for some lunch that did not have a clear purpose. The trips she did take to Washington were brief and surreal, with quick stays in her husband's nearly furniture-less apartment and fellow spouses offering advice she didn't want. (You need to move here and keep an eye on your handsome husband, one told her, according to Jarrett.) During her rare visits, her husband often skipped events on his schedule to spend time alone with her, sometimes offending a group that expected him at their gala. It was an early hint of the Obamas' lack of appetite for tactical Washington socializing.

The most important event on the Washington-spouse circuit was the annual Congressional Club luncheon, a large banquet held in a hotel ballroom, thrown by the spouses every year since 1912 to honor the first lady. It was not exactly a favorite among first ladies: Jacqueline Kennedy tried to make the event pass more quickly by singing show tunes under her breath, and Laura Bush trashed the ritual in her memoir, saying the organizers were so demanding they regularly reduced her staff to tears. The hosts asked that the first lady stay at the event for a full four hours. There were photo opportunities, a receiving line, a VIP reception before the lunch, and a walk across a catwalk with a military escort—the better for the other Washington wives to see the first lady, said Betty Ann Tanner, one of the recent organizers. But the first lady invariably attended; the event was a chance to cross party lines and create goodwill for her husband's agenda, as Anita McBride, Laura Bush's former chief of staff, put it.

The luncheon that took place on April 30, 2009, a few weeks after the London trip, was notable for its all-mint-green décor and a performance given by Blake Lewis, a runner-up on *American Idol,* and for how hard Michelle Obama tried to get out of attending.

When she inherited the list of annual Washington-spouse events from Laura Bush's office, she asked her staff if she could skip all of them, including the Congressional Club luncheon, and invite greater numbers of congressional and Senate spouses to a series of other White House events instead. "It's a lunch for the sake of a lunch and this is not a first lady who just does lunch," one of her advisers said. Besides, she had a generally low regard for Congress. It was one of the areas where the Obamas seemed to reinforce and stoke each other: the president's opinion of Capitol Hill legislators was low, and his wife's was lower.

The congressional wives refused the East Wing's counteroffer. The luncheon was the highlight of their calendar, a nearly century-old ritual, and every other recent first lady had attended.

The two sides went back and forth. The Congressional Club wanted the first lady to take photos with their corporate donors, but she was leery of lending her image to corporations, especially ones her office had not vetted. Most figures in public life were used to ceding some control over how they were represented. When you spent years and years trying to get elected, you shook hands and took pictures when required, Anita McBride pointed out. Because of their near-overnight success, the Obamas had more protective instincts—to guard everything that seemed to be slipping away from them. The first lady was sensitive about the use of her image and prone to feeling exploited, especially with bookstores and magazine racks filling with attempts to cash in on her popularity.

Weeks before the event, she agreed to attend, but in exchange she pointedly requested that a day of volunteer work for the spouses be added. Each year, the luncheon raised money for a different charity, chosen by the organizers and the first lady, but the donated funds usually amounted to twenty-five thousand dollars or so, which worked out to only about fifteen dollars per attendee. That was a relatively low figure for a group of well-off women, East Wing aides thought, especially given the effort the organizers put into flowers, tablecloths, and entertainment. "If she's going to take an afternoon out of her life to do something counterintuitive to who she is, which includes walking a catwalk, on the arm of a military man not her husband, then what she would like in return is something that's meaningful to her, a service event," one of the first lady's aides said.

On the appointed day, Michelle waited backstage at the Washington Hilton wearing a demure flowered dress. She was there for a very long time, because before she could walk out, there was a full thirty minutes of formal introductions and applause for others: spouses of congressional leaders, Supreme Court justices, and so on, including a few husbands. The luncheon was the polar opposite of the school visit in London: formal and ceremonial, with an audience that was mostly white and privileged. When the first lady finally strode out, she faced a sea of women who looked like they might have come from a different era. The daughters and granddaughters of club members served as "junior hostesses," wearing identical apple-green bridesmaidlike dresses and shoes in the same shade and carrying hyacinth bouquets. The tables were covered in a custom green toile print depicting eighteenth-century European figures frolicking in a pastoral setting, looking a little like Marie Antoinette and friends at the Petit Trianon. As their commemorative gift, the hostesses gave the first lady a needlepoint rendering of the White House.

In her remarks, the first lady updated everyone on her daughters ("the kids are settled in and getting good grades") and her mother ("she has an active social life"). She told everyone she felt right at home. "I feel like I've never left Chicago," she effused. Then her speech turned uncharacteristically gushy, as she rhapsodized about a safe topic, her family's recently arrived dog, Bo. "I have to say he is the best puppy in the whole wide world," she cooed. "I love him to death."

She thanked the spouses who had joined her for the volunteer event the day prior at a Washington-area food bank, where they had loaded two thousand grocery bags for hungry youngsters. The women should do even more, she urged. "Whether it's a food bank or a homeless shelter, there's so much need out there," she said, using the blandest possible language to register her critique of their tablecloth-and-centerpiece approach.

What she did not mention is that the food bank event had drawn widespread coverage for an unintended reason: to stuff the bags, the first lady had worn a $515 pair of sneakers by the French designer Lanvin.

Chapter Five

CAMPAIGN PROMISES

MAY–AUGUST 2009

O n the clear Saturday afternoon of May 30, the first couple emerged from the back of the White House and walked across the South Lawn to Marine One. The fringes on the first lady's black cocktail dress swayed and her heels stuck a bit in the soft earth. Sasha waved her parents good-bye from the balcony above.

The president was fulfilling a private promise he had made during the campaign. For years, through child rearing and commutes to Springfield, Barack and Michelle had maintained a sacred weekly ritual of Friday date nights. For the rest of her husband's time in Chicago, Michelle had to share him with law students and constituents, but at the end of the workweek he was hers. On Friday mornings, she would prepare by stopping at Van Cleef, a chic salon near Michigan Avenue, as early as 5:30 a.m. for "the working girl's special," her hairdresser's nickname for a manicure-and-hair appointment. The dates helped the Obamas keep their relationship intact while juggling two careers (three, if you counted Barack's two jobs serving in the state senate and teaching law), two small children, and significantly different opinions on what kind of life they should ultimately be leading. During the presidential campaign, the Obamas managed to slip away just a handful of times, and the candidate had promised his wife that when it was finally over he would take her to dinner and a Broadway show in New York.

Their evening out was the briefest of breaks in a frenzied spring. Just a few days prior, Obama had nominated Sonia Sotomayor to be the first Hispanic Supreme Court justice in American history and the third woman on the high court. A few days later, he would travel to Cairo to call for a more cooperative and peaceful relationship between the United States and Muslims abroad. The economy seemed to be stabilizing, if not quite recovering, and the president was pursuing two of the most pressing domestic policy priorities of his term, the health care and energy policy overhauls. The second was already moving through the House of Representatives, in the form of a bill to curb emissions and address global warming, though Democrats were nervous about it: Republicans were calling the potential legislation another example of heedless Obama overspending, saying it would hurt pocketbooks and send jobs overseas. Amid it all, unexpected issues kept cropping up like plot twists on an especially contrived episode of *The West Wing*. A rare form of influenza spread from pigs to human beings, sickening thousands worldwide and requiring a nationally coordinated public health response. The American captain of a cargo ship traveling off the coast of Africa was taken hostage by Somali pirates and freed only after the president authorized a successful, daring rescue by Navy SEALs.

For the president and the first lady, dinner and a Broadway show turned out to mean a helicopter ride from home, a flight to New York on a smaller-than-usual Air Force One, another, more spectacular helicopter ride over the Brooklyn Bridge, and a motorcade procession through streets closed to traffic and lined with cheering pedestrians.

The Obamas ate at Blue Hill, a restaurant known for its pricey farm-to-table cuisine, and then sped uptown to see August Wilson's *Joe Turner's Come and Gone.* The show started late, since every ticket-holder had to pass through security screening. When the Obamas walked in just before curtain, the audience gave them several minutes of applause.

The Obamas, enjoying their outing, had no idea they were being attacked for it in real time. The pool reports made the president's whereabouts public, and hours before the Obamas returned home, the Republican National Committee sent out a press release. "As President Obama prepares to wing into Manhattan's theater district on Air Force One to take in a Broadway show, GM is preparing to file bankruptcy and families across America continue to struggle to pay their bills," it read. "Have a great Saturday evening—even if you're not jetting off somewhere at taxpayer expense." The Obamas had paid for their own theater tickets and dinner, but the federal government had paid for their transportation, as it had for the excursions of their predecessors—after all, there was no other way for a president to travel. Still, the trip played right into the Republican story line that the president was profligate with other people's money and out of touch, and soon television pundits were debating whether the evening had been a mistake.

Usually the first lady responded more strongly to attacks than her husband, shadowboxing in private while he urged her to brush it off. But this time the president was the one who was annoyed. "If I weren't president, I would be happy to catch the shuttle with my wife to take her to a Broadway show, as I had promised during the campaign, and there would be no fuss and no muss and no photographers, and that would please me greatly," he said in an interview months later. "This was sort of a treat for her," he lamented.

Republicans had taken aim at what he considered a private area of his life, and a ritual that had once been so personal, so intimate—a night out with his wife—had now turned into fodder for attack ads and nationwide debate. Naïvely or arrogantly, whether for her sake or his, Obama still had the idea that he could declare his wife, or other swaths of his life, out of bounds from politics. "What I value most about my marriage is that it is separate and apart from a lot of the silliness of Washington, and Michelle is not part of that silliness," he said. "And I want to keep it that way."

But the incident also pointed to an even deeper conflict: what were the consequences of Michelle's taking on a role and way of life she would not have sought on her own? Could Barack Obama's attempts to make his wife happy—to compensate for his decision to pursue politics, to run for president—hurt his work as president? What if his attempts to reconcile the irreconcilable—Michelle and politics, but also many other issues—were impossible; what if the attempts themselves came with their own costs?

By Monday, the criticism was still unfurling, not just on the predictably negative Fox News but on programs like the *Today* show as well. When reporters in the briefing room asked Robert Gibbs about how much federal money the president and first lady had spent on the New York trip, his defense was less than vigorous.

"I think it's . . . lemme uh . . . ," he stumbled. He paused to consider a buzzing noise and whether it was coming from an air conditioner or a helicopter outside. "Uh . . . I, I, I think spokespeople have spoken to this over the weekend," he resumed, looking down. "Had the president—could he based on the Secret Service—he would have taken the shuttle, but I would say the costs are proportionate for [the] president. I would encourage you to look up previous travel costs because they're analogous." He did not mention that the Bushes, flying back and forth from their Texas ranch, did a lot more recreational travel on government planes than the Obamas, or that the Secret Service preferred the president to fly on the full-sized, more secure, more expensive version of Air Force One.

That evening, Katie Couric suggested on her newscast that the Obamas keep their next date night "a little closer to home." The first couple scaled back their excursions. They had little choice politically, but another escape route out of the White House had been sealed off.

ALL THROUGHOUT THAT FIRST SUMMER, the president had trouble with campaign vows, far beyond the one he had made to his wife. After four months in office, it was becoming clear to him that the visions with which he had inspired millions upon millions of people during the campaign were going to be very difficult to achieve, not just because of the economic crisis and the Republican opposition but for reasons he had not fully understood back when he was campaigning.

Ten days before his New York excursion, he had sat with his attorney general and top aides at the gleaming wood table in the Cabinet Room, facing a dozen well-known law professors and leaders of civil liberties groups. The encounter was uncomfortable from the start. The visitors felt betrayed by the president. Obama had vowed to end Bush-era detention policies and close the Guantánamo prison, which years after the September 11 attacks still held untried terrorist suspects. Contrary to conservatives who argued that the United States could not worry about legal niceties when dealing with dire threats, Obama had declared, even after being sworn in, that there was no conflict between security and liberty. It was a classic Obama statement, following the same theme as his 2004 convention speech about red and blue America: once again, he was promising to resolve what seemed to be irresolvable.

He wasn't saying that anymore. The one-year deadline he had set for closing Guantánamo was still months away, but it was already

clear he would not meet it. He had made that promise before administration officials read the classified files on the detainees, which showed
that many of the cases would be much harder to resolve than he had
anticipated. Congress certainly wasn't cooperating with the initiative
to shut down the facility, even voting to deny funds for alternatives; no
one wanted suspected terrorists housed in prisons in their states.
Meanwhile, on a host of related matters such as releasing photos
depicting detainee abuse, the administration seemed to be echoing
Bush policies or adopting them with slight revisions. Obama shared
little of the left's interest in prosecuting the former officials who had
sanctioned policies such as "enhanced interrogation techniques,"
including methods denounced as torture, because it could criminalize
those vital to counterterrorism efforts.

As would so often be the case in the years to come, the president
was taking fire from both sides: the left was angry at the administration for not taking a stronger stand, while the right, including former
vice president Dick Cheney, was calling the president naïve and weak
on national security. Many in the White House, including Emanuel,
worried that the fracas could hurt the president's efforts on health care
and other issues. That was why the Cabinet Room guests had been
invited, and they knew it: the president was going to share his private
logic in hope of making them less critical in public.

As the meeting began, Obama answered their queries directly,
barely reacting to the sharpest criticisms. He shared their constitutional concerns, he said, but Bush had left him a mess. Releasing the
wrong detainee could result in new terrorist attacks, he said, and none
of his options were comfortable ones. He urged his visitors not to overlook distinctions between Bush's policies and his own—for example,
his ban on harsh interrogation techniques and the modifications he
made to the military tribunal system set up by the former president.

But Obama didn't pull his punches. "When I was a senator running for office, I talked very firmly about what I thought was right based on the information I had," Vince Warren, of the Center for Constitutional Rights, recalled the president saying. "Now I'm the president of all the people, and the decisions I make have to be from that perspective based on the information I now have." His face emotionless, he told his guests that he was considering an indefinite detention policy, allowing authorities to hold certain suspects without charges. It was an *"oh my god* moment," one guest said later. The legal rule was so basic, everyone knew it: suspects were innocent until proven guilty, entitled to speedy and fair trials. For a Republican president to violate the rule in the wake of a national catastrophe was galling to the guests. But for a Democratic president, a former constitutional law professor who had campaigned on protecting civil liberties, to make it official policy was shocking.

Before the gathering, the visitors had decided not to confront the president, for fear that leveling accusations at him would backfire. But Anthony Romero, the director of the American Civil Liberties Union, was deeply upset by what he heard.

"Mr. President," he began, eyes fixed on Obama, "I am a gay Puerto Rican American from the Bronx. In my *entire* life, you are the only politician in whom I have placed genuine faith. If you proceed the way you're indicating, I fear you will sacrifice your legacy and disappoint a generation." It was a well-crafted shot, aimed directly at Obama's belief that he was not like other politicians, at the fact that he had been elected because of the faith he inspired in others.

The president reacted viscerally, the attendees recalled. His jaw clenched, and so did the rest of his body. "Tony," he said, even though Romero went by Anthony, and launched into a reply about how he was doing the best he could, adding that ACLU statements comparing his administration to Bush's simply were not helpful.

It wasn't the only time Obama snapped back defensively when

confronted with supporters' disappointment. It was a hint as to just how heavily his promises weighed on him that the seemingly confident chief executive might not be quite as assured as he looked. He was the president of the United States, and yet his statement indicated a sense of powerlessness: Congress is not cooperating, and there's not much I can do about it.

The encounter ran far over its allotted one-hour time period, unusual for the Obama White House. The president asked if anyone else had an urgent point to make before the gathering broke up. Romero urged Obama one last time to prosecute a Bush official. "Hunt one head and hunt it famously and bring it down to ensure we don't make the same mistakes again," he said.

"That's one man's perspective," Obama said dismissively, and the meeting was over.

BY MIDSUMMER, THE PRESIDENT'S PLEDGES to overhaul the health care system were starting to look questionable as well.

His self-imposed August deadline for passing the massive piece of legislation looked even more unlikely than his one-year deadline for closing Guantánamo. The White House's decision to let Congress take control of the health care bill looked like a mistake: it was languishing in the Senate Finance Committee, losing momentum day by day. He had quietly abandoned his campaign line that the overhaul would lower premiums by as much as $2,500 per year per family: the math was wrong, his economic advisers told his political advisers, and they had to stop touting that number.

Republicans, eyeing his vulnerability, moved in for the kill. Senator Jim DeMint of South Carolina told conservative activists that blocking the health care legislation would "break" the president. The proposed bill included funding for end-of-life counseling, meant to ease trauma and discourage expensive, fruitless treatments. Republican leaders, including House minority leader John Boehner, called it "government-encouraged euthanasia" for the elderly. It was a completely baseless, instantly effective line of attack.

The bill's final contours remained unclear, making it hard to defend. Many people were satisfied with their health insurance, and the overall message — that overhauling health care at a cost of nearly a trillion dollars would help the economy — sounded convoluted. "I'm a pretty good communicator," the president told aides. "Why aren't I breaking through?" Obama was having trouble fighting back effectively and knew it.

He further weakened himself when he gave a news conference to explain his health care efforts and stumbled instead into a defense of Henry Louis Gates Jr., the black Harvard professor who had gotten into a fracas with a white police officer in Cambridge. It was a rare and regrettable entry into a discussion of race. To many Americans, the president looked as if he was siding with a Harvard crony over an ordinary cop. Glenn Beck, the conservative television and radio host, proclaimed that Obama "has a deep-seated hatred for white people."

Rahm Emanuel saw a disaster in the making. He spent the final week of July mounting what another aide called a "nonstop campaign" to convince the president to scale back his efforts on health care. A full overhaul would not pass, he told Obama. If the president narrowed his approach, covering needy children and cleaning up insurance practices, he could always do more later. His years with President Clinton and in Congress had taught Emanuel to do things a little at a time, avoiding controversy and gigantic win-or-lose moments. David Axelrod showed Obama poll after poll indicating that the effort was costing him precious public support. Voters were beginning to think that Obama was too cerebral and distant, more interested in following his own preset agenda than in responding to their concerns. The unemployment rate, which his economic advisers had once predicted would stay below 8 percent, was at an alarming 9.5 percent. Making health care into a grand battle could mean just what DeMint said: a loss from which the presidency might not recover.

The president plunged ahead anyway.

Around that time, Obama gathered with a group of aides around a table in the office of Phil Schiliro, the legislative affairs director, to discuss the bill's chances.

Republicans were not going to support an incremental approach, the president had told Emanuel. They weren't going to embrace a smaller plan any more than they were going to embrace an ambitious one, and scaling back would mean infuriating the left, he explained to his aides. Besides, Obama stated, it was the wrong thing to do. "I can't in all conscience leave 32 million people uncovered," he said. If he had the chance to fill an essential gap in the safety net, he had to do it. When advisers brought up alarming poll numbers about the cost to his own popularity, Obama countered with stories about individuals: a woman he had met in Green Bay with Stage 4 breast cancer and two kids, headed to bankruptcy because of her medical costs, among others.

But none of that settled the practical problem Obama and his aides were dealing with that day: even if they could get the bill out of the Senate committee, they did not think it would have enough votes. The advisers in the room had dozens of years of legislative expertise among them, and they could not quite see a route to successful passage. A feeling of discouragement settled in around the table.

"You know what, I feel lucky," said the president, sitting at one end of the table. "This is going to pass."

I feel lucky? Barack Obama was highly rational and deliberative, and yet he was ending the meeting with a profession of blind faith. For five years, things had broken his way again and again; was he still able to imagine that things would turn out otherwise?

A few weeks before, Obama had more or less acknowledged to the civil liberties advocates that he was departing from a major campaign promise. Now he surprised some aides with what seemed like the extreme opposite move — pursuing a campaign promise even though some of his assumptions about it had been wrong in the first place, even though conditions in the outside world had changed and he had every reason to scale it back. "I don't care if I'm a one-term president," Obama told his senior staff. Forget the polls, he told political advisers. He had seen them. "I understood when I went into this that I was going to be spending political capital," he said. "That's what you do with political capital."

In Obaman terms, the choice to let Guantánamo go but defend health care made a certain sense: he and his aides felt they could not ask Congress for unpopular votes on both, so he was sacrificing the first to save the second. Detainee issues did not directly affect a large number of Americans — after all, only a few hundred suspects lingered in the Guantánamo cells. For someone who had taught constitutional law, the president had always been surprisingly uninterested in upholding abstract principles. Former law students remember him continually brushing away theoretical arguments to ask, How does this affect real people? Health care, in contrast, was a massive, systemic issue, a problem that Obama believed the country simply had to solve. As one aide put it, "POTUS believes that policy is a science (largely economics) and that maximizing the greatest benefit for the greatest number is the objective, and that there are 'correct' and 'incorrect' choices." It was the best and the worst of Obama: his insistence on thinking big-picture and long-term, his devotion, so rare in politics, to the underserved, and his eagerness to do the undoable, all coupled with a sense that he knew better than everyone else, from the public to his own advisers.

The Republican attacks that unfurled over the following weeks, and throughout August of 2009, were even more spectacular, led by the growing Tea Party movement, which was becoming a kind of mirror of Obamaism: it rose on the same wave of general discontent with Washington that had carried Obama to office, and its proponents used the same grassroots organizing principles he had employed in his presidential campaign, though far more confrontationally. Sarah Palin took up their charge, accusing Obama of wanting to put her son Trig, who had Down syndrome, in front of a "death panel." Congressional town halls, normally placid civic events, flooded with protesters who leveled angry accusations about what they called "Obamacare." Instead of merely criticizing Obama's approach to federal spending, Tea Partiers accused him of being a socialist.

The administration was unprepared for the assault. As his staff became more frantic, the president dismissed the claims against his plan. The death panel accusations were beyond false: they were ludicrous, a sign of desperation. "It's because we're getting close that they're going so crazy," he told aides. He also believed August was a bad-luck month for him. (In August of 2007, his campaign had been in the doldrums, and a year later, Sarah Palin had become a star Republican vice presidential nominee.) To survive both Augusts and win the presidency, he had relied on mantras that he now repeated: ignore the naysayers, even within your own party; don't overworry about whatever is being said on political talk shows; don't change course because of week-by-week turbulence, and the American people will eventually calm down and judge the argument on its merits. "August is just not my month," the president told aides. "We're going to get this done." It was not clear if he understood that the Tea Partiers were driven in part by a fear that no one in Washington was listening to them; to brush off their claims was to rouse them even further.

At night, once the tourists were gone and the girls were asleep, the

Obamas sat out on their new furniture on the Truman Balcony, which had become their favorite spot in the White House, and talked. The health care overhaul fit perfectly with their shared sense of mission — their joint idea that the president's career was not about pursuing day-to-day political victories but the kinds of fundamental changes they had sought since they were young. This was Michelle's most profound influence on the Obama presidency: the sense of purpose she shared with her husband, the force of her worldview, her passionate beliefs about access, opportunity, and fairness; her readiness to do what was unpopular and pay political costs. Every day, he met with advisers who emphasized the practical realities of Washington, who reminded him of poll numbers; he spent his nights with Michelle, who talked about moral imperatives, aides said, who reminded him again and again that they were there to do good, to avoid being distracted by political noise, to be bold.

All of these beliefs underscored and supported her husband's own. The president believed his election had a specific meaning: it was a declaration by the American people that they were ready to take on long-festering problems, he told others. Otherwise there was no way a black man with an unconventional background and an unusual name would have been elected. "There was such a huge desire for change, and he was [the] personification [of that] in many ways," David Axelrod said, describing the president's feelings. The months he had spent dealing with the financial crisis had been a necessary detour; he figured the economy was on the mend; health care was what he had been elected to do. Ever since his election to the U.S. Senate, he had been talking to historians about his work, asking them for advice; and what always came through clearly, said Doris Kearns Goodwin, was his desire to do something monumental, to leave a major accomplishment behind.

The first lady had been eager to help her husband sell the public on the health care overhaul. A few months before, she had met with Nancy-Ann DeParle, the president's top adviser on the matter, and as they sat and talked, Michelle had grown visibly excited. *This* was what she wanted to throw her support behind; *this* was where she would make her contribution, she told aides.

Working at the University of Chicago Medical Center, Michelle had seen the dysfunction of the system up close: the huge expenditures on heart disease and diabetes that earlier, cheaper interventions might have prevented; the gap between cutting-edge academic medicine and a population that needed help with basics like nutrition; the patients who didn't have coverage and those who were one pink slip away from losing it. One of her big projects at the hospital had been to divert the tide of uninsured patients from the emergency room into local clinics where they could get regular primary care. During the campaign, she and her husband had heard countless firsthand tales about the unfairness of the system: insurance companies denying coverage for arbitrary reasons, parents struggling with limited coverage for severely disabled children, even people who died because they could not afford treatment.

The first lady told an aide that she did not want to get drawn into the policy details. "I don't want to be Hillary Clinton, I can't be that person," she said, referring to the criticism her predecessor had earned for taking charge of her husband's failed reform efforts. But she could use her popularity to build public support for the effort. "Figure out how to use me effectively," she instructed. "I'm going to tell my team, this is my priority."

As the health care wars raged that summer, the West Wing did not fully take Michelle Obama up on her offer. She did a few events—for instance, visiting a health care clinic to discuss stimulus funds—but not the kinds of appearances that would have won major attention. The president's political advisers were certainly tempted to use her more heavily, Robert Gibbs said later. They knew that she was ready and

willing. But Michelle Obama was one of the most popular public figures in the country, with an approval rating significantly higher than
her husband's. The president was already sacrificing some of his popularity to the health care cause, and the last thing political advisers wanted
was for the first lady to risk losing hers. The idea that she could fight for
health care *and* remain popular seemed improbable to them. "We had in
the back of our heads other first ladies who had gotten deeply involved in
health care," Gibbs said, another reference to Hillary Clinton.

Her support for the initiative became a mostly private matter, the
subject of long conversations between the Obamas. The president was
spending his days speaking the dense language of health care premiums, exchanges, regulations, and subsidies; as always, Michelle's role
was to pull him back into the world of everyday concerns, telling him
what she believed regular people truly thought. "She gives me a good
read on what's penetrating her consciousness in terms of the news
because she's not following it all the time," the president said in an
interview later. "In some ways Michelle is similar to the audience
we want to be speaking to," he continued, "which is commonsense,
hardworking Americans out there who are not policy nuts and are
mostly focused on their own lives, but do have a stake in the success of
the country and making sure government is working for them." She
told him when the administration's arguments weren't clear enough,
when they were failing to address a criticism from the other side. That
summer, her concern was about families who were struggling under
the current health care system but were also afraid of potential
changes, he said. The administration needed to do a better job of
addressing their fears, she counseled her husband.

With the president's isolation increasing, with his own solitary
nature exacerbated by the loneliness of the presidency, Michelle's feel
for the emotional element of an argument, for what most Americans
cared about, was more essential than ever. But she lived in the White

House now; she had only a little more contact with everyday people than her husband. The fact that he was still relying on her as a barometer of public opinion was evidence of just how removed he was from it.

Indeed, neither Obama fully grasped the dramatic change in the public mood that had taken place in the months since he was elected, or the collective sudden panic about government spending. Obama was elected to lead "a rational, postracial, moderate country that is looking for sensible progress. Except, oops, it's an enraged, moralistic, harsh, desperate country," one White House official said later. "It's a disconnect he can't bridge."

Cut off from the texture and nuance of American daily life, the Obamas viewed the opposition to the president's agenda as a series of tendentious and ill-motivated allegations like the death panel charges, a continuation of the nastiest rhetoric from the 2008 campaign. Because of prejudice, some Americans were never going to accept anything he did as president, Obama told aides. As a consequence, it is not clear that the Obamas heard what was most valuable and true in the public resistance to the health care plan and its overall cost. In the rush to implement his agenda, to earnestly deliver on his campaign promises, they did not see that, as Emanuel argued, the timing was uncomfortable for the country and the presidency. Obama's case for health care reform was highly analytical, based on the kind of long-term thinking he prided himself on. But part of the job of the presidency was to bring the country along with you, to make your agenda everyone else's. Obama simply had not done that.

Tellingly, when the president talked to aides about his eagerness to pass the legislation despite the political costs, he cited his wife. "Michelle and I are perfectly comfortable if we're only here one term if we feel like we really accomplished something," he said.

AT THE END OF THE first week of August, the first lady insisted that the family visit Camp David for the weekend so they could relax. She liked spending time there; with no threat of being photographed, she could take a break from getting her makeup and hair done, and the girls could roam free. The president generally found Camp David a little artificial, cut off from real life. When the Obamas did go there, they liked to bring friends, because the place was like an expansive vacation resort, far too big to occupy by themselves. On this particular weekend, he could not figure out why they were going; no one was even coming with them, he protested.

As soon as they landed on Saturday morning, the president was summoned into the main lodge for an urgent phone call. The lodge looked strangely dark and quiet as he entered. "Hey, anyone here?" he called out, looking for his family or staff. No answer.

That was the cue the figures hunched in the dark had been waiting for. As the lights came on they started yelling: "Surprise!" "Happy birthday!" The most powerful man on earth looked flabbergasted. A dozen of the president's closest male friends surrounded him, representing nearly every stage of his life. They had all arrived the night before. His boyhood pals from Hawaii had flown in, and those from college, too. Marty Nesbitt and Eric Whitaker had come from Chicago, along with John Rogers and Alan King, members of the same close-knit group from the South Side. David Axelrod and Robert Gibbs came from Washington. Decorations made by the kids hung on the walls.

"You got me," the president said over and over again. "You got me."

The weekend in the Maryland mountains, the invitations, the emergency call—the first lady had organized it all. Her birthday gift to the new president was a weekend away from 1600 Pennsylvania Avenue, a chance to be Barack, the person he had been all his life, not the nation's new leader. Everyone at the party had known him before he became famous, before he started shouldering the weight of

Democratic dreams. That became one of Michelle Obama's jobs in the White House: to remove her husband from it. "It's very important to her that he get away, that she take control of the situation," Alan King said, and Michelle carefully selected the guests "so that everyone in the room can allow him to completely relax, let down his guard, and speak freely."

Unlike the New York trip, this escape took place completely out of public view. Camp David, with its rustic cabins and deck chairs nestled around a swimming pool, was set on a military base with a wide perimeter, so they could move around without security or press. The members of the disparate group already knew each other because they had gathered for so many big moments: the presidential campaign announcement, the Iowa caucus, election night, the inauguration. Now they were at the private presidential compound, staying in cabins where kings and prime ministers had slept. In the shots the men took that weekend with their iPhones, the president and first lady were beaming real smiles, not the stiffer ones they used in official photographs.

It wasn't exactly a laid-back weekend, though: Barack Obama's idea of fun was to compete and win. The president wanted to win every game he played—basketball, pool, golf, Scrabble. That was the way he operated: constant self-improvement, an attempt to be the best at everything he did. Such focus made him occasionally insufferable, friends and aides admitted. When he beat you in basketball, he'd let you know forever, and when you gained weight, he was liable to taunt you about the extra pounds. During the U.S. Senate campaign, he was asked to throw out the first pitch at a game of the Kane County Cougars, a minor league baseball team. Aides familiar with their boss's competitive streak arranged for him to practice on the pitcher's mound one night at an empty Wrigley Field. When the president recorded the audio of *Dreams from My Father,* he mimicked every character's voice perfectly—not because it came naturally, said the producer who worked on the project, but because he practiced and honed the accents and inflections. (He won a Grammy Award for the reading.) After an embarrassingly low bowling score became public during the presidential campaign, he practiced in the White House basement alley, his wife poking fun at him for wanting to stay for just a few more frames.

For the birthday escape, Marty Nesbitt set up an Olympic-style tournament, a weekend-long competition in which players would be assigned points based on where they ranked in each event. At the end of the weekend, the person with the high score would be crowned Olympic champion. The men golfed on the small course at Camp David and played basketball, pool, and shuffleboard. Nearly two years later, Nesbitt, just as competitive as his friend, was able to rattle off Obama's scores in every event offhand.

Some of Barack Obama's best moments of personal athletic performance took place at some of the worst moments of his presidency. Life in the political arena was chaotic and often unfair; there were no referees, and fouls often produced the desired results, with no penalties. But in sports, the rules were established, the competition was fair, and Obama could exult in the kinds of clear-cut victories that eluded him back at the White House.

Going into the last event of the weekend, bowling, the president was behind. As the match drew to a close, his friends watched in wonder as he made four strikes in a row. That put him even with the top scorers; with one more strike, he could win the entire competition.

He swung back his arm and released the ball, which collided solidly with the pins, leaving one standing. The final pin wobbled, wobbled some more, and toppled. "Maybe the Secret Service blew it over," someone joked.

PART TWO

STRUGGLE

Chapter Six

THE WALLS CLOSE IN

SEPTEMBER–OCTOBER 2009

One day in fall 2009, Michelle Obama sat upstairs in the private family quarters of the White House, alone, frightened, and unsure of what to do next. The president was at an event across town, and the first lady had just received an email from Valerie Jarrett telling her that there had been a minor security incident. Don't worry, Jarrett had written.

The first lady's mind reeled anyway. What did minor mean? For several years now, she had been living with threats to her husband's life, but by the end of the summer, criticism of his health care plans had taken on an increasingly nasty, threatening edge. Protesters had brought guns to his rallies, and when members of Congress showed up to town hall meetings with their constituents, there were unnerving placards and signs, like two in Maryland that said "Death to Obama" and "Death to Michelle and her two stupid kids." In public, she wore a brave face, saying that you couldn't worry about these things, that the Secret Service had it covered. But in private, friends said, she dwelled on the threats.

Now she emailed Jarrett, who did not respond, which raised alarming possibilities. The butlers and ushers surely did not know anything, and Michelle did not want to panic them. Asking the Secret Service might create a fuss. "She's thinking, I don't want to be a distraction," Susan Sher recalled. But was there a reason no one was telling her anything yet?

The first lady emailed Sher. The minutes stretched by with no reply from her, either.

It was enough. She could not wait any longer. She picked up the phone and asked a White House operator for her husband.

He picked right up. "What's going on?" her husband asked, according to Jarrett. He was fine, he told his wife. There had been a tiny incident with his motorcade—the Secret Service had discovered what looked like a bullet-sized hole in one of the other cars, not his, but the agents had dismissed the incident and it barely registered with him. Jarrett had not written back because she and the president were in a meeting, nothing more. Sher had been working out so she had not checked her messages, either. Everything was okay.

The false alarm could have been worse. September 11 put authorities on high alert for terrorist attempts on the White House. Late on the evening of the attacks, the Bushes had finally fallen asleep in their White House bedroom when Secret Service agents pulled them out of bed, shouting that the house was under attack. It was not, but the same thing kept happening for months afterward. Laura Bush wrote in her memoir that she would be sipping a glass of wine or chatting with a friend when alarms would force her to flee to the bunker underneath the house. The Obamas were luckier; that had not happened to them so far. Yet here was Michelle, in another bunker of sorts upstairs, fearful and alone.

The first couple's experiences in the White House, so radically different from each other's in many ways, were becoming parallel in one unexpected respect: neither felt as powerful as he or she looked, aides said. While Barack Obama had spent the summer struggling with the limits of presidential influence, Michelle Obama was struggling with the limits of life inside the White House. To the outside world, she seemed like a modern, confident first lady, but as her momentary panic over Jarrett's well-intentioned message about the security incident showed, she was living in a confined, old-fashioned universe, and she had not yet found the escape routes.

For Michelle, the simple act of walking out the door was not simple. The official Secret Service policy was to accommodate whatever the president and first lady wanted to do, but the practical reality was different. Whenever anything happened on the grounds—a presidential statement outside, a Marine One landing—an email went out to a small group of aides, including the president and first lady's personal assistants. Before anyone in the Obama family ventured outside, they generally checked with someone on the list to make sure the coast was clear. "She can't even go walk her dog in her backyard without finding out first if there's a [media] pool movement or a Rose Garden ceremony," an aide said. Her daughters did not just run out to the swimming pool or tennis courts; they had to see what was happening first. The warmer months of the year were hardest, because they brought more outdoor events and visitors, which meant less freedom for the family.

The first lady's garden was one of the loveliest spots on the property, but, like her recent predecessors, she did not use it, because the tours passed right by. (Sher had to call a handyman to unseal the door that led from the East Wing offices to the garden; no one had gone from one to the other in years, she realized.) A good chunk of the Truman Balcony, the most immediate place for Michelle to breathe fresh air, was visible from the public corridors that led into the East Wing. If she took a book and a blanket to the edge of the balcony on a sunny day, tourists would be able to gawk or point cameras. Sometimes she exercised twice a day, she said later, because she spent so much time indoors that she wanted to compensate for all the steps she was missing. Once, she and Sher visited the Corcoran Gallery of Art. Michelle was surprised to discover that it was only a block from the White House; she had little idea what was in the surrounding neighborhood, because she could never traverse it by foot.

The president's confinement was far greater than her own; for him, private excursions to art museums were out of the question. But he was busy every day, with the most urgent work imaginable, while his family was left to cope with the life he had chosen. Nearly every one of them carried a different level of security and was permitted different amounts of freedom. The president was a virtual prisoner, while the first lady could sometimes slip out to restaurants (stores were more challenging: she often shopped online to compensate, using a card registered in another name and an off site delivery address to prevent tampering). The girls had far more freedom—they could go almost anywhere with a bit of planning and Secret Service agents tagging behind—but their parents often could not go with them.

Sometimes outings were deemed too risky or logistically complicated by the Secret Service, but sometimes Michelle declined of her own accord, because she did not want to cause a fuss. Before the inauguration, she had talked about wanting to take her girls to school every day, but she almost never did, because doing so caused traffic and distraction that inconvenienced other people and embarrassed her daughters. If the president or first lady attended soccer games, "there will always be one person who thinks it's their right to come and share all of their thoughts," Eric Whitaker said. The game would turn into a gawking session. Rather than risk the focus not being on the kids, she sometimes did not go at all, he said. The Obamas, who had campaigned in 2008 on being citizens of the real world, were growing

more and more cut off. "I don't think any of us contemplated how isolating this whole experience would be," Whitaker continued. "I don't
think this is a fun part about being the first family for any of them."

The Obamas worried about their daughters, missed their freedom, worried about how much they were accomplishing, and craved
escape from the perch they had given so much to achieve. As far back
as the presidential campaign, Obama had joked about how much he
was looking forward to being an ex-president. Life in the White
House was something to endure, not to luxuriate in, and he sometimes
discussed it with an undercurrent of anxiety. "If we keep that sense of
perspective, don't get full of ourselves, don't—take the work very
seriously but don't take ourselves too seriously, then not only will I end
up doing a better job, but what's most important is our family will
emerge from this process intact," he said in an interview at the end of
September. There it was, buried at the end of the sentence, the worry
that most politicians, presidents, and their families felt but did not
articulate, about just what this life could do to a person.

The Obamas had not been back to Chicago since their first trip in
February 2009, and, unlike many other first families, they did not
have an additional home that could serve as a refuge. Jacqueline
Kennedy passed a good chunk of her husband's term in Palm Beach
and at weekend houses in Virginia, and the Bushes, savvy about the
restrictions of White House life, built their ranch in Texas during the
campaign. The Obamas mostly had Camp David. Though they
spent a lot of time with the Whitakers and the Nesbitts, many of their
long-standing, more casual relationships withered. Old friends sometimes received invitations to an official event—a concert, a Cinco de
Mayo reception—and if the Obamas spotted them in the crowd, their
faces often lit up at seeing genuine pals among the sea of must-invites
and political contacts. Other times, however, the president and the
first lady looked stressed at evening events and only dropped in for

fifteen minutes at a time. No one had a manual for how to maintain a friendship with the president or the first lady. Did you need an excuse to get in touch, or could you just call to say hello? Everyone wanted to see the Obamas—to check on them, to pass along encouragement and gossip—but nobody wanted to intrude, overstep, or offend.

Michelle had the occasional friend to lunch in the upstairs residence—they weren't going out, she laughed—where she also gave tours, her normal voice falling into tour-guide cadence. Some of her friends and relatives, though, never heard back from staff when they emailed. What did that mean, they wondered—had they lost favor? No one warned them that harried White House staffers tended to reply to only a fraction of the email that came in.

The president's dawning sense of political powerlessness, the first lady's sense of personal powerlessness: the two were not entirely separate. The fears about safety, the lack of personal liberty—it was tolerable to the Obamas as the cost of what they wanted to accomplish. Michelle had said it countless times to audiences during the campaign: their old lives were wonderful, this was difficult for them, and it was worth doing because her husband would create real change. They had made their original decision to run for the presidency based on the idea that he would be able to do great things in office, not on the possibility that his presidency could get stuck.

But the president's agenda *was* slowing down: a momentary development, he hoped, that he would be able to overcome. When Obama reflected privately on the presidency that fall, he often spoke about the limitations of the office, the way circumstances, mainly the economy, had forced his hand. Instead of setting a precedent for tackling other big issues, as the president had once hoped, the health care overhaul was impeding the progress of much of the rest of his agenda. Support for the measure was middling, and the congressional votes so uncertain that the administration feared that any more conflict could capsize things. Thanks to energetic White House wrangling, the energy bill had passed the House over the summer, but that meant nothing until the Senate passed it, which would not have a chance of happening until the health care question was resolved. The president was optimistic, but climate change experts inside and outside the White House were queasy with worry.

That fall, Tea Party and Republican protesters staged a revolt against a planned "back to school" speech by the president, even though his predecessors had given such routine addresses and he only planned on urging young people to study hard. "As the father of four children, I am absolutely appalled that taxpayer dollars are being used to spread President Obama's socialist ideology," said Jim Greer, the chair of Florida's Republican Party. (Some school districts, caving to parental concerns, made viewing the speech optional for students.) It was the same argument Republicans had been making for months, this time penetrating all the way to middle school cafeterias: the president wasn't the centrist, commonsense leader he claimed to be, but a big-government ideologue who could not be trusted around the young, the old, and everyone in between.

The developments raised a question about the overall Obama project: if the health care overhaul wasn't moving forward, if the president couldn't even tell schoolchildren to do their homework, if Republicans were able to block them at every turn, then why were they living like this?

The Obamas never complained publicly; they emphasized again and again that their opportunities were a privilege. They tried to make the best of their confined new lives, to take advantage of the things they could do. Michelle created "Camp Obama" for her daughters over the summer, taking them to historical sites like Mount Vernon and Charlottesville. The girls accompanied them on a diplomatic trip to Europe, where they met the pope (all Sasha noticed was the shape of his thumb, her parents laughed later). The president was finally able to read to his daughters at night; that fall, he and Sasha enjoyed Yann Martel's *Life of Pi*.

Because they couldn't leave town, they brought people to them. The Nesbitts had rented a house in Washington for the summer, and the president's sister, Maya Soetoro, a free spirit who taught peace education, temporarily moved to town with her husband, Konrad Ng, who became a visiting scholar at the Smithsonian, and their two young daughters. They rented an apartment and slipped quietly in and out of the White House gates, and on weekends, the two families watched movies and slaughtered each other at Scrabble.

Sasha resumed her tennis lessons, this time on the outdoor courts behind the White House, so much more exclusive than the scruffy one where she had played in Chicago, and her mother and sister took lessons, too. When Michelle was younger, she had been too competitive to play organized sports, according to Craig Robinson, her brother. Now she took lessons as well, thwacking away as Bo, the first dog, often bounded over to the court, attracted by the balls. (The Obamas were competitive with each other even at tennis: "He beats me," the first lady said. "For now," the president added.) They improved at tennis the way British prisoners in the Second World War became skilled birdwatchers: they were confined, so they did what they could.

They were still working to make the upstairs residence feel like their own home. The public rooms downstairs might be a museum, decorated in the style of an era when African Americans had few legal rights or social standing, but at least upstairs could reflect how the first couple saw and experienced the world. Every first family was allowed to borrow art from Washington's museums, and inside the residence, the Obamas chose colorful abstract works by Alma Thomas, who was barred from museums as a child because she was black and had begun painting full-time at age sixty-nine, and *Black Like Me* by Glenn Ligon, which used text from John Howard Griffin's memoir about darkening his skin and traveling through the South to experience segregation firsthand. Another painting, *I Think I'll...*, by Ed Ruscha, seemed like a sly joke about the decisiveness and clarity demanded of a president, the words "MAYBE...YES..." floating against a blue and burnt-orange background, along with "MAYBE...NO..." and "WAIT A MINUTE" and "ON SECOND THOUGHT." The art didn't cost anything, and it helped tremendously.

Word passed quietly among aides and close friends: the adjustment has been quite difficult, and the first lady feels very claustrophobic. But no one else knew, which was part of the reason the public still had a largely fairy-tale vision of the White House: no president or first lady, while in office or after, wanted to seem ungrateful, and so almost no one ever talked about the confinement or disorientation. Visitors saw the glamorous bits of the presidency: the pristine grounds and gardens, the historic rooms and legions of staff, and, perhaps most appealing of all, the magic of a truly spectacular White House party.

The Halloween bash the first couple threw on the final day of October 2009 was a case in point, a celebration that looked dazzling on the outside and generated considerable anxiety on the inside.

Not surprisingly, children of politicians often got the short end of Halloween; in 2004, John Edwards's kids were reduced to trick-or-treating on the campaign plane. But the Obamas had always been big Halloween people. In Chicago, Michelle had decorated the house and supervised the costumes; her husband took the girls trick-or-treating. In 2007, Barack had worn a mask, allowing him to roam his neighborhood blissfully undetected, but the following Halloween, their last at home, had been a little odd, because it took place just a few days before the election. He insisted on escorting Sasha, dressed as a ghost, around Hyde Park/Kenwood. When television crews began to follow them, the neighborhood asserted its protective powers: local kids yelled at the cameramen to leave the two alone.

For the Obamas' first celebration in the White House, Desirée Rogers and her team turned the building into a spooky wonderland, with orange spotlights, thousand-pound pumpkins, and musicians dressed like skeletons. Stilt-walkers and performers dressed like butterflies flapped their wings inside giant clear bubbles on the lawn.

The Obamas stood on the front portico, handing out sweets to thousands of Washington-area schoolchildren who had lined up to trick-or-treat. The president wore a sweater and slacks, ducking the awkward sartorial question of what sort of costume the leader of the free world might wear. The first lady wore a leopard sweater, cat ears, and sparkly eye makeup. Some of the younger children tried to pet her, and she did not seem to mind. Even by the standards of baby-kissing politicians, the Obamas loved children, seeking them out at events, finding joy and relief in their company. The president could be introverted or occasionally even icy with associates, but around kids he was playful, even goofy.

Inside the house, at an invitation-only party, children of military service members and administration officials mingled with characters from the *Star Wars* movies—not knockoffs, but the real Chewbacca and company, personally dispatched by George Lucas for the occasion. The children of commerce secretary Gary Locke were dressed as pint-sized Secret Service agents, in dark suits, sunglasses, and earpieces, and when the president heard about their costumes he called a photographer over for a photo with his tiny protectors.

The party's pièce de résistance was the State Dining Room, decorated by the movie director Tim Burton in his signature creepy-comic style. His film version of *Alice in Wonderland* was about to be released, and he had turned the room into the Mad Hatter's tea party, with a long table set with antique-looking linens, enormous stuffed animals in chairs, and tiered serving plates with treats li

meringue cookies. Fruit punch was served in blood vi

Burton's own Mad Hatter, the actor Johnny Depp, presid

scene in full costume, standing up on the table to welcome eve

character. The Obama girls sat at the table, surrounded by a gag

their friends, and then proceeded to the next delight, a magic show

the East Room.

From all appearances, the party was a dazzling success. Internally
it was not. This time, the in-house debate about entertaining had
resulted in an awkward stalemate. White House officials were so
nervous about how a splashy, Hollywoodesque party would look to
jobless Americans — or their representatives in Congress, who would
soon vote on health care — that the indoor party was not discussed
publicly, and Burton and Depp's contributions went unacknowledged.
The media covered the trick-or-treating outside but not the party
inside. Rogers and the East Wing had put a great deal of effort and
creativity into the party, but the more they did, the more internal anxiety they caused. A few weeks later, Rogers would preside over a disastrous state dinner, and she did not leave the White House until March,
but by the time of the Halloween party, aides said later, her fate was
effectively sealed.

The biggest disappointment of Halloween 2009, however,
occurred a few miles from the White House, where Malia and Sasha
had attempted to go trick-or-treating that afternoon. They wanted to
circulate from house to house, just like other kids. Going with their
parents was out of the question: the group would attract too much
attention. So Maya Soetoro and Konrad Ng, along with the Nesbitts
and the Whitakers, took Malia and Sasha and their own children to
what seemed like a promising residential neighborhood. The adults
hoped that between the costumes and the other kids roaming the
streets, the Obama girls would blend in. For a little while the plan

g, neighbors began texting neighbors,
eras surrounded the girls. "People
them," Whitaker said later. "It was
l to the White House earlier than
on the porch greeting children
uld not: walk around Washing-

upbeat and composed during the party, as she
ways did in public. What almost no one knew is that even as
she was chafing at the constraints around her, she was beginning to
reassess her whole approach to her role.

SHE HAD STARTED THE SUMMER BEFORE, by firing Jackie Norris, the
chief of staff she had selected only a few months earlier, and asking her
old friend and former boss Susan Sher, who had come to the White
House as a lawyer in the counsel's office, to take over. The first lady
and Sher were a study in outward contrasts, one tall, attention-getting,
and capable of being quite vehement, the other short, unassuming, and measured. They knew each other inside and out, and though
Sher was an outsider to Washington, she was an Obama insider:
a close confidante of Valerie Jarrett's, trusted by the president
and David Axelrod as well. Sher stepped into the job quietly, with
few outsiders aware that she was on a turnaround mission: to
establish better relations with the West Wing, put a meaningful
agenda in place, and somehow make the job of first lady work for her
old friend.

Sher also had the awkward task of managing Desirée Rogers, who
was quickly losing favor. Many of the events Rogers planned were
inventive and fun: astronomy lessons for children with NASA astro-
nauts and telescopes on the South Lawn, and a luau at which members
of Congress plunged administration officials like Robert Gibbs and

Peter Orszag in a dunking booth. But as the unemployment rate climbed and the health care fight continued, Rogers and her splashy approach lost ground.

She had not made many friends among administration members. She tended to articulate things out loud that the Obamas left publicly unstated—their frequent disdain for Washington custom, the sense that the White House was in some ways fusty and outmoded. Concerned staff members who had initially assumed that there was a close friendship between Michelle and Rogers, and who were consequently afraid to tell Michelle about their problems with Rogers, started to let her know. Rogers also hurt her own cause considerably when she appeared in May on the cover of the *Wall Street Journal* magazine in earrings that were identified as costing $110,000. Outside of the White House and political circles, the profile and accompanying photos did not provoke much notice; inside, it was like the $87,000 Merrill Lynch rug all over again, except this time a member of the administration was wearing the offending object in a major publication. Staffers from both wings were aghast: they had all been worrying about looking clueless and insensitive during a time of economic pain, and this was how Rogers responded?

In a way, the change in Rogers's fortunes was not entirely about her; it was also a measure of how much Michelle Obama herself had begun to change since November 2008, when she had asked Rogers to take the job. Back then, the first lady had barely attended any White House events; now her office supervised several per day. A year prior, she had had little understanding of the diorama quality of White House life; now she did. And by fall 2009, the first lady was no longer a newcomer to Washington. She had watched her husband get torn up mercilessly over the summer, her date night had been dissected on television, and she was growing far savvier about the rules of her position—from arcane matters such as which foreign royals were to be addressed as "Your Highness" and which as "Your Royal Highness" to which congressional officials mattered and why.

The first lady's attitude toward fashion and style was also shifting. Putting herself on the line as a role model and using her clothes and even her body to send a message turned out to have an unexpected downside: suddenly *everything* she wore carried meaning. She was picked apart for wearing anything too fancy, like the Lanvin sneakers, but wearing clothes that were too everyday provoked criticism, too. Early one summer morning she had walked Bo, the new family dog, on the White House grounds, dressed the way people dress to walk dogs — baggy madras shorts, no makeup, bra strap peeking out a little. Someone managed to snap an unofficial photo, and within hours, pictures of her looking slightly unkempt were all over the Internet.

A few weeks later, when the first family visited the Grand Canyon, they were warned to dress in light clothing, because temperatures on the canyon floor could climb dangerously high. Michelle wore a pair of unremarkable-looking shorts. Another flurry of pictures hit the web, and Robin Givhan, then the fashion critic of the *Washington Post*, wrote a column deeming the shorts "common." The first lady approached Robert Gibbs afterward, worried and contrite: had she committed a faux pas? He felt sorry for her, he said later: she was trying so hard, and was so concerned about making a mistake. For months, Gibbs had been making the case for the Obamas looking approachable and down-to-earth, and now that the first lady had dressed like a regular mom, she was being picked apart for that, too. "You're never going to please some of these people," he told her.

She was tired of being known for what she wore, she told aides, and though she still dressed glamorously, she pointedly refused all fashion-related requests and invitations. As some of her advisers had predicted earlier, she ultimately didn't want to be known for which designers she wore; she and her husband had come to Washington to change the country. If her husband's initiatives were stuck, if he and his aides weren't going to incorporate her into the presidential strategy, she would find another way.

ALL THROUGH THE FALL OF 2009, her husband was trying to move his health care overhaul plans along, with a combination of earnest public argument and frenzied behind-the-scenes dealmaking. In meetings with his team, he was analytical and upbeat: he did not want to hear recriminations about what had gone wrong over the summer. "What we're here to discuss today is moving forward," he would say. "How do we fix this, how do we change it, what is the plan?" In September, he gave a long, reasoned speech to a joint session of Congress, making argument after argument in favor of his efforts, sounding like a lawyer presenting arguments to a jury. "We are the only advanced democracy on Earth — the only wealthy nation — that allows such hardships for millions of its people," he said. Parts of the speech had a *why-don't-you-get-it, I-can't-believe-I-have-to-address-this* quality. He ticked through assurances that he was not planning a government takeover of health care, panels to execute infirm senior citizens, taxpayer support for abortions, or coverage of illegal immigrants. (Just after he got to the immigrants, Joe Wilson, a Republican congressman from South Carolina, called out, "You lie!" as Obama glared back at the insult and breach of etiquette.) Michelle, privately so concerned about whether his arguments were registering with the public, watched over him from the balcony.

Eager to dismantle barriers to the legislation's passage, Rahm Emanuel and Jim Messina, a deputy chief of staff, had cut a quiet deal with pharmaceutical industry lobbyists: in exchange for supporting the legislation, the administration would guarantee that it would cost the companies no more than $80 billion. Many White House aides were surprised and alarmed: Obama had campaigned as a reformer who would fight lobbyists and pharmaceutical companies, and now he was cutting a backroom deal with them that looked like a giveaway? David Axelrod and Emanuel, the closest of friends and allies, went back and forth, Emanuel saying that he needed to do what had to be done to pass the bill, Axelrod protesting that this was exactly what they had campaigned against. But Obama, his competitive juices stoked and his most important initiative on the line, did not halt his chief of staff's horse trading. That was their deal, another aide said: Rahm would try to pass Obama's bill, but the president had to accept that it wouldn't look pretty.

At the same time, Michelle Obama was starting to work on a health care initiative of her own, a campaign to reduce and prevent childhood obesity. Her initial progress was very slow, and at first she was stuck on small efforts: the White House garden, a new farmer's market on Pennsylvania Avenue, hula-hooping with youngsters on the South Lawn. ("You're doing *what?*" Emanuel had asked Sher one day at his 8:30 morning meeting; by late afternoon, the pictures of the first lady swiveling her hips were everywhere, more evidence that she knew the power of an image.)

But Michelle didn't want her anti-obesity work to be "just another first lady initiative," as one aide put it, meaning a polite public-interest campaign. She wanted real change — to take on a seemingly intractable public health crisis, attack it hard, and win. Still, though her staff had accumulated mountains of research and suggestions, no actual program had really cohered.

Around Halloween, Sher called Stephanie Cutter and asked her to take a look at the situation. In Obamaworld, Cutter was known as a crisis counselor and rescue artist: the blond Smith graduate, a veteran of the brutal fights over John Kerry's image in the 2004 presidential campaign, had engineered the turnaround of Michelle Obama's reputation during the 2008 campaign. She was one of the few aides on equally good terms with the East and West wings.

Cutter quickly realized that while numerous government agencies had authority over nutrition, exercise, and childhood-related issues, they did not work in concert. "The U.S. Department of Education has access to students and teachers and gym teachers and parents, but they don't control the lunchrooms," she said, offering just one example. Those belonged under the Department of Agriculture — and on and on, with different government authorities controlling nutritional labels on packaged food, farm subsidies, and other food, as well as childhood- and education-related programs. It was an alphabet soup of bureaucracy without unified goals. Public health officials and private foundations had worked on the problem for years, to little avail: one-at-a-time adjustments, like adding more recess time at school or eliminating soda machines, did not help much, because dozens of factors influenced a child's nutrition and fitness. The only hope of real progress, the experts said, would be to take on the entirety of a child's environment, from school meals to recess and playgrounds to the grocery store to restaurants. The war had to be fought on all fronts at once, and it needed a powerful spokesperson, someone to advocate and fight for it in public.

The first lady, with Cutter's help, decided her role would be to unify the existing anti–childhood obesity efforts and add new ones, bringing federal, state, and local government efforts into alignment, working with nonprofits, chefs, and pediatricians, and lobbying the corporations behind supermarket food and restaurant chains. Everything would be tied together with a catchy name: Let's Move!

True to her organized, disciplined nature, the first lady felt strongly that the campaign needed structure and a clear goal. After months of *not* being able to do things, of looking attractive and smiling at photo opportunities, she craved credibility and a tangible sense of progress. The question was how ambitious the goal should be.

Very ambitious, the first lady told her staff. She decided she wanted to try to end childhood obesity within a generation, meaning that children born in 2010 would grow up without the same burden of obesity that had afflicted the group before them. Advisers worried a little about whether the use of the word "obesity" would be a turnoff, and about the wisdom of touting organic vegetables in a bad economy. But the goal seemed politically safe, in part because by 2028, she would be sixty-four, nearly her mother's age, out of the White House for twelve years or more. The program launch was planned for the following January.

With Let's Move!, Michelle Obama planned to finally move away from some of the roles she had taken on so far in the White House — lavish entertainer, subordinate of the West Wing — and strike out in a direction more her own. To deflect any criticism that she was getting too deeply involved in policy decisions — the Hillary Clinton problem again — advisers referred to her publicly as the point person on an administration-wide initiative, even though it was really her own. She would have no real money to spend and no official policymaking position, just the support of her husband and his team, her own popularity, and her own ability to inspire and persuade.

At the broadest level, the president and first lady's separate health care efforts shared common goals: to improve the overall well-being of Americans and fix the badly overstrained health care system. An end to or even a decrease in childhood obesity would mean fewer cases of diabetes, heart disease, and hypertension, which would mean less medical intervention, which would mean lower health care costs and healthier Americans, two of the most widely agreed-upon but hardest-to-legislate goals of health care reform.

Aides insisted that Let's Move! and the health care overhaul had nothing to do with each other, but together the projects illustrated a stark, telling contrast between husband and wife. Barack Obama, as he had for decades, was trying to change things by passing laws. But Michelle Obama had never trusted legislatures, or even governments, to change people's lives for the better. She was going straight to doctors, schools, food manufacturers, grocery chains, parents, and kids to ask them to alter their environment and behavior. "This is important irrespective of what happens with health care," Sher said a few months later. "She has less appreciation for the political process to actually accomplish things than he does. Which is part of why he's a politician and she isn't."

Overtly, the president and first lady's initiatives may have been separate. Yet with the passage of health care reform uncertain, Michelle Obama was complementing her husband while also pitting her philosophy and approach (targeted, not solely governmental in approach) against his (sweeping, government-mandated). The two programs, health care reform and Let's Move!, were a continuation of the conversation the Obamas had been having since they first met, this time played out with higher stakes than ever, on a gigantic new stage.

AT THE SAME TIME, the first lady sent the West Wing a strong message about what she thought about the way advisers there treated her.

She was facing a classic political-spouse question: when should she agree to her husband's advisers' requests for her to appear in public? Politicians' wives were often their husbands' best surrogates; few understood their husbands better or represented them with more authenticity. Some of them, like Betty Ford and Laura Bush, were more popular than their husbands. As a result, their husbands' staffs liked to deploy them—as fallbacks when their spouses couldn't make an event, as charming facilitators for potentially awkward encounters, to attend ribbon-cuttings or make speeches as payback for political favors. And because their husbands' aides were often, by the nature of their jobs, frantic, improvisational, and willing to agree to almost anything, the women were sometimes booked without any consultation, as if they had no say in the matter at all. If they refused to go, political aides sometimes saw them as high-maintenance, unwilling to help with key tasks and willing to disappoint supporters; if they always said yes, they lost independence and control, precious commodities for any political spouse. Being dispatched without consent had proved maddening for more than a few political wives over the years, including Hillary Clinton and Michelle Obama. During Bill Clinton's first term, Emanuel, then a young but high-ranking aide to the president, put together a last-minute dinner with members of Congress and scheduled Hillary Clinton to attend without checking with her office. She refused; she had her own private plans that evening. She *has* to go, Emanuel urged her staff. She called Emanuel and lit into him. He groveled, begged her to attend. When he swore it would never happen again, she at last relented, but not before making it abundantly clear that her husband's staff had zero power to preempt her own plans and commit her to a political event without her knowledge. Shortly afterward, the first lady tried to fire Emanuel. The dinner was not the main issue — her husband's White House was chaotic, and she wanted more experienced hands — but it did not help. Emanuel stubbornly remained in his office, coming to work each day, refusing to go unless Bill Clinton told him to. Within a few years he had the office next to the president, but he had learned his lesson, he told others: stay out of the first lady's way.

Prior to arriving in the White House, Michelle Obama had often taken even tougher stands. During her husband's failed congressional campaign in 2000, he could not make one of his own fund-raisers because he was stuck in Springfield for a vote. Dan Shomon, the campaign manager, asked her to step in. The event was in her neighborhood, hosted by someone she knew. "We pleaded with her," Shomon said. She would not do it. "Michelle is sort of like, you made your bed, go lay in it," Shomon said. It wasn't her fault her husband was stuck in Springfield, she told him.

Four years later, when Barack Obama won the Democratic primary for the U.S. Senate, his schedule was even more jam-packed. One day staffers called her in a bind: he could not appear as promised at an award ceremony only two days away; could she come instead? She lost her temper with the aide who made the request, swearing "like a sailor," he said later. Emil Jones Jr., the president of the Illinois state senate, appeared instead.

But in the White House it had happened again. In June, as the White House desperately pushed to pass the energy bill in the House, Allen Boyd, a Democrat from North Florida who was threatening to vote no, asked Emanuel to send the first lady to do an event with him for a campus volunteer organization. Boyd was white, but many of his constituents and a potential primary challenger were black, and an appearance with the first lady would send a strong, helpful message. Making a commitment on Michelle's behalf without consulting her first could be perilous, but Emanuel needed Boyd's vote on the critical piece of legislation, and he saw his job as delivering that vote. Without calling the first lady's office, he told Boyd that he could make the visit happen. Boyd voted for the legislation.

Emanuel's chief of staff, Sean Sweeney, told Susan Sher about the commitment, who told the first lady, who was extremely unhappy about it.

In October, Michelle flew down to Florida and spoke at the event, introduced by Boyd. He got his picture and his hug with her. East Wing aides never told Michelle she was being used to head off a potential black challenger for Boyd's seat—they did not know that themselves. Her staff did know that Boyd was planning on voting against the health care bill, but they did not tell her so, they said later, because they were too afraid of how she would react.

The West Wing was starting to send her other requests to appear on behalf of members of Congress. She was the most popular figure in the administration, especially now that her husband's numbers were slipping, and because of her mom-in-chief image, she was perceived as appealingly apolitical, above the fray. But she now sent a message to the West Wing: no more one-off requests, even in advance. She wasn't doing one little thing here, another event there. Implicit in her message was a warning: she didn't flat-out refuse to campaign in the midterms the next fall, but she made it clear she would not be an easy sell. If the West Wing wanted her out there for the midterms, she said, they would have to ask her properly, to make the case for how she fit into an overall strategy, to be far more organized in their approach.

She had been burned in the 2008 campaign, she felt, sent out in front of audiences with little support, and she was not making that mistake again. She did not want to put herself on the line for members of Congress she knew little about and might not agree with. Her message carried an implicit critique, too: she thought the West Wing was too disorganized; that they didn't plan well enough. She had been saying so for years, first during the campaign and then in the White House, and now she was reinforcing the message, with more leverage than ever before.

Emanuel found her reluctance maddening. Michelle Obama was a key asset, he told others in the West Wing. House and Senate Democrats were going to need her help with voters, and the White House needed to build goodwill with them too. He didn't push her directly, but he wanted the president to convince his wife — to make her understand, to explain the urgency. The president, however, hated asking his wife for political favors. It was a genuinely worrisome situation: was the White House going to have to go to bat for midterms without the president's own spouse?

David Axelrod counseled giving the first lady some time. The midterms, after all, were still a full year away.

Chapter Seven

Twenty-Six Hours in Wonderland

OCTOBER–DECEMBER 2009

One fall evening, Mark Leibovich, a reporter at the *New York Times*, was working late at his desk when the phone rang: it was Valerie Jarrett, calling from Air Force One. Leibovich was working on a story that would explore whether the Obama administration was a boys' club, with men dominating the political, economic, and national security teams, led by a president who spent spare moments watching ESPN and weekends playing basketball and golf with male buddies. Jarrett was calling to tell Leibovich that his case was overstated, "a Washington perception that has nothing to do with the reality on the ground," and to list all the women Obama had appointed to high-level posts, starting with Hillary Clinton. Her tone on the phone was defensive, insistent.

Unbeknownst to Leibovich, the story was being managed behind the scenes by none other than the president, who was personally dictating talking points to the aides who would speak to the reporter. The still-to-be-published story was causing high anxiety in the West

Wing; this presidency was supposed to be different, inclusive, more than the usual club of white males. Obama's defeat of a potential first female president in the 2008 Democratic primary, not to mention his heavily female electoral base, only made the charges more fraught. The president was dreading days of cable news chatter on the topic, and on the weekend the article was published, he invited Melody Barnes, his chief domestic policy adviser and a skilled golfer, to join him, the first time he had included a woman in his foursome. The gesture caused a collective cringe among some women in the West Wing, because it was so transparently triggered by the story.

Ten days after its publication, Obama sat down for a White House dinner meeting quite unlike any in recorded presidential history: he was the sole man present. Around him sat the highest-ranking women in the West Wing: Barnes; Nancy-Ann DeParle, who directed health care reform; Carol Browner, the energy chief; Christina Romer, chair of the president's Council of Economic Advisers; Mona Sutphen, a deputy chief of staff; Alyssa Mastromonaco, the president's scheduler; Anita Dunn, the communications director; and Jarrett, the only woman among Obama's closest aides. Jarrett had convened the dinner, not the first time she had arranged a meeting in which Obama would hear frank views she felt he needed to hear. Contrary to what she had told Leibovich, she was concerned. "Early on, some women did not have a direct relationship with the president," she said later. "I felt direct interaction, where they could speak freely, would help." The first lady did not attend, but she was an invisible presence: for years, she had urged her husband to open himself up to a more diverse array of advisers, including by gender, and she quietly let it be known that she thought the story raised important questions.

The attendees couldn't quite tell if Obama really wanted to be there. He began by glancing at his watch and effectively said, okay, we have this much time, according to one attendee. That's how he was, always on schedule, always crossing an item off his to-do list, rarely falling into open-ended conversations. "Are there genuine concerns that I need to know about?" the president asked, looking around the table.

There were, although not exactly the ones he may have expected. The women were divided on how necessary the gathering was from a pure gender point of view. A few, like Romer, felt strongly that they were excluded from an internal boys' club, but others were indifferent: they had been around Washington a long time, risen to powerful positions, and did not care who the president invited to play golf. As the women went around the table, taking turns speaking, they did not exactly cut loose. "It was an awkward, silent dinner where we were given one glass of wine and a piece of fish," one participant said.

But many of them agreed on a more central concern. The *Times* article and the dinner were an excuse to gently tell the president that they had serious concerns about how his White House was run in general. Their real worry wasn't that the guys were causing them great personal offense, several later said: they were worried the guys were screwing everything up.

The situation wasn't anything like, say, the abject disorganization and careening quality of the early Clinton White House, where even getting the president to a meeting on time was a challenge. But there was little flow of information in the West Wing. Too much was secret even from insiders, and one team did not always coordinate well with another. Rahm Emanuel's 7:30 a.m. meeting for top staffers, which the president never attended, did not have an agenda — it often seemed driven by what was in the newspaper that morning. Some senior staffers, like Barnes, were not invited; and when decisions were made at these meetings, they were not shared in a systematic way outside the small group in attendance. Sometimes others in the West Wing only found out about the decisions when they were put into effect. Larry Summers was supposed to be a mediator of economic ideas but repeatedly cut out other people, for instance, giving colleagues little time to comment on memos going to the president. Summers had gotten in hot water at Harvard for asking if women had less innate scientific ability than men, but it was hard to say he was sexist, exactly, because he could be dismissive to everyone.

A few of the women had been quietly trying to pull things together: Dunn had put together a weekly coordination meeting, and Browner had urged more long-term planning efforts, but their attempts only went so far.

The dinner was a delicate situation: the women wanted to alert the president, but they were worried about sounding like they were griping. So they left some concerns unsaid, such as the president's own daily meeting with his senior advisers, which had no agenda, either. Axelrod, Gibbs, Jarrett, and the rest just went around the room and brought up what they felt was most important, often focusing on the crisis of the day. The attendees in that meeting were like a soccer team, one aide said, where every player ran for the ball instead of remaining in position. The sessions were "dangerously reactive," she added, with little long-term planning.

"There was almost no process on anything," a former economic adviser, not at the dinner, said later, meaning no structured way of making sure decisions were reached. "It was really remarkable."

Any White House was a series of competing power centers, but Obama had more than usual: Biden, Emanuel, Axelrod, Gibbs, Jarrett. He actually liked being surrounded by a set of wildly disparate influences; he had supreme faith in his own ability to mediate and extract the best from all of them, and he did not seem deterred by the cost of that approach to others or, ultimately, to himself. "He believes that he can set up a structure whereby he can police that and get the best possible and available information," Gibbs said later. "It's how he tests his own arguments out."

Even Emanuel's allies admitted that his style was scattered: "schizophrenia," as one said. His philosophy was to put "a point on the board," meaning some small advance or victory, each day, to eventually win the match. That made a certain amount of sense tactically: long-term planning was sometimes futile in Washington, because things changed so fast that it was nearly impossible to predict what would happen months ahead. But it often made less sense to the public: Even if the White House was winning a point on education, and then on Social Security, and then on Afghanistan, those points would not necessarily add up, because there was no overall strategic message. "Yes, you've won that day, but you've so confused the American people about what you're talking about," the aide said.

Others were concerned about Emanuel's outbursts, a growing tendency to lose control of himself, to take out his frustrations on members of the staff. Later, some aides said it was hard to pinpoint a specific instance of his verbal abuse, because it was so frequent. But one instance stood out in their minds: one morning the previous spring, at the 8:30 meeting for senior White House staff in the Roosevelt Room, Emanuel had ripped furiously into Jason Furman, an economic aide. The week before, the president had announced that the major banks were repaying government bailout funds, but within a week Citigroup announced a setback to that plan, an embarrassment to the White House that had made front-page headlines. Emanuel "unleashed on Jason in a way that was completely unhinged," one attendee said. "I can't fucking believe that we didn't know about this," he fumed. "How can we fucking run this place if people aren't going to know about big news? What do I have to do to find out what's going on around here?"

The odd thing was that Furman, one of Summers's deputies, had nothing to do with Citigroup. Relationships with banks were under the jurisdiction of the Treasury Department. Timothy Geithner, the Treasury secretary, was absent that day, Furman happened to be sitting in his chair, and so Emanuel chose to rip Furman apart. "Just because you're sitting your sorry ass in that chair I will yell in your direction," one attendee recalled him saying, his performance almost theatrical. Furman sat calmly, letting the storm pass.

At the dinner, Obama was almost an entirely closed book; he was genuinely listening, said several of the women, but it was hard to tell what he was thinking. He sounded almost apologetic about Emanuel, telling the women he needed him. He ended with reassurances, telling the group not to measure influence by how often someone appeared in his office or how often they seemed to get the last word. (It was an implausible thing to say: presidential access was *the* ultimate measure of West Wing influence.) Just because a senior adviser told him something in a meeting, Obama said, didn't mean he believed it. He asked the group to report back to him soon. They never did. They had said their piece, and they were uncomfortable going much further.

Though Obama never tipped his hand, the concerns could not have been news to him. He had been telling others for months that he worried that Emanuel was too focused on the day to day at the expense of the long term. And the women were, knowingly or not, repeating some of Michelle's points to him. But later, another adviser said the president did not grasp the full measure of the problems. "Any president's isolated, and he was isolated in the Oval Office," the adviser said. "He never really appreciated why people would be so frustrated by this, and he didn't have time to dwell on it because he was learning to be president. He's never really run a big operation before, and he probably didn't appreciate or understand the depth of it. He's not an organization guy."

Besides, the president did not have the luxury of taking time to think about how his White House could be better organized. The West Wing was enmeshed in a fiendishly difficult set of decisions, and his I-feel-lucky optimism of the previous summer had been replaced by a sense of mounting pressure. In October, Attorney General Eric Holder announced that the administration had decided to try Khalid Sheikh Mohammed, one of the planners of the 9/11 attacks, in civilian court in New York instead of in a military tribunal at Guantánamo Bay, a victory for civil liberties advocates who had visited the White House in the spring. Republicans cast it as a dangerously naïve attempt to protect terrorists' rights. Hundreds protested in downtown Manhattan. The day of the women's dinner, a Muslim American army psychiatrist, Nidal Malik Hasan, killed thirteen people in a shooting rampage on a Texas military base. The shooting appeared to be the breakdown of a disturbed man, not an al-Qaeda–organized event, but Hasan had previously expressed extremist views and exchanged emails with Anwar al-Awlaki, a radical Islamic cleric in Yemen. The nightmare of regular domestic terrorism attacks seemed more and more likely, which sent tremors through the entire West Wing, not just its political precincts: there was *no* higher presidential priority than keeping the United States safe.

Just as the health care bill approached a crucial vote in the House, the president had to decide on his Afghanistan strategy, a pairing that aides compared to simultaneously landing two airplanes on a single runway. In September, when Obama had started a complete review of the situation, his team was badly divided. If he did not dispatch significant numbers of American troops to beat back the Taliban and al-Qaeda, the military brass warned that he could face what they termed "mission failure." But if he did agree to more soldiers, advisers including Biden and Emanuel warned, the United States could be mired in Afghanistan, sacrificing troops and facing local resentment. Even if the United States prevailed there, neighboring Pakistan, a supposed

Barack and Michelle Obama emerge from their daughters' school in November 2008, a few days after the presidential election. He was already plunging into the work of the presidency, but Michelle, unbeknownst to the public, was considering staying behind in Chicago with her daughters for the rest of the school year. *(Stan Honda/AFP/Getty Images)*

The Obamas initially found the White House grand but archaic and strange. (The phone lines did not work normally; a military valet did the president's laundry but not the first lady's; the carpets had stains from the Bush pets.) They planned to escape frequently to Chicago, but their first foray back, shown here, was awkward and they did not return for over a year. *(© Kevin Lamarque/Reuters/Corbis)*

On that February 2009 trip, their familiar home—pictured here in 2008—came to resemble an armed camp. The Secret Service, unaccustomed to protecting presidents who lived in cities, dropped black curtains over two sides of the house. *(Melina Mara/Washington Post via Getty Images)*

Barack Obama found that the presidency transformed nearly every aspect of his life—even what kind of sports fan he was. At his first White House Super Bowl party, he cheered avidly for the Pittsburgh Steelers, a favorite team; later, with reelection on the horizon, he remained neutral. *(Official White House photo by Pete Souza)*

Marian Robinson, the first lady's mother, initially resisted moving into the White House with her daughter and son-in-law, saying, "When you move in, you just hear a little bit too much." She became indispensable because she could take Malia and Sasha Obama on everyday excursions that their parents could not. When no one recognized her as she shopped alone at the Filene's Basement near the White House, she laughed: "They think I'm just another person who works at the mansion." *(Mandel Ngan/AFP/Getty Images)*

When Michelle Obama broke away from official spouse duties on a trip to London to visit a girls' school, above, she saw the potential of her role for the first time. But her first few months in the White House were difficult: she had a tense relationship with some of her husband's advisers, and she found the setting disorienting and confining and the job of first lady vague. She had a low regard for Congress and tried to get out of some ceremonial duties, like a yearly lunch with Capitol Hill spouses and daughters, pictured below. *(Mandel Ngan/ AFP/Getty Images; Official White House Photo by Samantha Appleton)*

The Obamas depart for a date night in New York in May 2009. Though many outsiders admired the glamorous images of the first couple, inside the White House they were drawn into an uncomfortable debate about how they should look and live. Michelle Obama, eager to change stereotypes, wanted the first black first family to look beautiful and chic; Robert Gibbs, the press secretary, was concerned about public resentment during a time of joblessness and disapproved of many of her clothing, entertaining, and decorating choices. *(Aude Guerrucci—Pool/Getty Images)*

Barack Obama at the July 2009 meeting at which he told skeptical aides that he "felt lucky" about his health care overhaul passing. His commitment to the unpopular measure came from a shared sense of mission with his wife. She wanted to drum up public support for the initiative, but West Wing aides stopped her, fearing she would appear too much like Hillary Clinton, whose own health care efforts as first lady had gone badly. *(Official White House photo by Pete Souza)*

For Halloween 2009, the Obamas handed out candy to schoolchildren on the North Portico, but the party inside—featuring decorations by the director Tim Burton and an appearance by Johnny Depp—was kept quiet. When Malia and Sasha Obama tried to trick-or-treat in a residential neighborhood, they were thronged by onlookers. *(Official White House photo by Pete Souza)*

The administration expected Obama's trip to Oslo to accept the Nobel Peace Prize in December 2009 to be awkward, but it passed like a brief, happy dream—a return to the acceptance and acclaim the president felt during the campaign. The Obamas, along with close aides and friends, came to believe that the American public did not appreciate their exceptional leader. *(Official White House photo by Pete Souza)*

Michelle Obama with Susan Sher, the close friend who became her chief of staff. Relations between the president's and the first lady's teams were so difficult that Michelle Obama and her staff went on a retreat to discuss the matter, and she held out on agreeing to campaign for midterms for nearly a full year, causing anxiety in the West Wing. But with Sher's help, the first lady became more content and more powerful, starting a widely admired campaign against childhood obesity. *(Chip Somodevilla/Getty Images)*

Though Michelle Obama played it safe in public, she was watchful and protective of her husband and sometimes privately critical of the White House's organization and message. After Democrats let Edward Kennedy's Senate seat slip into Republican hands, she was upset with the president and his advisers; by the late spring of 2010, she told him and others he needed a new team. *(Damon Winter/New York Times)*

Michelle Obama addressing the 158 graduates of Anacostia High School in 2010. She made her own work a smaller-scale answer to the problems of the presidency. As her husband had trouble giving inspiring speeches or connecting with audiences, she excelled in those areas. *(Jahi Chikwendiu/ Washington Post via Getty Images)*

The president with Robert Gibbs (left), his longtime press secretary, and Rahm Emanuel, his first chief of staff. When Emanuel ran for mayor of Chicago, he won a near-endorsement from Obama. But unbeknownst even to many West Wing aides, their relationship was difficult at times, and in early 2010, Emanuel secretly offered to resign. *(Official White House photo by Pete Souza)*

The president and his advisers prepare the text of his Oval Office address about the Gulf oil spill. As the midterm elections loomed over the White House in the summer of 2010, Obama's once close-knit team fractured, with internal blowups over a speech on immigration, the president's remarks about the proposed Islamic center near Ground Zero, and how much support the president was lending to Congressional Democrats. *(Official White House photo by Pete Souza)*

When the Obamas traveled to the Gulf to show that its waters were safe, the president surprised aides by asking them to release this photograph of him and Sasha. The Obamas were fiercely protective of their girls, but as the president struggled to connect with the public, he often cited his daughters, contrasting their sincerity and innocence with what he called the cynicism and self-interest of Washington. *(Official White House photo by Pete Souza)*

Once Obama had enjoyed pickup basketball on public courts; now uniformed White House butlers inflated his basketballs (below). "When I leave office there are only two things I want," the president joked to friends. "I want a plane and I want a valet." For his birthdays, friends and aides staged elaborate sports competitions. He celebrated his forty-ninth birthday with a basketball tournament with Joakim Noah and Derrick Rose of the Chicago Bulls (pictured here), LeBron James of the Miami Heat, Maya Moore of the University of Connecticut, and other stars. Though the president disliked the idea of anyone going easy on him, he just happened to win the 2009 and 2010 tournaments. *(Official White House photos by Pete Souza)*

The president spent most of his social time with two friends, Marty Nesbitt (above) and Eric Whitaker (below), very much like him: high-achieving, sports-loving African American men from modest backgrounds, with strong commitments to their families and to social change and little trust in Washington. The two men said they made a point of never criticizing or questioning Obama on his actions as president. *(Harry E. Walker/MCT/MCT via Getty Images; Jewel Samad/AFP/Getty Images)*

Obama in his private upstairs office, where he often worked late into the night. A solitary figure, ambivalent about politics, he told an old boss he was still a community organizer, talked to friends about looking forward to the post-presidency, and refused to miss dinner with his family more than twice a week. *(Official White House photo by Pete Souza)*

As the president's poll numbers flagged, Michelle Obama's popularity with the public gave her more leverage inside the White House. The Obamas denied marketing their marriage for political gain, but in a fall 2010 Oval Office meeting, political advisers showed the Obamas the power of their joint appearances. A few weeks later, images like this one, from a joint appearance in Ohio, were used in campaign literature for the midterm elections. *(Doug Mills/New York Times/Redux)*

Left to right: David Axelrod, Valerie Jarrett, and Robert Gibbs were three of the president's closest advisers, but the relationship between Jarrett and Gibbs, tense for years, imploded in August of 2010, as Gibbs showered expletives on Jarrett (and the absent first lady) out of frustration that they did not appreciate his work. *(Alex Wong/Getty Images)*

Obama almost never shared his emotions with the public or even with his own advisers. A rare, deep frown at a press conference after the fall 2010 midterms prompted a quiet debate among White House aides: was it a genuine show of contrition or an offering for the cameras? *(Doug Mills/New York Times/Redux)*

The shooting of Arizona congresswoman Gabrielle Giffords, a presidential favorite, captured the Obamas' worst fears about public life. Michelle Obama and Giffords's husband, astronaut Mark Kelly, watched the president give one of his best speeches at a memorial service for the victims. *(Kevork Djansezian/ Getty Images)*

Unlike her husband, who resisted the power of presidential images, Michelle Obama worked to create memorable pictures that sent a consistent message: if she could become first lady, then children who were outsiders and underdogs could grow up to achieve anything they wanted. Here she plays hopscotch with runaways and orphans in Mumbai in fall 2010. *(Official White House Photo by Chuck Kennedy)*

Eager to update the White House residence, the Obamas eased out Rear Admiral Stephen Rochon, the chief usher, in favor of a new hire with a background in hospitality. *(© Jonathan Ernst/Reuters/Corbis)*

At the beginning of the administration, the first lady had wanted a greater role in communicating the presidential message, but by 2011, she had created her own operation, running it more like a nonprofit organization than a political one. *(Official White House Photo by Chuck Kennedy)*

A rare instance of Malia and Sasha speaking in public, reading *The Cat in the Hat* at a community center in South Africa in June 2011. At difficult moments for the administration, the first lady tried to produce upbeat images to counteract the depressing news from Washington. *(AP Photo/ Charles Dharapak)*

The Tea Party's success in using the debt ceiling showdown to slash government spending, coming just at the start of his reelection campaign, left the normally even-keeled Obama in a funk over the summer of 2011. In private meetings, advisers saw his sadness at the decline of his public support, his anger that others did not seem to appreciate his accomplishments. "I'm running against the Barack Obama of 2008," he admitted at a fund-raiser. *(Saul Loeb/AFP/Getty Images)*

A rare photograph of the first family in the private residence, watching the women's World Cup soccer game, released by the White House as the debt negotiations stalled in July. With the economy potentially headed back into recession, the president's advisers planned to rely heavily on his personal appeal in the 2012 election, showcasing images of his wife and family. *(© Pete Souza/ White House/Handout/The White House/Corbis)*

U.S. ally, was quietly cultivating ties with the Taliban as a hedge against its archrival, India. The president inhaled memos and studied maps all fall, and here he did put in place a formal decision-making process: he presided over dozens of meetings on the matter himself, interrogating his military and national security teams, jotting notes on a yellow legal pad. His final decision was a short-term, thirty-thousand-person swell in forces, a "surge" not unlike the one General David Petraeus had led in Iraq, intended to produce a quick turn-around in the war. The administration would keep close tabs on the effort, and the troops would probably start to come home by July 2011 — in time for the 2012 election, everyone noticed. Before announcing the decision, Obama asked every member of the large team to pledge their consensus, and they all did, a sign that he had successfully managed the difficult decision.

At the same time, Obama was watching his economic team become paralyzed and riven by dysfunction. The recession was technically over, a real achievement, but by November unemployment was at 10.2 percent, the highest level in twenty-six years. Thanks to the tax cuts George W. Bush had enacted, plus the impact of the recession, the stimulus, and the inherited wars in Iraq and Afghanistan, the federal deficit was a stunning $1.4 trillion, the most red ink that post–World War II Washington had ever seen. Obama's advisers were divided between raising government spending to reduce unemployment, which would swell the deficit, or cutting government spending, which would lower the deficit but risked raising unemployment.

On the campaign trail Obama had promised to let the Bush tax cuts expire for people making over $250,000 a year: the wealthiest Americans had grown wealthier than ever before, and yet they were paying a lower share of the national tax bill than ever before. Ending their cuts would take a big bite out of the deficit. But the administration was nervous about a measure that the Republicans would surely pounce on as the latest in Obama's socialist advances, and some outside economists argued that ending the tax cuts for the rich would hurt the economy. "You're crazy," Emanuel yelled at one of the president's most experienced outside economic advisers when he called to recommend passing a bill to eliminate the cuts above the $250,000 income line before they would expire a few weeks later. "You're not saying we should vote in a tax increase *before* an election, are you?"

At meeting after meeting, economic advisers contemplated the same questions with little progress: which to prioritize, jobs or the deficit? Everyone agreed it was a bit of a false distinction—they had to attack jobs immediately, the deficit once the economy recovered—but they could not figure out what to do in the medium term. Their indecision weighed on the president, adding yet more pressure to his load. The critics who accused him of being unfeeling about economic suffering were wrong, numerous aides said. He felt it deeply, reading letters every night from parents who could not buy their children school notebooks and from people who had sent out hundreds of résumés with no results. Now he also had to face the fact that it was not clear internally, or to the outside world, what his overarching economic strategy was. Worse, the team members were sniping among themselves about matters like who would attend which meeting.

At a late fall gathering in the Roosevelt Room, Obama snapped. Once again, his team was debating what action to take, whether more stimulus was possible, and what to do about a spending freeze. The advisers had come to an unsteady consensus, but once the president began asking questions, their tenuous agreement fell apart, according to several people who were in the meeting. The president had already heard the same arguments again and again. The advisers had all taken those positions in prior meetings.

Obama lost his patience. "We have now been through this exact same discussion with exactly the same people saying exactly the same thing six times, goddamn it. *Six times.*" He rose and walked out, with twenty-five minutes still on the meeting clock. Several of those present said they had never seen him like that before. Axelrod, Rouse, and Gibbs rose and followed him in solidarity. Only the economic advisers were left.

More than anything, Barack Obama stood for consensus and common ground, the idea that reasonable, well-intended, smart people could come together to solve the country's problems. But he had not been able to do that with Republicans, and now it wasn't even happening on his own team. In theoretical terms, all the advisers believed in short-term stimulus and long-term deficit cutting, but, as in a bad marriage, the team had become polarized into two camps, and common ground had disappeared, as one of the infighters later put it. The president had repeatedly ordered his team to come to consensus, but they could not, and he seemed unwilling to choose sides himself. As another aide pointed out, Obama's explosion wasn't a sign of his impatience: it was a sign of his patience, because many managers would have cut the discussion off after two rounds, not a half dozen. The economic team's failure to resolve their differences, and Obama's failure to decide a course of action, would linger in the West Wing. The administration would be hamstrung by the stimulus-versus-cuts debate, in one form or another, for many months to come.

All hell broke loose in the room. Romer grew visibly upset and raised her voice while Orszag fled. "I do not understand what just happened here," Geithner protested. Austan Goolsbee, the president's longtime economic adviser from Chicago, sat holding his head in his hands. Rob Nabors, the deputy budget director, pointed frantically to the open door facing the Oval Office: could the president hear the screaming?

FOR THE FIRST SEVEN YEARS of Obama's political career, he had felt underappreciated, struggling over whether voters beyond Hyde Park would understand him: whether he was too lofty a thinker, whether his name was too foreign and his background too unusual, whether he was too Harvard to win on the South Side. From 2004 to 2008, the answer was the loudest, widest affirmation imaginable: People read *Dreams from My Father* and found their own experiences and observations reflected there; local chapters of Obama for America sprung up with little guidance from headquarters; rallies drew as many as seventy-five thousand people. Obama had opponents and critics during that time, of course, some of whom spread false rumors about him. But he also experienced what only a few people in the world ever have: a sense of connection with millions upon millions of people who had faith in him.

Now, during his presidency, he was experiencing a slow descent back into feeling misunderstood. Later in the first term, there were points when the American public seemed to be giving up on Barack Obama. But the relationship went both ways, and there were many times the president seemed to be giving up on the public, too, convinced Americans would never understand his point of view.

The nonstop attacks were taking their toll, but so was his failure to explain his own policies in a clear, engaging way. The stimulus Congress had passed in February 2009 contained a middle-class tax cut, but the administration had not advertised it, and Republicans incorrectly alleged again and again that Obama was raising taxes. During a routine meeting near the end of the year, the president and his economic team went through the results of a survey on the public's understanding of the cut. Something like 40 percent of respondents said the stimulus had not affected taxes, Goolsbee remembered later. About another 50 percent said that it had *raised* taxes. Less than 10 percent correctly said that taxes had been cut. The economic advisers were aghast: the communications and press people had to fix this somehow! The president held his arms out wide and gave a fatalistic shrug, a gesture of helpless surrender. Almost no one understood that he had lowered their taxes, he said slowly, as if he was trying to make the advisers accept what he already believed: Yes meant no, up meant down, and there seemed to be no chance of restoring truth. He had been in office less than a year, and he was already low on faith that others would understand his work.

The president was an elitist, but an unusual kind. He often showed a sweeping disdain for entire categories of the powerful — members of Congress, bankers — and a natural attraction to underdogs, to anyone he saw as vulnerable, ignored, or left behind. Being in the White House seemed to intensify one of his best traits, his natural seriousness, along with one of his worst, his conviction that he was more serious than anyone else. There was a gap between the way Obama consumed information — in orderly, high-level briefings — and the way nearly everyone else in the country did, and it could often turn him derisive.

He took his frustration out on the media, which he largely viewed with condescension bordering on contempt. Obama was a writer — in his twenties, that was how he identified himself to others, and he only ran for office after *Dreams* failed to have much impact — and it sometimes seemed that along with being his own speechwriter, political director, chief of staff, and so on, he also wanted to be his own White House correspondent. In an interview with Jonathan Alter, Obama grew animated talking about his encounter in South Korea during the fall of 2009 with President Lee Myung Bak, who told him that parents in his country were so devoted to educational excellence that they demanded he import English teachers. "And then I sit down with U.S. reporters and the question they have for me in Asia is have I read Sarah Palin's book?" It was a double swipe, at Palin and the media, and Obama shook his head for emphasis. "True story." The president was perversely fascinated by cable news — he liked to see "what the idiots are paying attention to," in the words of one aide—but he preferred to lose himself in the *Economist* and the *New Yorker*.

He wanted the media to be more of a referee; to put unfair Republican charges to rest. He could brush off the wildest, most baseless attacks themselves, he told Jarrett, along with Marty Nesbitt and John Rogers, at lunch in the little dining room next to the Oval Office that fall. What galled him was when they gained mainstream credibility despite distortions of truth. Rogers had just noticed a new book by the conservative columnist Michelle Malkin called *Culture of Corruption: Obama and His Team of Tax Cheats, Crooks and Cronies.* Among many other allegations, Malkin wrote that Michelle Obama—the president's "bitter half"—was secretly running the country in Lady Macbeth–like fashion. Malkin even took a hatchet to long-dead Fraser Robinson, arguing with no evidence that his job at a water plant made him part of the "Chicago political corruptocracy." The book debuted at number one on the *New York Times* nonfiction bestseller list and stayed there for weeks.

One day that fall, Emanuel was glancing through a sheaf of polls regarding whether voters thought the country was headed in the right or the wrong direction. He had been feeling uneasy for months, but now the results he saw, said Patrick Gaspard, the political director, made "the hair on the back of his neck stand up." Emanuel knew congressional seats better than anyone else in the White House, and he had a kind of clairvoyance about elections. Months before others in the West Wing said so, he saw what was coming: unless the administration quickly changed course, the midterm elections coming up a year later were going to be a bloodbath.

ON DECEMBER 9, THE PRESIDENT, preoccupied by the health care legislation, flew to Oslo to collect the Nobel Prize for Peace, which had been announced a few weeks before. He and his aides hunched over the conference table on Air Force One, writing his address through the night. It was one of the more important speeches of his presidency, but things had been frenetic back in Washington and they were crashing it anyway.

They were unsure what sort of ridicule might await the president for accepting the award. The Nobel committee chose Obama because his election broke a racial barrier and because he turned the page on the Bush era, but the timing was awkward. He would be honored for furthering world peace just as he was preparing to send tens of thousands more troops to Afghanistan. He was still ordering drone attacks there and in Pakistan, killing suspected terrorists but also some civilians. Indefinite detention was still on the table, too. And though he was about to be inducted into a pantheon that included Nelson Mandela and Elie Wiesel, he could not pass his legislative priorities at home. The award seemed to underscore an idea Obama chafed against: the main accomplishment of his presidency might be his election. When subordinates congratulated the president, he said, "I just want to pass health care."

The Obamas and their advisers knew the jeers to come might be even louder than they were when the award was announced. Normally Nobel Peace Prize winners were celebrated with three days of banquets, receptions, press conferences, and a television interview, plus a concert and museum exhibition honoring the recipient. To avoid the appearance of Obama's celebrating with European royals while Americans suffered at home, the White House had clipped the festivities short ahead of time, warning the committee that the president would be able to come to Norway for only about twenty-six hours.

But amid the bad news and pressures of late 2009, the trip unexpectedly passed like a brief, happy fantasy for the president, a Nordic alternate reality where citizens were learned and pensive, discussions were thoughtful, and everyone was a fan. "It wasn't hero worship," said one adviser who accompanied them. "Okay, it was."

For one day, the Obamas lived the dream version of his presidency instead of the depressing reality. At meals and receptions, they mingled with the members of the Royal Academy — government officials, academics. Instead of false rumors or specious charges, the first couple found respectful Scandinavians who were surprisingly well versed in the president's work. "They had read the president's books," Susan Sher said later in amazement. "They knew more about some of his policy ideas than I did." They asked the same question the president had asked Congress: how could a country as rich as the United States not provide health care for its citizens?

The president and first lady were deeply touched, proud that they had improved America's reputation abroad, and, in some sense, they felt better understood than they did in Washington. "I was struck by how well read and how knowledgeable every person I met with was," recalled Eric Whitaker, one of a coterie of friends the Obamas brought with them. In contrast to the well-informed people they met in Norway, "Americans have no idea what's going on in the rest of the world," he said. "This was a room that represented the better angels of our nature," David Axelrod echoed. In one set of remarks, the president mentioned his mother, an anthropologist and idealist who had worked in dozens of different countries and had raised her children to prize the same sorts of universal, humanist values as the ones extolled by the Nobel committee. He gestured to Maya Soetoro, his sister, who had come, too. Axelrod noticed the president was fighting back tears.

A small crowd of protesters gathered around Oslo's city hall, site of the ceremony, claiming that Obama was not a figure of peace — a novelty for a president often accused by Republicans of being too soft to keep the country safe — but a far larger crowd assembled to cheer. From their hotel window, the Obamas peered out at thousands of

people assembled for a torchlight parade in the president's honor—
"candles as far as the eye could see," Whitaker said. It was hard to
think of a time since the inauguration that the Obamas had received
that kind of shower of appreciation.

The president gave a ponderous acceptance speech meditating on
the contradiction of giving a peace prize to the leader of a nation at
war. He spoke of nothing less than the history of war in humankind.
"War, in one form or another, appeared with the first man," he said,
and continued to World War II, the founding of the United Nations,
the cold war, the rise of terrorism, and how "to build a just and lasting
peace."

He also laid out standards that he privately must have known he
would not reach. "The United States of America must remain a standard-bearer in the conduct of war," he said. "That is why I ordered the
prison at Guantánamo Bay closed. And that is why I have reaffirmed
America's commitment to abide by the Geneva Conventions." He did
not acknowledge that the effort to close Guantánamo was failing or
address the questions about whether his detention policies violated
those guidelines. "We lose ourselves when we compromise the very
ideals that we fight to defend," he said. It was as if he had pressed
some sort of rewind button to 2008.

The trip spurred a thought the Obamas and their friends would
voice to each other again and again as the president's popularity continued to decline: the American public just did not appreciate their
exceptional leader. The president "could get 70 or 80 percent of the
vote anywhere but the U.S.," Marty Nesbitt told Eric Whitaker
indignantly.

CONSIDER, FOR A MOMENT, the ideal holiday setting. A home full of
family and friends, away from meetings and deadlines. That would
not be the Obamas' experience in December 2009.

A few weeks before, Michaele and Tareq Salahi, participants in the reality television show *Real Housewives of D.C.*, had waltzed into the first White House state dinner without invitations, clearing two security checkpoints and shaking hands with a smiling, unknowing president. The results were days of fevered headlines, multiple investigations, questions about the competence of the Secret Service and the social secretary, and yet more distractions from the critical work of the administration.

The state dinner disruption, which took place a few days before the final installation of the White House's holiday decorations, pretty much ruined Christmas. The state dinner had been for just a few hundred people; in the ensuing days, fifty thousand were invited to troop through the house for holiday parties. The East Wing was supposed to be the fun part of the White House, and the first lady hated the idea that an unforced error partly under her management had cost the administration weeks of negative press. The gate-crashing incident also supplied new grist for her fears about safety; what was the point of living in virtual lockdown if anyone could slip through? Everyone put on a brave face for the parties, but one aide summarized the prevailing yuletide sentiment as: "Let's make a gingerbread cake for Christmas next year and be done with it."

Even the ornaments on the indoor Christmas trees were under scrutiny. The White House had sent old ones to community centers around the country for people to redecorate (in the recycling spirit) and return. A conservative blogger published grainy images of a few of the more saucily decorated results: a portrait of a transvestite entertainer named Hedda Lettuce, an image of Mount Rushmore with President Obama's face added. It was the kind of irritant that arose weekly in right-leaning media and went largely unnoticed by most voters, but it contributed to the White House's sense of embattlement and unease. "There really isn't much margin for error," Susan Sher said later, after she returned to civilian life. "That's the thing that kept me up at night. There was no issue that was too small. It wasn't paranoid."

West Wing aides ducked quickly in and out of the holiday parties, but they were in overdrive. The president, Emanuel, and congressional leaders were finally managing to bring the health care bill for a vote in the Senate, the second-to-last step before final passage in the House. To seal the crucial Senate vote before winter recess, they made a deal late on Friday evening, December 18, with Democrat Ben Nelson of Nebraska, a holdout on supporting the measure. The arrangement promised to give his state a better deal on Medicaid funding than any other, to the tune of tens of millions of dollars. Many other administration members did not know about the deal until the next morning, when Republicans started attacking it as the Cornhusker Kickback. The arcana of the health care overhaul had been difficult for voters to understand, one former aide who objected to the deal pointed out, but the Nebraska deal was easy because it looked like simple extortion and a willingness on the president's part to make questionable backroom deals.

Obama, who wanted nothing more than to pass the plan, was willing to live with the actual deal, according to several of his close aides. It was "the optics issue," as one put it — how awful it looked — that concerned him. He had run for president promising to put the health care negotiations on television, to get away from the usual Washington horse trading and renew bipartisan cooperation. Now he was attempting to pass health care via secretive deals with the pharmaceutical industry, fat benefits in exchange for votes, and no bipartisan support. (Though lawmakers had for months tailored the bill to her specifications, Republican senator Olympia Snowe walked away at the final moment.) It was not clear, as Obama smiled stoically and waved his way through the holiday parties (sometimes even two a day), whether he fully absorbed that the deals were diminishing his reputation as a reformer, a vital reason voters were so drawn to him.

Because the president disliked grip-and-grin photos, the Obamas did relatively few of them compared to their predecessors. "Even people who claim he was born in Kenya want a picture" with the president, Whitaker said. "They say crazy things on TV, they still want to get invited to the Christmas party." At most of the receptions, the Obamas did not mingle with the crowd. At some, they stood behind a security cord, reaching their hands across the rope to greet those lucky enough to get near them.

When the Obamas saw their real friends in such settings, however, they lunged for them. At one party that December, the president spotted his old community organizing boss. Jerry Kellman had first made Obama a Chicagoan and an organizer, giving him a job a few years after college, training him, spending long evenings discussing who held power in society and why. When the president glimpsed Kellman, a slight man with thinning gray hair, at one reception, he pulled him across the rope barrier so that he could have a word with his old mentor and friend.

"I'm still organizing," Obama told Kellman.

The statement was absurd on its face. Was the president in denial about who he had become? Was it wishful thinking, or had he completely failed to confront the fact that he really was a politician who, like all politicians, made ugly choices in order to pass legislation? The crowd pressed closer around the two men and Secret Service agents pressed back.

"I know you are," Kellman replied. He did not know what else to say.

AT LEAST THE OBAMAS WOULD have a decent vacation. Their Chicago escape the previous February had not gone as planned, date night in New York had been ruined, and Senator Edward Kennedy's death and funeral and Ben Bernanke's reappointment to the Federal Reserve had landed right in the middle of their Martha's Vineyard trip the summer before. Their departure for Hawaii had been postponed on account of the Senate health care vote, but right after Democrats exhaustedly collapsed across the finish line, their vote successful, the Obamas finally flew off.

As Air Force One headed west, Bill Burton, the deputy press secretary, passed on a special message from the president to reporters: relax. Don't expect any announcements or newsmaking events.

Everyone, no one more than the president, desperately needed a break. More than any other place on earth, Hawaii was his real home, and his yearly vacation there was a sacred ritual. He played basketball with high school buddies, took his daughters for shave ice, and had visited his grandmother, Madelyn Dunham, until she died in the fall of 2008. Michelle liked to say that you couldn't really understand her husband unless you had been to Hawaii. In recent years the Nesbitts, the Whitakers, and Valerie Jarrett started coming along, too.

The sanctity of the Hawaii trip was also the result of years of negotiation between the Obamas. During what he later called the low point of his marriage, when he challenged Bobby Rush in 2000, Obama had been in Hawaii over the holidays when an important gun control vote, one he would look terrible missing, was called in the Illinois State Legislature. Malia had a fever and Michelle refused to fly home early, not for a race that she had not wanted to embark on and that her husband was already losing. Barack could have flown home alone, but he stayed, missed the vote, and, when he returned to Chicago, gave explanations about a sick child that bombed with reporters. Jarrett said later that those public statements were really aimed at Michelle—a sacrificial offering. Maybe he was showing that he was willing to pay a political price, even to be humiliated in public to satisfy her; or maybe he was also making a point about the cost of stubborn inflexibility.

Now the Obamas had a rule: as much as possible, they tried to keep work away from vacation. Jarrett vacationed with them, and more than a few other aides in the West Wing found it unusual that she shared their getaway. But Jarrett and the Obamas had an informal rule against discussing work on vacation unless necessary. "I would read the daily briefings, he would read the daily briefings, we would not discuss them," she said of their trip to Martha's Vineyard in August 2009. When the president had to break away for daily updates or other business, he did, and then rejoined the group when he was done; the others did not change their plans or sit around waiting for him.

Christmas 2009, a Friday, was the Obamas' first full day in Hawaii, and for a few hours, the president's quest for a real vacation went well. The group settled into their airy rental house with white-beamed living spaces and spectacular views. Their holiday tradition was to work on talent-show acts throughout their vacation, presenting them right before they left. The women did one number, the men another, the kids their own act. This time, the women were working on "I Will Survive," the men on "Lean on Me." (The president could really sing, said Cheryl Whitaker, a pianist, even comparing his voice to Otis Redding's.)

The group was belting out carols when a military aide walked in with news: a young Nigerian man had tried to ignite explosives on a flight from Amsterdam to Detroit, and only the quick actions of the passengers and crew had saved the plane from disaster. The president decided to say nothing in public. Statements by Robert Gibbs and Janet Napolitano, the Homeland Security secretary, would be enough, he decided. He had long objected to what he saw as George W. Bush's overly aggressive casting of terror threats — "the color-coded politics of fear," he had called it during the campaign, yet another of his objections to politics. He did not want to hype a botched attack in which the most severe injury was the bomber's burns. He held regular conference calls every day with his national security team but otherwise continued his vacation.

As the situation became clearer over the weekend, the president continued his silence. The accused bomber, Umar Farouk Abdulmutallab, had managed to board a U.S.-bound airplane with no special screening, even though he paid for his ticket with cash, had no luggage, and was listed in a terrorism database. His father, alarmed by his son's radicalism, had even alerted the U.S. Embassy in Nigeria, but his visa had not been revoked. Napolitano blew her television moment, saying that "the system worked." Americans on vacation grew jittery about flying home. As news outlets related all of this, many also mentioned that the president was in Hawaii enjoying sports and beach picnics, and some even ran photos of him in the waves. Republicans eagerly joined the chorus of disapproval. It was one of many moments when Obama chose to register a high-minded objection to political maneuvering—in this case, a critique of how his predecessor communicated—instead of understanding how terrible he was making himself look, or how nervous Americans felt.

On Monday the president conceded that he needed to make an appearance, donned a suit—the valets always made sure he had clothes for any occasion—and headed to the marine base outside Honolulu where his press corps was set up and read a prepared statement. "This incident, like several that have preceded it, demonstrates that an alert and courageous citizenry are far more resilient than an isolated extremist," he said. The statement was proved wrong almost instantly. The bomber was not acting on his own: the Yemeni branch of al-Qaeda claimed responsibility for directing Abdulmutallab, which meant a whole new arm of the organization was now threatening Americans on their own soil. That evening the president's advisers learned that the National Security Agency had collected hints about Abdulmutallab's plans but had failed to share them with other agencies. Now the president looked out of touch *and* the government looked incompetent. In a final maddening touch, the secure phone lines installed at the house did not work well, and his calls to national security officials in Washington kept being dropped.

In light of the new information, Obama needed to make another appearance; he could not let his inaccurate, out-of-date words stand. He was so frustrated that he grabbed a laptop on which one of his aides had been typing a fresh statement and pounded out the rest himself.

The group of vacationers—the Obamas, the Nesbitts, the Whitakers, and nine kids among them—had been planning to leave the house for a snorkeling trip. Everyone and everything except the president was assembled and waiting in the motorcade. The procession consisted of lead cars, separate cars for the president, his Secret Service detail, military aides, the presidential doctor, the counter-assault team, the countersurveillance team, and the press, followed by a handful of vehicles whose functions were classified, an ambulance, and a spare presidential car. A bunch of adults and kids stood around in bathing suits, holding plastic snorkeling gear. In order for Obama to get to the hotel to give his statement, it would all have to be untangled. Staff began rearranging the motorcade so that the president could get to the hotel and everyone else to the beach. As the single convoy became two, Michelle stood to the side and waited without complaint, watching what her life had become in the eleven months since inauguration.

At the base, the president, suited and tieless, read his statement to the cameras, acknowledging a "systemic failure" in security, while his daughters, wife, and friends played in the waves. He headed to the beach as soon as he was finished, seeking a moment of peace. Soon he was snorkeling in the familiar blue-green Hawaii ocean of his youth, letting the waves rock and carry him. The surrounding beach and water had been cordoned off for the occasion. No one was there other than the presidential party. As he floated, the president was ringed by Secret Service agents wearing official-looking wet suits and yielding aquatic weapons.

Chapter Eight

THE BIGGEST MARRIAGE ON EARTH

JANUARY–MARCH 2010

Every few months Michelle Obama liked to crash a White House tour. Generally the first family hid from the tens of thousands of visitors per year who coursed through the museum parts of their home. But once in a while, Michelle's staff would arrange for her to materialize in one of the formal, empty rooms, a living, breathing first lady amid the historic marble-topped tables and candelabras. The appearances were photo opportunities — events that took place mostly for the pictures and stories they would generate — but she liked the mischief and surprise of them anyway.

On January 8, 2010, Michelle waited in the Blue Room, wearing a lemon-colored top and navy skirt that matched the décor. "Hey, come on in," the first lady gestured to the first arrival, an unknowing young blonde woman. The visitor looked stupefied, her cheeks very pink. Was it a mistake? Michelle flung her long arms out for an embrace and the woman fell into them, then drew back to look again. "This isn't you," she said in wonder. She reached out and lightly touched the first lady's shoulder, as if to check, and Michelle jokingly mimicked the gesture, touching the visitor's arm back. An Italian family walked in. "I *love* your country," the first lady said, heartfelt. "My children want to *live* there," she added. "In the U.S. Embassy." She reached down to embrace a tiny girl, then turned to her bigger brother. "Do you give hugs or are you too cool for that?" she asked and swooped in. A young man entered the room, so tall he towered over her. "Regular height guy!" she exclaimed. "This is sort of what I'm used to!"

This was where Michelle Obama was a far better politician than her husband. When he met strangers, he often offered them the smallest rations of himself, just a brief handshake or quick word. His wife offered new comments for each person, little jokes, big gestures, a momentary sense of connection, and not just handshakes but hugs.

She was still new enough to public life to enjoy the idea that people were excited to meet her. Though her hugs seemed like the essence of spontaneity, like everything else Michelle Obama did they were thought through: the attempt of a nearly six-foot-tall, world-famous woman in designer clothing to render herself approachable. (When you're big and scary, you give hugs, she once explained.)

A curly-haired woman in a red jacket approached, and as soon as Michelle said, "Welcome, it's good to see you," she realized the visitor was deaf. The first lady raised her hands to her face and switched to sign language: "My name is M-I-C-H-E-L-L-E." She looked pleased with herself—sure, it was just a tour visit, but she was acing it and she knew it.

Before the group departed, an aide brought Bo, the first dog, in. He was the perfect White House ambassador, because unlike the rest of the Obama family, visitors could rub their hands all over him and he didn't care. "The rest of the tour is just as exciting!" the first lady teased and swept out.

*　　*　　*

MICHELLE WAS PLANNING A FEBRUARY LAUNCH for her anti–childhood obesity project, and on January 20, 2010, she gave a speech to mayors from around the nation asking them to join in her efforts, ahead of a larger kickoff planned for a few weeks later. As she strode onto the stage at a hotel ballroom a few blocks from the White House, the mayors gave her a thunderous round of applause.

Unlike the president, who gave little hint of his inner state at most public appearances, the first lady was easier to read. The mask of public life, the carapace that most political figures wear at podiums and on cable television, did not yet cover her face. Sometimes when she sat through speeches by her husband or other officials, her face grew still and her eyes went blank, like a television with the power snapped off. But when she spoke, her hands and eyes jumped back to life and conveyed currents of feeling: enthusiasm, wariness, or sly amusement.

As the applause from the mayors faded, she launched into her prepared remarks. The speech was written in the peppy, athletic-coach language she generally used when discussing activity and nutrition. "It's going to take all of us — businesses and nonprofits; community centers and health centers; teachers and faith leaders; coaches and parents; and particularly all of you, our nation's mayors — all working together to help families make commonsense changes so our kids can get, and stay, healthy," she said. She praised mayors who distributed pedometers to kids to track their steps and started farmers' markets in neighborhoods in need of fresh produce.

This was supposed to be a proud day for her, another step in telling people about her big project. But the words coming from Michelle's mouth were at odds with the drained, dejected look on her face. She seemed exhausted and visibly irritated. Taking in her speech was like listening to the dialogue from one movie and watching the images from another. Only her expression acknowledged what everyone knew: the night before, Scott Brown, a Republican and novice to national politics, had won a special election for the late Edward Kennedy's U.S. Senate seat, yanking away the final, crucial vote of the Democratic supermajority that was supposed to enable the passage of the health care legislation, along with the rest of the president's agenda.

It was an unthinkable loss: Massachusetts was one of the bluest states in the nation, and Kennedy's seat was sacred, passed down to him when his older brother John won the presidency. Ted Kennedy had smoothed Obama's road to the White House by endorsing him at a critical moment in the Democratic presidential primary, and the passage of health care reform had been his final wish. By the time the White House learned of the impending disaster with his seat, it had been too late to do much but send the president on a depressing, last-minute campaign trip for Martha Coakley, a candidate whose seeming sense of entitlement and consistent missteps had transformed a sure thing into a Democratic disaster. No one had really thought it was possible for a Republican to win Kennedy's seat, no one had ever questioned that assumption, and no one understood how Obama's political team could have let such a thing happen.

The mood at the White House was so dark the day after the election, one former aide remembered, that the usual frenetic passage of email slowed, as if the entire organization was paralyzed. Just like that, it looked as if the health care overhaul was probably dead — certainly most of the senior staff, including Rahm Emanuel, David Axelrod, and Robert Gibbs, privately feared so, and some prominent Democrats on the outside were publicly saying the same thing. Emanuel once again urged the president to scale back his efforts, arguing that they did not have the votes for passage. Many congressional Democrats who had been warning the White House for months that the legislation was unpopular had spent the holiday recess hearing from constituents angry about the Senate deal. The president was willing to spend his political capital on health care, but "there are people in Congress who felt it wasn't just his political capital but theirs," David Axelrod said later. Pushing the legislation forward could mean failure on the president's most pressing priority, the one into which he had poured so much of his effort.

While Robert Gibbs prepared for his daily briefing, an aide asked him how he would respond if reporters asked whether the health care legislation was finished. Axelrod brought his fingers to his lips and made a gentle shushing noise. "Tell them it's not dead. It's just *sleeping*," he said.

The president had few public appearances on his schedule in the days after the election, and even inside the White House, aides did not know whether he was going to try to salvage the full bill or follow Emanuel's recommendation. In meetings, the president did not dwell on the Brown loss or lash out at his political team. "I have never known him in all the years that we've worked together to look around in a bad moment and say you guys screwed up," Axelrod said. He meant it as a compliment. "His attitude was, 'Okay, how do we get there now?'"

As her appearance before the mayors had hinted, Michelle was reacting differently. She was fuming, not only at the president's team but at the president himself. "She feels as if our rudder isn't set right," Obama told his aides. They had the sense that was not the actual language she had used.

The Obamas' dispute was private, but its effect on the president was clear. He usually seemed so emotionally constant, so free of downs and doubts, and throughout a brutally difficult autumn he had mostly maintained his stride. But his wife had an ability to bore into him, to shake him up emotionally, in a way that almost no one else could. In strategy meetings, he talked about moving forward, but his closest aides could see he was downcast.

To her, the Scott Brown victory provided grim evidence for what she had been saying for months, in some cases years: he had been leaning on the same tight group of insular, disorganized advisers for too long; they were not careful planners who looked out for worst-case scenarios. After their long, hard fight, health care was going to end in failure. Michelle was not particularly easy on mistakes in general, and to her this was an unfathomable instance of malpractice, said several aides. Plenty of Democrats on the outside were making similar charges.

But it was more than that. The loss in Massachusetts propelled the Obamas' long-standing disagreements about politics, suppressed in the glow of the 2008 victory, back to the fore, vindicating Michelle's accumulated anxieties and doubts. The health care situation epitomized everything she disliked about politics, everything she had been arguing about with her husband for going on two decades: her skepticism about whether true change could be accomplished through the legislative process, the way serious ideas devolved into craven horse trading, the way you could risk and give so much and end up with nothing. When her husband was largely winning, Michelle had been able to mostly put aside her concerns about his chosen career, but now they were losing, and she took the failure much harder than he did. "He's got that cold-blooded ability to move on which she's never had," an adviser said.

Barack Obama tended to see his close advisers in their best light, many aides who had worked for him over the years said, and he was confident that he could forgive and compensate for their flaws and weaknesses. The habit ran deep; he was the son of an arrogant, self-absorbed father who abandoned him and a loving mother who nonetheless sent her young child to live across the ocean from her. To hold those around him to strict standards would have left him with no one, and he learned to rely heavily on himself to compensate for his parents' failures and absences.

The man who had partly raised himself tended to have a soft spot for anyone whose help had proved crucial during his rise. Some of the Obamas' friends had been dubious about the Reverend Jeremiah Wright Jr. ever since he officiated at their wedding, making what some found to be an overlong, inappropriate speech that included references to the new couple's sex life. But he backed Barack in the failed 2000 race, and Barack stuck with him for a full year after the minister's public statements caused controversy, until the unrepentant Wright, who continued to embarrass Obama, finally forced the candidate to break ties with him in 2008.

The president's loyalty was even greater toward those who had sacrificed for him, moving cities or spending time away from their families, even those who benefited greatly from their association with him. Axelrod was the member of the national political establishment who had first seen Obama's potential and translated it to the public in the Senate and presidential races. Gibbs had gotten him that 2004 convention speech and protected him from the media onslaught for years. Emanuel had given up his position in the House leadership and sublimated his own aspirations to the president's. Given the demands of his job, the president was hugely dependent on all three of them. The first lady, in contrast, graded people less sentimentally—on results, her aides said. She was the daughter of parents who had every reason in the world not to achieve—racial prejudice, physical disability—but held themselves to such high standards that they sent two children to Princeton anyway. There were no excuses in the Robinson family, and where Barack tended to analyze failure in systematic terms, avoiding personal judgments, Michelle was much quicker to lay blame.

Scott Brown's victory also marked the public loss of something vitally important to Michelle: the idea that the president was a transformational figure, above the ways of Washington. The public outcry from the Nebraska health care and pharmaceutical deals had been angry and loud, and polling and focus groups from the Massachusetts

Senate race showed that Brown's win was in part a protest against such bargains. Voters now saw Barack Obama as part of the problem. Like many first ladies before her, Michelle was fighting for *her* defining vision of her husband to prevail, to protect their longtime joint mission, and in that sense, she was losing as much as he was.

Emanuel saw the president's dejection and repeated the first lady's criticisms to others in the White House with an air of indignation, according to three aides he spoke to. Later, he denied that he was annoyed at the first lady; he said he was just upset about the loss of the Senate seat. But Emanuel hated it when people criticized the administration from lofty perches—sure, the first lady was intent on getting the health care legislation passed, but she wasn't the one who actually had to get it done herself. She was criticizing them even though she was holding out on agreeing to campaign for members of Congress herself.

Rahm knew that the first rule of an effective White House was to hang together and avoid finger-pointing. His team was flagellating itself for their mistakes, they were already in bad straits, and on top of everything else, they had to deal with her accusations. He and other aides wanted Michelle Obama to be the warm, welcoming first lady who greeted tour groups and a partner who buoyed the president's spirits rather than deflating them. After what her husband had been through all fall and what he was facing now, how could she lay into him like this?

More fundamentally, the chief of staff was trying to convince the president to scale back his health care efforts, but the first lady wanted him to push forward. Emanuel wanted to win by the standard measures of presidential success: legislative victories, poll numbers. Michelle Obama had more personal criteria: Was her husband fulfilling their mission? How much good was he doing? Was his progress worth their family's sacrifice and risk?

Obama had positioned himself in between the two. He was a hedger by nature; his interviews and *The Audacity of Hope* were full of on-the-one-hand, on-the-other thoughts. That was a comfortable role for him, the mediator between different worldviews: uniting conservatives and liberals on the *Harvard Law Review*, splitting weeks between Springfield and the University of Chicago Law School. (Two nearly opposite figures in Illinois state politics mentored him at the same time: Abner Mikva, a liberal good-government lion, and old-time operator Emil Jones Jr.) Now he was a president with a wife and a chief of staff who were philosophical and temperamental contrasts, pulling him in two different directions.

Strangely, Michelle and Rahm were not entirely unalike: near opposites, they were also mirrors. They each knew how to deploy their gigantic personalities to bring everyone around them up or down, as the occasion suited. Both were feared inside the White House, yet each had passionate defenders who insisted that their barks were worse than their bites. They both believed that they were more in touch with the public mood than many others in the White House. Emanuel was in constant contact with officials on the Hill, who were finely attuned to their constituents; the first lady felt her modest roots and non-Washington background made her, in the words of one aide, "the Department of 'Let's Get Real.'" They each tried to protect Barack Obama, and they each struggled with his solitude and introversion. They were like first and second spouses with one thing in common: they had each married the same man, and each been driven a little crazy by him.

PERHAPS THE STRANGEST THING ABOUT the relationship between the president, the first lady, and the advisers was the sheer expansion it measured in the Obama union. That was the singular quality of presidential marriages: the way a once wholly private relationship between two people could stretch out, accordionlike, until public events and policy decisions and parts of the federal government were contained within its span. The back-and-forth between Barack and Michelle, their debates and differences in approach, had once played out within the span of a not very large condo apartment in Hyde Park, with consequences that did not extend much beyond the two of them. Now their date nights and home redecoration were matters of public debate, their different philosophies about government had resulted in two separate approaches to fixing health care problems, and they differed over not neglected household chores but a neglected Senate race.

The first lady's complaints about the president's team in the White House tended to sound a lot like Michelle's personal complaints about her husband over the years. Not planning, not keeping her informed, focusing on his own needs, taking on risky projects without seeing their potential for failure—these were all concerns she had shared with him since the beginning of their union. Some of her objections to her husband's advisers—to Rahm's dealmaking, Gibbs's reminders of what the public would think—sounded like they were really objections to her husband's choice of career. The differences in power between the East and West wings had institutionalized the equality issues Michelle had been struggling with for so long. The official launch of Let's Move! took place a few weeks after the Massachusetts loss, on a snowy, chaotic morning when the president was attending an important bipartisan meeting on health care that would include a televised statement. East Wing aides realized, almost by accident, that the president and first lady were scheduled to speak at nearly the same time, colliding awkwardly on cable television, and called their counterparts in the West Wing, who seemed annoyed that they had to adjust his schedule. The East Wing aides took the whole thing as more evidence their counterparts were not paying attention to what they were doing. By March, the situation was bad enough that the East Wing held a strategic planning retreat at Blair House, across the street from the White House, led by Patricia McGinnis, an expert on leadership and government, to discuss what they perceived as lack of coordination and respect from the president's staff. Equality had been an issue in the Obama marriage from the beginning; now daylong retreats and leadership experts were involved.

Likewise, the president's advisers said things about Michelle that her husband would not. Though Barack Obama liked to joke about his wife's intensity, as if he wanted to let people know about her formidable force, the comments were always accompanied by a chuckle; he never breathed a word of protest about her in public. But his advisers' grumblings about Michelle being overcritical mirrored the few he had expressed over the years. In *The Audacity of Hope,* he wrote that during the most difficult period of their marriage, "he didn't see what she had to complain about" and resented how hard she was on him. Now his advisers were saying the same thing for him.

When strains arose, advisers often wished the Obamas would just work things out themselves. Take conflicts over scheduling: the president's days were put together by a thirty-three-person department, and problems frequently cropped up. The president's foreign trips would grow too jam-packed, or the Obamas wanted to bring the girls on a foreign trip but found that it was not scheduled during their school break. Sometimes Sher or Jarrett would raise the first lady's objections, but on occasion Michelle sent emails directly to Alyssa Mastromonaco, the president's director of scheduling, that were so stern that Mastromonaco showed them around to colleagues, unsure of how to respond to her boss's wife's displeasure. (The messages were unusual, an aide said, because most people in the White House kept their written communications mild and indirect, knowing they could leak or be released, but Michelle did not speak like a Washingtonian.) The fault didn't lie with Mastromonaco, other aides said: she had the thankless task of parceling out the president's time, sometimes the president would forget to mention things to his wife, and the Obamas could have avoided the whole situation just by settling the issue at hand with each other. The advisers could feel helplessly caught between husband and wife. "You're unintendedly in the midst of that quarrel even if you don't have a stake in it," Gibbs said.

This expanded version of the Obama marriage was awkward for everyone: for the aides, for the president, who had sought to keep his personal life separate from his political one, and for the first lady, who, with scheduling and other matters, was sometimes cast as yet another petitioner for the president's time, attention, and agreement. Though East Wing aides tended to dwell on her lack of power in the White House, the West Wing regarded her as very powerful indeed. "My staff worries a lot more about what the First Lady thinks than they worry about what I think, on a full range of issues," the president said in September, half joking, half not. It wasn't that different from what he had said countless times about family life: "I believe in the general theory that if mom is happy, everybody's happy."

But if the president was sometimes uncomfortable with Michelle's criticisms, he also relied on her. "She has very much got his back," Axelrod explained. Michelle Obama wasn't like Nancy Reagan or Hillary Clinton, involved in the day-to-day business of the West Wing. Though she could grow annoyed, she almost never got really angry on her own behalf; it was almost always when she felt her husband, so conciliatory, so quick to say yes, was being taken advantage of or badly served. "When she thinks things have been mishandled or when things are off the track," Axelrod continued, "she'll raise it, because she's hugely invested in him and has a sense of how hard he's working, and wants to make sure everybody is doing their work properly." It was the same Michelle Obama who had counted the campaign petition signatures all those years before.

He still needed her to play the enforcer. "That is something about the president's personality in general," one Obama aide said. "He likes to have people to play the bad guy." Many presidents and countless politicians had needed the same: Ronald Reagan, George H. W. Bush, and Bill Clinton were all married to women widely considered by White House aides to be more exacting and less forgiving than their husbands. With the press, the bad guy was Robert Gibbs; with his advisers, it was Michelle Obama.

So some of the same qualities that appeared to fit poorly into her husband's political life—her idealism, exactitude, unwillingness to settle for less than what they wanted—were also qualities on which her husband depended, especially when things were going badly. "She possessed not only an ability to share the good times," Maya Soetoro once said about their partnership. "She would be there when things got tough, when he was in need of some forward propulsion."

A few days after the Scott Brown victory, at a town hall meeting in Elyria, Ohio, the president announced his renewed intention to pass the health care overhaul. White House aides were startled; the president was departing from his prepared remarks. "I want to say one last thing," he said. "None of the big issues that we face in this country are simple," he said. "Everybody wants to act like they're simple. Everybody wants to say that they can be done easily. But they're complicated. They're tough. The health care system is a big, complicated system, and doing it right is hard. We can't shy away from it, though. We can't sort of start suddenly saying to ourselves, America or Congress can't do big things; that we should only do the things that are noncontroversial; we should only do the stuff that's safe. Because if that's what happens, then we're not going to meet the challenges of the twenty-first century. And that's not who we are."

The decision to push ahead on health care reform belonged to the president, not his wife. It did not even feel like a decision, some advisers said later: there was no evidence the president ever seriously considered giving up during that period, and he just kept moving forward, trying to find a way through. Nancy Pelosi, the leader of the House Democrats, pushed him, too. To stop or scale back would be to accept defeat—to end the story with the unsavory Senate deals and invalidate his efforts of the prior year.

But Barack Obama *had* made a choice in the contest of the worldviews that surrounded him, between his chief of staff's point of view and his wife's. His decision to pursue the health care overhaul later seemed to mark the beginning of the end of Emanuel's tenure in the White House. The president could have done things Emanuel's way, narrowing his plans, stemming his losses, and deferring to the urgent concerns of congressional Democrats. Instead, the president once more rejected his chief of staff's vision of the presidency, just as he had the summer before when deciding to go forward with his health care plans, and instead pursued one more in line with the one he shared with the first lady.

Emanuel, having lost his case, began to make it clear in the outside world how much he disagreed with the president's decisions. Some of his colleagues thought he was trying to save his own reputation; others felt he just couldn't help himself; he treated some journalists like friends, even like therapists. He told the *New York Times* he differed with the president's decision to try Khalid Sheikh Mohammed in civilian court. "Arguably, Emanuel is the only person keeping Obama from becoming Jimmy Carter," Dana Milbank wrote in the *Washington Post* in February, praising the chief of staff for resisting the president's attempts to pass the health care bill and close the Guantánamo prison. No one knew the exact source for the column; everyone suspected Emanuel, who denied it, or an intermediary. Either way, a chief of staff was publicly disagreeing with the president he served—it was a shocking breach. "When you have a major setback and it appears that the chief of staff is trying to separate himself from the president, that's troubling," Axelrod said later.

Obama was amazed that his chief of staff thought he could get away with such a thing; he knew exactly what Emanuel was doing, he told advisers. Shortly after the Milbank story appeared, Emanuel went to the Oval Office to apologize to the president. He knew the stories were terrible, Axelrod said later.

As the two men talked alone in the Oval Office, Emanuel offered Obama his resignation. "Rahm understood that those stories were very, very negative for the president and felt bad about it," Axelrod said. "He understood that the stories were an embarrassment and felt like he owed it to him to offer his resignation." The move made sense for another reason, too: if Emanuel's vision of the presidency was different from Obama's, what was the point of staying?

"I'm not accepting it," Obama replied. "Your punishment is that you have to stay here and get this bill done. I'm not letting you off the hook."

The president was too focused on passing the health care legislation to consider changing his chief of staff. "He had basically no interest in major dislocations or switching horses, and Rahm was a very deft legislative strategist," Axelrod said.

But a few weeks later, in February, the president asked Pete Rouse, his low-key but widely trusted adviser and old Senate chief of staff, to draft a plan for a reorganization of the West Wing to fix the problems on the economic team and throughout.

Emanuel worked tirelessly on the passage of the health care legislation. He still went on angry tirades, but the president quietly chastised him, other aides said, and he began to apologize for them afterward. One March day, he melted down at the 7:30 a.m. meeting, spraying invective at the advisers seated around the table in his office. But a few hours later, at the president's daily session with his senior advisers, Emanuel apologized, the others surprised and glad to hear his contrition. Meanwhile, Obama drove his chief of staff relentlessly on the health care efforts. The president even had a few things for him to take care of on the day of his son's bar mitzvah, and Emanuel did as he was told.

AROUND THIS TIME—the precise date is unknown—the president of the United States smoked his last cigarette.

He had been smoking since he was a young man, outside the stately brick buildings of Harvard Law School and the stark modernist ones of the University of Chicago Law School. In their old apartment, Michelle had exiled him to the back porch to smoke. After he vowed to her, at the start of the presidential campaign, to quit for good, she had tried to recruit the press to her side, asking them to report her husband if they caught him. "Please, America, watch," she said. "Keep an eye on him, and call me," she said laughing, "if you see him smoking."

Though he chomped Nicorette, he couldn't stop altogether. As president, he never smoked inside the White House; his spot was somewhere outside on the grounds. For a man relentlessly focused on self-improvement, who prized control and tried to achieve virtuosity in every area of his life, it was his one apparent bad habit. He hated to even admit he smoked. Though the national press covered it, bringing it up in person was taboo, and friends made a point of not asking him about it. Even his wife eased up on him in the White House. "To try to quit smoking in one of the most stressful times of the nation's history is sort of like, you know, okay, he's going to struggle a little bit," she said later. "Once he made the commitment to quit, I left him alone because it's a very personal thing."

Now he finally gave his wife the one thing he promised her when he embarked on the presidential race. Later Michelle said he quit because their kids were getting old enough to figure things out. But her husband knew how much this meant to her. And though quitting as president seemed especially difficult, in some ways, his was a classic quit scenario. Everything else was out of control. He did not know if he had the votes to pass the most important legislation of his presidency. He had disappointed his wife and his chief of staff had humiliated him in public. But somewhere on the White House grounds, he flicked away his last cigarette butt and enacted his own tiny, personal piece of health care reform.

SUNDAY, MARCH 21, 2010, the day of the final House of Representatives vote on the health care bill, was the climactic moment of the Obama presidency to date. Barack and Michelle Obama spent it apart.

Originally the first couple was supposed to travel on a state visit to Indonesia with their daughters, but the trip was postponed once it became clear that the health care vote might take place. To make it up to the girls, and to prevent them from hanging around the White House with nothing to do over spring break, the first lady took Malia and Sasha on their first visit to New York City. Because the president wasn't with them, they were able to travel around the city relatively unobtrusively, without the fuss of the date night excursion. As the hour of the vote approached, they ate brunch at Mesa Grill, a Southwestern restaurant, and saw *Memphis,* about an interracial romance during the era of segregation.

A few hours after the show's final curtain dropped, the president and his aides gathered in the Roosevelt Room to watch the vote on television. When the 216th vote came in, meaning the bill would pass, everyone applauded and high-fived: they had done the seemingly impossible. Rather than return upstairs to an empty house, the president invited everyone who worked on health care reform, even the assistants, to come upstairs. It was the most triumphant night of his time in office and he wanted to celebrate.

For many staffers, it was the first time they had been inside the residence, because of the strict separation the Obamas tried to maintain between their official lives and their private ones. As everyone milled around the Yellow Oval Room and the Truman Balcony, drinks in hand, the president turned emotional, talkative, even huggy. His tie was gone. "Who's up for the Lincoln Bedroom tour?" he called out after someone asked to see it.

For over a decade, the president, so sensitive to criticism, had faced a recurrent charge that he was underqualified and overhyped, precocious but untested, with his greatest accomplishment his own climb. "What's he ever done?" Representative Bobby Rush had said of his congressional challenger in 2000. "The Messiah," Mike Madigan, the speaker of the Illinois House of Representatives and a Democrat, called him once. "Maybe one day, he will do something to warrant all this attention," Michelle whispered to Jeff Zeleny, a reporter, as the new senator walked through the U.S. Capitol for the first time, trailed by a large entourage. During the presidential campaign, Hillary Clinton's supporters accused him of being a lightweight and Republicans turned the messianic charge into a campaign commercial complete with swelling music.

Now Barack Obama had done what none of his predecessors had been able to: he passed universal health care reform legislation, covering the largest remaining gap in the American social safety net. The law would require most Americans to purchase insurance, cover thirty-two million uninsured people, prevent insurers from turning down people with preexisting medical conditions, and subsidize families making up to $88,000 a year to pay their premiums. Never again would anyone be able to say that Barack Obama had not accomplished much beside his own rise. Later, an outside adviser said, the president reacted defensively to the private suggestion that he had pursued the health care passage out of personal insecurity over his accomplishments. But that night, he exulted. "Winning the election only gives you the chance to do something," he told Axelrod that night. "Here we've actually done something."

Obama was sure the bill would finally become popular now that it had passed, according to several aides. He thought voters would begin to see the legislation as he did: not as an expansion of government, not as the watered-down result of excessive horse trading, but as a series of consumer benefits that would result in more accessible care, fewer people without insurance, and healthier Americans overall.

In a way, it was fitting that the first lady was not at the party, given that almost no one knew the private role she had played. She had eased up on her husband, at least momentarily, according to an aide. She did not *want* to be the person constantly prodding him, even if she sometimes couldn't resist. She had said her piece; it was his presidency.

Michelle watched the television coverage alone in her suite at the Waldorf Astoria, according to an aide, as her daughters slept. She exchanged upbeat email messages with aides at the White House, but she exuded less giddy triumph than exhausted relief. "She has a lower tolerance for Congress than her husband does," the aide said.

"She was like, finally, finally the American people are getting it," the aide continued. "At that point, she was just like, you guys have now caught up with where we've been all along."

Chapter Nine

THE BUBBLE WITHIN
THE BUBBLE

MAY–JUNE 2010

Two months after the passage of the health care overhaul, the Obamas returned to Chicago for Memorial Day weekend, their first trip home together since their disappointing initial foray thirteen months prior. Their old neighborhood had become a bit of a shrine to them. Portraits of them hung over the bar and behind the booths of Park 52, a stylish bistro, and the city hummed with speculation about whether the president would attend the Blackhawks hockey game that weekend. Obama was still enormously beloved in Chicago, and all of the city seemed to be wondering why he and his family had stayed away.

The trip was easier this time. The Obamas stayed mostly out of sight, with no disruptive visits to downtown restaurants. Wedding guests at the synagogue across the street from their house all had to go through security, but by way of apology the Secret Service sent over presidential trinkets for the bride and groom: cuff links and a letter opener. Reporters covering the trip spotted the first lady in her backyard in yellow rubber gloves, as if after months under the care of the residence staff she was making a small counterstrike into the domestic sphere.

A few days ahead of time, family members received a message: you are invited to the Obamas' home on Friday for a barbecue. The Obamas had been trying not to lose touch with the first lady's many aunts, uncles, and cousins, scattered over the South Side and its suburbs.

This was the second time the Obamas had summoned them since the inauguration. The first had been six months before, when the family was invited to the White House. The president and first lady had always hosted Thanksgiving in Chicago, and they wanted to continue the tradition. On the holiday, a few dozen visitors from Chicago had filed across Pennsylvania Avenue, through Secret Service checkpoints and into the formal entertaining rooms of the White House, where they found a grand holiday setting, including a traditional Thanksgiving spread with an African American spin—turkey, collard greens, oyster stuffing, macaroni and cheese. The kids in the family gathered under a portrait of George Washington for a photograph: a picture of how far the nation had come and how long the journey had taken.

The visitors were regular Chicagoans, mostly a generation or two into the middle class, schoolteachers, engineers, and government workers. Some had to scrape to make the journey to Washington, even with the hotel discounts the White House had arranged. They were awed, excited, and a little intimidated by what they saw. After using the bathroom, one elderly guest confessed to another that he had pocketed a paper towel with the White House seal as a souvenir. Was that stealing? "If it's there to wipe your backside, it's probably okay to take it," the other said. Some of the young people wanted photographs with the president—so they could prove they knew him, one uncle said—but Obama, photo-weary as usual, resisted until the end, when he finally spent a few minutes posing.

Six months later, the family gathered again in Chicago, lining up at security barriers again, this time at the end of the Obamas' street. How to speak to the first couple had been a big topic of conversation in the family since the election; the relatives were afraid of saying the wrong thing to the president or first lady, and only now were they settling on an informal code of conduct. The key was to follow the Obamas' cues, they decided. It was important not to bring up the president's work unless he did or to ask for favors. Complaining about anything was a bad idea, the relatives decided, because then the Obamas might think you were requesting something even if you weren't. So as the family milled around the backyard, greeting the first family, they kept the conversation light.

There wasn't a lot of positive White House news to discuss anyway. That spring, the president's feelings of being misunderstood and underappreciated were continuing to mount. Americans were still unenthused about the health care legislation, and Republicans were threatening to block implementation, force repeal, and/or run against the law for years to come. Obama's own defenses of the law were sometimes rambling or filled with exactly the kind of dense policy-speak that Michelle was always warning him against. He had bet nearly everything on health care, managed to win, and yet was still losing. "This is a historic accomplishment and nobody knows about it," the president told an aide back at the White House, his confidence and drive giving way to frustration and plaintiveness. "I really need this."

After an exploded drilling rig called the Deepwater Horizon began spewing oil into the Gulf of Mexico in April, he was drawn into a bizarre public standoff: pundits demanded he show more emotion over the spill, and Obama, unwilling to emote on demand, continued his usual tone of cool analysis while he and aides worked nonstop to manage the disaster from Washington. "He absolutely has an aversion to manipulating people and to acting," Jarrett said a few weeks later. "He is not going to play on people's emotions in a way that's insincere." It was another of Obama's principled objections to the practice of politics. But no one was asking him to say anything fake, just to share more visibly in the pervasive sense of loss and anxiety, to say something *real*. Other presidents, particularly Bill Clinton, had used vulnerability as a tool; by letting the public in on their struggles, they won people to their side. Obama, the former memoirist who now allowed others almost no access to his emotions, appeared diligent but remote, introverted, and stubborn.

The health care legislation, the Gulf coast spill: one was a long-sought victory, the other an unexpected tragedy, and yet both demonstrated the president's weakening connection to the public, the evaporation of the trust, the mutual sense of recognition, he had established with voters during the campaign. Obama's relationship with the public wasn't just a problem of the summer and fall of 2009 and the winter of 2010 — by the spring, it was becoming a clear problem for his presidency. He had passed an extraordinary amount of legislation since January 2009: health care reform, the stimulus, Ted Kennedy's national service bill, new credit card reforms, a fair pay act for women, the expansion of the Children's Health Insurance Program, and student loan reform, just to name a few. But he seemed to be succeeding at a cost to himself, still dogged by the perception that he was following his own agenda instead of filling the pressing need for jobs.

He was still bashing pundits, saying he wanted to talk to regular Americans instead, and in the family milling around his backyard that day, Obama had a potential asset that George Bush did not: relatives whose lives resembled those of many voters. "Whatever's happening out here in America, it's happening in this family," said one uncle — job losses, depleted retirement savings accounts, foreclosures. But on the rare occasions the president and first lady saw their extended family, the conversations steered clear of the personal toll of the sputtering economy, two relatives said, because the family was intimidated and the Obamas so clearly craved a break.

So the talk stayed light that Friday. The president and Craig Robinson joked about buying a basketball team once the Obamas left the White House, high-fiving each other with excitement at the idea. Michelle patiently answered relatives' questions about life there. She didn't brag or talk down to them, they later said appreciatively. She was matter-of-fact: yes, there were a lot of people who worked in the White House, cleaning and taking care of the mansion.

One relative told her it was hard for him to connect the Michelle he knew — first a fat-cheeked baby, later a hardworking wife and mother — with the new version. "When I see you on television you look like a glamour queen," he said.

"Well, I have to put on my mask," she said.

THE OBAMAS SPENT THAT WEEKEND visiting familiar haunts, like the girls' former school, and they caught up with old friends at a Sunday barbecue in the backyard of Valerie Jarrett's parents, James and Barbara Bowman. But as usual, they gravitated toward the two couples with whom they spent the majority of their social time: Marty Nesbitt and Anita Blanchard, and Eric and Cheryl Whitaker.

As president and first lady, the Obamas led a social life that was circumscribed in the extreme. They ate at home with their daughters most nights, avoided Washington dinner parties and most galas, and rarely even went out on date nights anymore. Instead the Obamas burrowed ever deeper within a tiny, preexisting circle. Their behavior was on the far side of introverted, Washingtonians noted; even when the Bushes retreated to Crawford they entertained there a lot. Any first couple were isolated by definition, but this was something different, more like self-imposed exile.

If the presidency is often referred to as a bubble, sealed off from the rest of society, the Obamas and their closest friends created an even smaller bubble within the bubble—an intimate, alternative world in which the president and first lady could count on total understanding, constant sympathy, and unconditional love. Around the Nesbitts, Whitakers, Jarrett, and select others who were sometimes allowed into the fold, the first couple had a remarkable ability to let the presidency fall away—indeed, the Obamas *wanted* it to disappear, the friends said. It really didn't matter much what was going on in the news or the administration. This was their time to escape, and to be messier, funnier, edgier, more frank, and altogether more themselves than they were in the public eye. The Obamas gossiped about the people they used to know at home, argued playfully, and sounded different, too, using more African American slang. Naturally sarcastic, the Obamas, Nesbitts, and Whitakers made outrageous jokes—far too outrageous to repeat to a reporter, the friends said. "You can let your hair down and not worry about whatever you talk about being in the press," Whitaker said. Barack became Barack again, shedding his stiffness and defensiveness.

Nesbitt and Whitaker were so close with the president that they did not wait for invitations to visit the White House; they just sent him a message they were coming. Often they dropped in alone, just for a weeknight. Sometimes Nesbitt and the president played a late game of pool at the table on the third floor as the first lady and the girls slept in the bedrooms below. (As with every other game, the president liked to win, and bragged mercilessly when he did.)

Like Michelle's relatives, the Nesbitts and the Whitakers almost never asked the president about work. Every once in a while, Cheryl Whitaker could not resist asking him a policy question, she said, for the sheer pleasure of a private tutorial. But "I don't want to feel like I'm spitting out the news to them," she explained. "They get enough of that." Nesbitt said the same: "We talk about Washington when he wants to, not when I want to." And Whitaker put it most strongly of all: "My job, I'd say, is *not* talking about that stuff," he said. "I'm pretty good at my job."

Instead they found encouraging stories to relay back to the president, an alternative narrative to the one in the media. Nesbitt was on a flight where he saw someone in first class give up his seat to a passenger in a military uniform. He emailed Obama about it, adding that he had noticed people behaving with a lot more kindness and altruism since he had been elected. Later the president mentioned the story to Nesbitt as an example of just the kind of behavior he didn't see enough of in Washington.

Being with the Nesbitts and the Whitakers was one of the first couple's chief coping mechanisms, first against the newness of the presidency and then against its trials and disappointments. No one could have reasonably expected them to come to Washington and make a boatload of close new friends. But the way the Obamas clung to their most comfortable relationships seemed a mark of how badly they sought relief and protection. That spring, the Obamas' time with them had the quality of going to ground. Unable or unwilling to explain his work or to share his true feelings with the outside world, the president retreated to an inner one.

In that safe inner world, the president did sometimes permit himself a bit of vulnerability. One late night over the White House pool table, when the oil in the Gulf was still spewing, the president told Nesbitt that trying to plug the leaking well cap was like bringing a very sick child to the emergency room. He felt helpless because all he could do was sit and watch the doctors, or in this case the engineers, work. There it was again: the powerlessness of the presidency, the gap between what President Barack Obama was supposed to be capable of and what the forty-eight-year-old man clicking at colorful balls felt he was able to do.

The emergency room image was a potent analogy, tying the complex underwater mechanics of the leaking well into a succinct phrase that every parent could relate to. It was just the kind of thought the president might have shared with the nation, to let Americans know how seriously and personally he took the problem. But Barack Obama chose to share it only with an audience of one.

WATCHING THE PRESIDENT WAS WASHINGTON'S SPORT, and the time the Obamas spent with the Nesbitts and the Whitakers, chronicled in pool reports, aroused curiosity. What was it that drew the three couples together? Another question, too, was often asked off the record: there was nothing parochial about the Obamas, so why was it that their best friends were black?

The answer was in their life stories. Though they didn't meet until they were in their twenties and thirties, the three couples were almost perfectly matched in terms of life experience, or as perfectly matched as anyone could be, given a couple with as singular a story as the Obamas. Like Michelle, they were the children of parents of modest means—steel and sawmill workers, nurses, bus drivers. Cheryl Whitaker, who grew up on the black side of town in tiny Washington, Georgia, told her parents at nine years old that she wanted to be a doctor, with little idea of what that meant. "Even though I had top grades in school, they didn't think a poor girl could do this," she said later. To make money, she learned to play the piano and worked as a church choir accompanist from age thirteen.

Like Barack Obama, Marty Nesbitt and Eric Whitaker grew up more or less without their fathers, who were bogged down in career and personal problems and paid little attention to their bright, hardworking sons. Nesbitt's father, laid off from a steel mill, only became interested in him when he became a star basketball player in high school, his son recalled. The one time Barack Obama Sr. visited his son in Hawaii, he left him with a basketball. "Up through probably my midtwenties the biggest driving motivator for me was to not be like my father," Nesbitt said, echoing some of the president's statements about trying to avoid becoming like his own embittered father.

However, each of the friends also had parents who believed in education as a means of advancement and as a response to prejudice. When the president was growing up in Indonesia, his mother roused him at 4:00 a.m. for English lessons; in Chicago, Marian Robinson bought reading and math workbooks so her children would always be a few steps ahead in class. "My mother would say, 'When you acquire knowledge, you acquire something no one could take away from you,'" Craig Robinson said. Eric Whitaker, Nesbitt, and Blanchard won scholarships to private school. A high school biology teacher referred the teenage Cheryl Whitaker to a federally funded summer program that helped black students learn about medicine as a career. "That summer changed my life," she explained. "I was able to see someone like myself in medical school." For college and graduate school, the six students made it to some of the finest universities in the country. At Northwestern, Blanchard urged the other members of her African American sorority to study hard and found tutors for the ones who fell behind.

One day Obama was eating breakfast at his apartment near Columbia University when he received a phone call saying that the father he barely knew had died. Nesbitt was preparing for a business school exam at the University of Chicago when he picked up the phone for his own version of that call.

On their rarefied campuses, each relied on the few students from similar backgrounds for commiseration, company, and support. Barack Obama and Eric Whitaker met as graduate students at the Harvard gym. "When you come up through the elite schools there's not a lot of diversity, and on the basketball court was one place where you could bond and find black men," Whitaker explained. A few years later, Nesbitt befriended Craig Robinson, then a fellow student at the University of Chicago's business school, more or less the same way. Nesbitt started dating Blanchard, who was studying medicine across campus, as was Eric Whitaker. Together the two doctors-in-training found a mentor in James Bowman, Jarrett's father.

Sometimes the students faced outright prejudice: Michelle's original roommate at Princeton moved out when her parents pressured her not to share quarters with an African American. But for the most part, in their education and careers, the friends said they did not face as much overt discrimination as their parents had a generation earlier. Instead they experienced something different: resentment of affirmative action. They arrived on campus when such policies were coming under fierce debate, and though they thrived academically, they often felt underestimated and resented, treated as if they were less than qualified. No matter how bright they were or how hard they studied, they felt lingering suspicion about whether they belonged. "I wasn't supposed to have my own successful career," Michelle once said. "They said my achievement must have been the result of racial preferences." Together the friends were different not only from more privileged students but also from their own parents and relatives, who had never had the chance to weigh which medical residency or law firm job to take. Their experiences resembled no one's so much as each other's.

When Michelle met Cheryl Whitaker in the late 1990s, the circle was complete. Soon the couples had something new in common: they were two-career pairs, trying to figure out how to balance home and work, how to succeed and yet give their children a sense of what had come before. The Obamas convinced the Whitakers to have kids—they had been hesitating because of their busy medical careers—and Blanchard, who had a thriving obstetrics practice, delivered nearly all the group's babies. The friends became godparents to each other's children, and in addition to basketball games and dinners, the group shared swim parties, playdates, and car pools. On the weekends in Chicago, the men took the children to tennis lessons, where they sat together on the sidelines, lay on the ground, read newspapers, and talked. They wanted similar things for themselves, one of which was being better fathers than their own had been.

As they climbed in their various fields, watching the flow of money, opportunity, and power up close, they became ever more convinced of how uneven the landscape was, how advantage and disadvantage seemed to reinforce themselves. When Craig Robinson took a job in Dean Witter's training program, he quickly noticed that the most lucrative investments were in the hands of white investment professionals. The few top-earning African Americans at the firm all had degrees from elite business schools—a credential their white counterparts didn't seem to need.

All of them were acutely aware of their good fortune, and they worked to provide others with the kinds of opportunities that had benefited them. Michelle had dropped out of corporate law to work for nonprofits and then the university. As a young doctor, Eric Whitaker founded a South Side medical clinic with a barbershop that offered free haircuts to lure black men to get health care. Cheryl Whitaker specialized in hypertension, which disproportionately affected African Americans. As John Rogers put it, they had been born too late for the civil rights movement, but like the Obamas, they saw their generation's mission as evening out the pervasive disparities they saw every day. "The way I look at health is more broad than just having access to a doctor and a clinic and a hospital," Whitaker explained. "To have a healthy community you need to have a viable economic base, you need to have the education system work, you need to have those clinics and hospitals." It was the medical version of the Obama vision of systemic change.

Even with their university years behind them, the group still felt the stigma of affirmative action, a sense of being underestimated even if others didn't directly discriminate against them. The better they did professionally, Whitaker said, the more powerful that presumption became. "You can be excellent and people still are going to think you got there because of your race," he said. "There's a presumption that somehow you took a shortcut."

Their response was to work harder, to show that they were smarter and more industrious and more generous than anyone else. Even by Barack and Michelle's standards, Nesbitt was a spectacular over-achiever: a great athlete, father of five children, an increasingly successful businessman—he proposed an idea for an airport parking company to the Pritzkers, the Chicago real estate family, they backed it, and he became wealthy as a result, too—and with too many civic commitments to name. (Jarrett was the same way: she was on a dozen boards in Chicago, as if three or four were not enough.) Even the vacation and birthday sports tournaments Nesbitt set up seemed like a response to the invisible critics: he and the president simply could not stop showing how good they were at everything.

When Obama ran for Congress in 2000, Bobby Rush had derided him as an overeducated outsider—charges that appalled the friends. "Rush basically mocked Barack with the worst anti-intellectualism that flew in the face of everything that we as young African Americans had been told to aspire to," Eric Whitaker said. After the defeat, a serene, upbeat, and relentless Nesbitt worked the phones to wipe out his friend's campaign debts and told him that his political career was far from finished. Two years later, when Obama decided to run for the U.S. Senate, Nesbitt helped secure the backing of Penny Pritzker, which in turn helped Obama secure other donors. The night Obama spoke at the Democratic Convention in Boston in summer 2004, Nesbitt was by his side. In the space of a few years, he had helped drive his friend from his lowest career point to his highest.

Most people rise in politics by making friends. As George H. W. and Barbara Bush wound their way across the South in the early 1970s, Barbara created an index card for every new relationship they forged. Soon she had four or five thousand, and a decade later the Bushes were sending out thirty thousand Christmas cards annually. But when Barack Obama shot to fame in 2004, his new popularity created such widespread desire on the part of others to know and help him that the Obamas, intent as ever on authenticity and self-protection, decided to limit their friendships to the circle of those to whom they were already close. New allies, donors, contacts — they wanted all of those. But their social life was something else. "No more new friends," as Craig Robinson put the rule a few years later, at the start of the presidential campaign. "You don't know what people's real agendas are."

When the Obamas got to the White House, Michelle repeated the same credo.

THE NESBITTS AND THE WHITAKERS and Valerie Jarrett saw, in a way few others could, the utter complexity of becoming the first black president and first lady.

Every first couple experienced certain common emotions: the thrill of arrival; the responsibility of being role models; the disappointment of not being able to fix problems like joblessness or poverty;

the fear that some nut might try to physically harm you. Being black only heightened those sensations. Asked what they thought it was like to be the first African Americans in their positions, several aides reached for the same word: exhausting.

Once upon a time in Chicago, the Obamas discussed race frankly. Doing so was part of their jobs. The president's signature legal course was on racism and law. He assigned readings by Frederick Douglass and W. E. B. Du Bois, as well as graphic accounts of lynchings, and pushed his students to contemplate difficult questions: Was life better under segregation? Did special public schools for black men violate the precepts of *Brown v. Board of Education*? Once in a while, Professor Obama even imitated the way clueless white people talked. "Why are your friends at the housing projects shooting each other?" a student remembered him asking, in a mock-innocent voice not his own.

The old Barack could be slyly funny about race, too. One morning during the Senate campaign, he did not show up to a meeting with donors — he sometimes disappeared like that, switching off his phone, looking for escape even back then — and after a frantic search, a white staffer named Peter Coffey called Obama's barbershop to find that, yes, he was there. A few hours later, the candidate walked into the campaign office and made a beeline for Coffey. "The relationship between a black man and his barber is sacred," Obama bellowed for all to hear. "They are closer than man and wife. For failing to understand this truth, your punishment is to watch the movie *Barbershop*. And for further punishment, you will then watch the sequel, *Barbershop 2*."

Michelle's professional life involved race as well. At Public Allies, she had frequently pushed participants to talk through racial and ethnic conflict in the group. "I hate diversity workshops," she said in an interview during the presidential campaign, referring to the mandatory, once-a-year discussions held in many schools and corporate settings. "Real change comes from having enough comfort to be really honest and say something very uncomfortable."

Since the start of the presidential race in 2007, the Obamas had been quietly figuring out the job of being the first African Americans to lead the country—testing, refining, watching how other people reacted. In public, Obama usually preferred not to dwell on race, but his advisers were anxious about it and he could be, too. The night before Chris Rock, the comedian, performed for him at a fund-raiser at the Apollo Theater in Harlem, Obama told one of the organizers he was so nervous about what Rock would say that he wondered if he should call the whole thing off. He ended up loving the performance and thanked Rock the next day. When Reverend Al Sharpton was supposed to travel to Iowa just before voting began, the Obama team grew nervous; when Sharpton canceled out of fear he would throw white voters off the candidate sounded relieved, those who spoke to him about it said. (Later, when Obama's old pastor, Rev. Jeremiah Wright Jr., continued to make the kinds of incendiary public statements that had hurt Obama's candidacy but had stopped communicating with Obama and his team, it was Sharpton who finally convinced him to quiet down.)

In the White House, being the first black first couple could be a source of inspiration and sustenance at times. "There is a reservoir of pride that they know African Americans feel for them," said Michael Strautmanis, an aide who handled much of the White House's outreach to the black community. At speeches in front of the National Association for the Advancement of Colored People (NAACP) and the Urban League, the president fed off the crowd's energy. "So much about the presidency creates distance," Strautmanis said, but with black audiences, his connection was more intimate. The Obamas delighted in showing respect to earlier generations; when Maya Angelou or Dorothy Height attended an event at the White House, they took special care to greet them. During a concert of songs from the civil rights era in the East Room, the president had a rare expression on his face: relaxed, proud.

But the question of what a black president could and could not say was confusing. When fellow African American Eric Holder, the attorney general, called America a "nation of cowards" for refusing to discuss race honestly, the president gently rebuked him in public and Rahm Emanuel tried to install a minder at the Department of Justice. The one time Obama spoke instinctually about race in public, expressing his frustration with the white policeman who had arrested Henry Louis Gates Jr., had been a disaster, necessitating an awkward "beer summit" with the parties. Michelle Obama was the great-great-granddaughter of slaves, but she did not discuss the meaning of that legacy: the closest the Obamas got was the annual Passover seder they held, the guests mostly Jews or African Americans, the holiday a rare chance to safely discuss oppression and liberation.

The presidency brought a surreal twist to Barack Obama's own lifetime story of race. For the first half of his life he had wondered how he fit in the African American community, and even at the start of the presidential campaign, some critics had repeated the "not-black-enough" charge. Now, as president, he was treated as blacker than ever before. Some of this was decidedly positive: he was understood as a historic African American figure, the apotheosis of black success, the heir to Martin Luther King Jr. But he also experienced racism on a larger and more profound level than ever before, with people mischaracterizing him, stereotyping him, calling him a thug or a chimp on the Internet, even threatening to kill him.

The charges that Barack Obama was a secret Muslim or not a U.S. citizen or a hater of white people all drew in one way or another on the idea that he was different, foreign, other. By April of 2010, a *New York Times*/CBS poll showed that over half of Tea Party supporters believed that "too much has been made of the problems facing black people." (Asked what they didn't like about Obama, many Tea Partiers would not name a reason; they just didn't like him, they said.) When Representative Joe Wilson shouted "You lie!" during the president's address to Congress, when Bill O'Reilly interrupted Obama on television, even when Jon Stewart called him "dude," black aides worried that a white president would not have been treated the same way. The issue was respect: "At the end of the day, there's a fear you're just an N," one said.

The president never talked about it publicly. After the Henry Louis Gates gaffe, the Obamas spoke about race only in decorous, feel-good ways: a Martin Luther King Jr. birthday celebration here; a Black History Month event there. Michelle's old rule about making people uncomfortable was long, long gone. "The first black president doesn't want to give any insight into being the first black president," a member of the Chicago group of friends said with a chuckle.

Obama and his advisers knew there was no political upside, and tremendous risk, in calling out racially tinged attacks. But it was also a matter of personal ethos. Obama lived by Fraser Robinson's rules of not lashing out over unfair treatment; of working hard, carrying on, and hoping people would see you clearly. "There is a dignity about it, a reservation about it, a reluctance to present it as a grievance," one of his advisers said.

But that didn't mean the president was oblivious. He saw the poll numbers on Tea Party members' racial attitudes; he knew the sound of what his advisers called "dog whistles": the statements, like calls to "take back our country," that weren't explicitly racist or xenophobic but subtly appealed to people who already thought that Obama was too black, too foreign, too strange. He believed there were always going to be some Americans who were just uncomfortable with him in office, no matter what he accomplished, said one African American aide who discussed it with him.

The Whitakers, the Nesbitts, and Jarrett talked about race and the presidency with the Obamas, but not incessantly. They didn't need to. In the Obama presidency, the friends saw projections of patterns and experiences they had known their whole lives. They knew what it meant to feel incredible achievement on the one hand and persistent barriers on the other. Being the first black person to do something was Jarrett's family business: her great-grandfather was the first black graduate of the Massachusetts Institute of Technology; her father, the first black tenured professor in his department at the University of Chicago. Cheryl Whitaker, who had a distinguished medical career, refused to attend her own high school reunions back in Georgia because they were still segregated all these years later, with separate gatherings for black and white members of the class. The growing birther movement, which alleged that Obama was not really a U.S. citizen despite overwhelming evidence to the contrary, reminded them of the suspicion with which high-achieving African Americans were sometimes viewed: you could win the highest office in the land and still some people would assert that you were not qualified.

Cheryl Whitaker said she actually had a pretty hard time even broaching the subject of racially inflected attacks with the first couple. It was too painful; it cut too deep.

THE NESBITTS AND THE WHITAKERS were well-liked figures around the White House because they calmed the president and first lady and struck aides as decent, down-to-earth, and funny. But the friendships, which the president had originally said would help him stay connected to the rest of the world, seemed to foster disconnection as well, reinforcing his and Michelle's day-to-day isolation instead of counteracting it. The group was self-contained, with little trust beyond its own boundaries. They made continual fun of the absurdity of the White House and Washington to each other, even the crucial question of how well the president was communicating with the country. "What statement is he trying to make by having a glass of lemonade?" Nesbitt said, mimicking the way pundits talked about the president. "What is he trying to say to America? He's trying to say he's thirsty? What did the president *mean* when he said Merry Christmas? I *think* he meant Merry Christmas, but I'm not sure."

Of course the Obamas and their friends laughed about these things: who wouldn't? But their laughter seemed to leave the rest of the world at an ironic distance, and their closeness seemed to inhibit fresh perspectives. The group's experiences were so close to one another's, their ties so interknit. Their understanding among themselves was so perfect that it seemed unlikely that anyone else would understand.

At the same time, it was hard to name more than one or two Republicans with whom the president had a close, trusting relationship. That was a problem that perhaps no cocktail-party canapé could solve: the Republican strategy was still one of total opposition. Nevertheless, Tom Daschle, the former Senate majority leader who was a close outside adviser to Obama, and other experienced Washingtonians advised the president to keep investing in small gestures toward Republicans, even with no immediate reward; he was surely going to need some of the congressmen later. It was hard for Obama to do, advisers said, because his charm offensive in the early days of the administration had gotten him nowhere, because he hated to waste time, and because schmoozing—like making emotional speeches— was another part of politics he seemed to have decided was mostly fake. George and Laura Bush had made a point of hosting Daschle, then the Senate minority leader, and his wife for dinner at the White

House, but in spring 2010, the notion of the Obamas inviting the Boehners over for an intimate meal seemed as fantastical as a supper between Lady Gaga and the Pope.

The president was losing Democrats that spring, too, allies who considered themselves friendly truth-tellers but found themselves frozen out. The Obamas "feel overassaulted," said one longtime friend and fund-raiser who felt cast out then. "The closer you are, the harder it is for them to hear" any criticism, he said.

At the same time, the president's derision toward Congress was reaching new heights. When Judd Miner, his old boss from the civil rights law firm where he once worked in Chicago, visited the president in the Oval Office with his wife, Linda, the president unloaded on his former Senate colleagues and their counterparts in the House. "This is the greatest job; I spend all my time thinking about things that really matter," Obama told them. "The one thing I don't like is that I have to scratch the backs of these legislators," he told them. "They're no better than the aldermen at home," he said, referring to the notoriously self-interested Chicago city representatives. "They're smarter but their values are the same." He was willing to say almost as much in public. On an April visit to Iowa, he stopped at a corn stand that accepted payment on an honor system. The setup could work, the president said, "as long as no members of Congress come by." The clip was actually advertised by the White House, posted on the website as part of a weekly video.

As the weather warmed, the president started playing golf on weekends again. It was a meditative escape, a chance to be outdoors. Years before, Obama had started playing in part to ingratiate himself with strangers in Springfield. Now his main golf partners were a press assistant, the trip director, and other aides unlikely to raise substantive or challenging topics. He rarely if ever invited cabinet members or elected officials to join him, let alone opponents. It was the same pattern the guests at the very first Super Bowl party had seen over a year before—the president was willing to give a lot of his time, a lot of himself, over to politics, but only so much.

"I think he thinks ninety-nine percent of [work-related socializing] is pure bullshit," said an outside adviser who urged the president to do more of it. "It doesn't have to be phony."

Politics was ultimately a public calling, not a private one. "It might have been a good thing," said the adviser, "if those of us who cared about his candidacy had more frank discussions with him about not just what you're going to have to do during the campaign but after to be successful."

THAT SPRING, MICHELLE OBAMA WAS still having trouble with the confinement of first ladyhood, and her relationship with the West Wing had improved just slightly. But her work was a solace, and consciously or not, she was making it into an answer to the problems of her husband's presidency. If the health care overhaul was not going as originally planned, she would work toward related goals in a completely different way. If his goals had been too sprawling, she was going to make hers extremely targeted. If she felt the West Wing was disorganized, she would fill the East Wing with strategy sessions and long-term planning meetings. And if Barack Obama wasn't connecting well with audiences, she was going to be their best friend.

In early June, she stood in front of the 146 graduates of Anacostia high school as they screamed in excitement, for her and for themselves. Most first ladies did not speak at high school graduations— they went to universities, where they could speak to thousands of graduates and their families. But Michelle and her staff had had their eye on that school from their first days in the White House. It was located in a Washington, D.C., neighborhood whose name was synonymous with urban problems, and the first time she visited, in March 2009, the graduation rate was just around 50 percent. A few months later, it was converted to a charter school, and the 2010 ceremonies a little over a year later were a true celebration: 79 percent of students were receiving diplomas, and all but a few of those were headed to college.

The graduation happened to take place at the Daughters of the American Revolution Constitution Hall, where, in 1939, the then all-white organization refused to host a concert by the African American contralto Marian Anderson, sparking the outrage of then first lady Eleanor Roosevelt. (She invited Anderson to perform at the White House instead.) Now Michelle Obama took the stage, wearing a pale blue dress and a double strand of pearls, to shouts of "Love you!"

She spoke of the history of Anacostia, drawing a direct line between its segregated past — in certain parts of town, it had long been illegal for African Americans to own land — and current problems. But she also rewrote the usual negative images of the place, talking about the students' perseverance and the high school's distinguished graduates, including Frederick Douglass.

"Maybe you feel like your destiny was written the day you were born, and you ought to just rein in your hopes and scale back your dreams. But if any of you are thinking that way, I'm here to tell you, stop it. Don't do that," she declared.

Until Barack Obama became president, many of his speeches were similar: rousing calls to hope, written entirely or worked on extensively by him, with few concrete policy details to weigh them down. Now he often delivered several sets of remarks a day, pounded out by a large speechwriting team who pasted together old material from his books and prior speeches. He rarely spoke extemporaneously because of potential gaffes. Diplomatic and policy speeches were often written in a kind of code, less for regular people watching at home than for various congressional leaders or constituent groups who might be listening for the presence or absence of specific words. And there was something a little archaic about the formality of presidential speeches and weekly radio addresses in an era of Facebook updates and TED talks. Only once in a while did the sensitive, empathic side of Obama come through: at a White House bill signing that summer for a law strengthening sexual assault prosecutions, Lisa Marie Iyotte, a rape survivor who was to introduce the president, broke down as soon as she reached the podium and could not continue. The president saved her, striding out before his cue, resting a patient hand on her back until her story of being beaten and raped as her two little girls hid was through. But that was a rare moment.

The lackluster, rote quality of many of his speeches suggested something about his own never-discussed true feelings about the presidency. There was a basic rule of thumb with Obama speeches, advisers agreed: when he was excited and inspired by what he was saying, he was a good speaker, even a great one; when he was just saying things out of political necessity, because he had to, his delivery was terrible, no matter how hard he worked on the speech.

The more the president's voice disappeared, the more the first lady's emerged. Unlike the president, she labored extensively on every one of her speeches herself, even the ones for small groups like the Anacostia graduates. "I remember my parents sacrificing for us, pouring everything they had into us," she recalled in her speech to the Anacostia graduates that day, her voice wavering on the verbs, her hands bouncing up and down in emphasis. "Being there for us, encouraging us to reach for a life they *never*"—she shook her head no—"knew." She was choking up again, just as she had at the girls' school in London:

once more, she saw herself in the kids' eyes, saw what she meant to them. It didn't matter that her parents had been the essence of stability, and it was hard to imagine young Michelle goofing off in class, let alone becoming a teenage mother, as some of the young women in the audience had. She was erasing the distance between herself and her audience, convincing everyone in the room, despite all immediate evidence to the contrary, that she was one of them.

Later, Jocelyn Frye, the first lady's policy director and a friend since they were among a small group of black women at Harvard Law School, told her it was the best speech she had ever given.

"You just think that because I got all teary-eyed," Michelle shot back.

FOUR DAYS AFTER THE FIRST LADY'S graduation speech, the president sat at his desk, cameras zooming in for high-definition shots of the grave expression on his face. He was addressing the nation about the still-worsening oil spill, not from his usual podium but from the Oval Office.

The setting had been a matter of internal dispute. An Oval Office address was the most solemn kind of presidential speech, saved for times of national disaster: the 1962 Cuban missile crisis, the 1986 *Challenger* space shuttle disaster, the attacks of September 11, 2001. At their best, the speeches conveyed authority *and* intimacy, building an electronic bridge between the president's office and viewers' living rooms at home.

Though he had given many statements already, Obama knew he had to say something more to the nation about the spill. Pundits were calling it "Obama's Katrina," underwater cameras turned the leaking oil into a television spectacle, and his political advisers, alarmed, wanted him to reach for the most powerful tool available. Jarrett was against it. Obama spoke best with an audience present, drawing on the energy and live connection. "This is not going to go well," she warned other aides. The president sided with the political advisers and practiced hard beforehand.

As he spoke, Obama tried to sound resolute about the terrible state of the spill. Family photos—he and his bride on their wedding day, Malia and Sasha at his presidential announcement—sat on a table behind him, and the green leaves outside the office swayed a little behind him in the evening light. Stopping the disaster "has tested the limits of human technology," he said. "There will be more oil and more damage before this siege is done." He acknowledged that just before the spill, he had approved more offshore drilling, thinking it was safe; he didn't mention that he had made the compromise in order to calm opposition to his still half-finished energy bill.

He laid out what he called a battle plan—containing the spill; making British Petroleum, the owner of the rig, pay for the cleanup; putting stricter safety regulations in place; nurturing the Gulf coast back to life; and, most important, moving forward on his bill, which would lessen American dependence on fossil fuels. He decried the "lack of political courage and candor" on the issue. Yes, changing American energy production and habits would cost money, he said, but "the long-term costs to our economy, our national security, and our environment are far greater." He ended with an uncharacteristically hokey story about God watching over the Gulf.

The speech didn't work, his advisers knew, though they disagreed as to why. He wasn't really saying anything new, one thought. Another theorized that the speech suffered because his wife and daughters were on vacation in California. ("He's such an introvert, they're the only ones who really draw him out," she said.) David Axelrod later said he had been wrong about using the Oval Office; they had given in to hysteria over the spill, and the speech was "a wasted bullet." They did not mention that the form and content of the speech were fundamentally at odds: Oval Office addresses were supposed to make presidents look powerful, but the truth about the spill was that there was ultimately a limited amount Obama could do.

Instead of showing how connected the president was to the American people, the speech demonstrated the opposite. Sitting all alone behind that big desk, Obama looked entombed, cut off.

Chapter Ten

MALIA'S GREAT ESCAPE

JUNE–JULY 2010

In the summer of 2010, a luminous, oversized photograph hung in the East Wing, showing Malia and Sasha Obama riding on Air Force One. Each sat in a seat stitched with her name in white embroidery. An untouched bowl of fruit and a stack of magazines rested on a table in front of them. Malia, who turned twelve that July, stared out the airplane window, looking lost in thought. Sasha, almost nine, sat beside her sister, but upside down, her head dangling off the seat's bottom cushion, her legs over the headrest. Their parents were nowhere in sight.

It was a picture to stop and stare at, a portrait that hinted at the questions and contradictions of its subjects' young lives. The photograph showed the enviable opportunities available to the first children, with their own seats on the president's plane, the chance to tag along on diplomatic trips. It captured how appealing the Obama girls were — Malia graceful and pensive, Sasha full of comic relief, both of them free of the awkwardness and embarrassing behavior of some prior presidential children. It also underlined just how young Sasha was, still too full of antic energy to sit still on a flight. And while the photo wasn't exactly private—it had been taken by a White House photographer and hung in an office corridor—it wasn't entirely in the public domain, either, because it had never been released or reproduced.

That was also the indeterminate position of the Obama girls: not entirely private figures anymore, but certainly not public ones like their parents. When their parents tallied what they most wanted to keep their own, to protect from the intrusions and poisons of public life, the girls were at the very top of the list. Little was more vital to them than letting Malia and Sasha grow up as naturally and sanely as possible. Yet by that summer polls were showing that Obama's family was more appealing to voters than his policies, and the president could not seem to stop mentioning his daughters in speeches.

It was a sensitive question: to what extent did Barack Obama use his children for political gain? By the time the Air Force One photograph had been snapped, the Obama family had already been dealing with the issue for a long time.

FROM THE BEGINNING, the Obamas had been anxious about combining parenting and politics. In 1999, when Malia was about a year old, her parents brought her along to a dinner party in Hyde Park. Barack and Michelle were so besotted with their daughter that they did not want to leave her at home with a sitter, remembered the host, Elizabeth Brackett. Barack was three years into his state senate career, and the couple was filled with angst over how to succeed in politics while raising healthy, well-adjusted children. What, they asked those around the dinner table, did they think? "They had never met the other guests but they were totally open," Brackett said, "almost to the point where it was uncomfortable." The Obamas' concerns seemed so urgent that they could hardly contain themselves.

Initially, Malia and Sasha, born in 2001, were adorably indifferent to their father's work. On the night of his U.S. Senate primary victory in 2004, Malia, not yet six, watched the cheering but, hours later, had a question for her parents. "Did we win?" she asked, according to Kaleisha Page, a staffer. No one had realized she could not tell.

After their father's keynote speech at the Democratic convention a few months later, the Obama family went on their first campaign trip together, across downstate Illinois. The excursion was designed to connect the candidate to the heartland and to address any lingering fears that Barack was too much of a typical black politician. (The night of his primary victory, aides kept an eye on Reverend Jesse Jackson to make sure he wouldn't hold Barack's arm aloft in victory, an image that might make the next day's front pages.) The family would travel in an RV to communicate how nice, how ordinary, how deeply Illinoisan they were. "Obama begins his 'family vacation' on Saturday July 31 and ends the trip on his birthday August 4 with a barbeque party," read the press release. The planners mixed in ribbon cuttings with stops at a carnival, parks, and eccentric local attractions like the grave of an elephant once killed by lightning. Voters were invited to every stop.

"The concept of it being a family vacation, that was never a popular one to begin with," Kevin Thompson, who stayed by the candidate's side as his personal aide, remembered. "Michelle was just really incredulous." When the candidate returned from Boston, exhausted, and learned about the marathon trip in store, he came the closest aides ever heard him to a meltdown. "What the hell are you doing to me here?" he screamed over the phone to Jeremiah Posedel, who planned much of the trip. Nothing could be changed. Everything was booked.

When Obama landed at the Springfield airport to begin the tour, he was greeted by a single supporter, a little kid holding a tattered sign. His body slumped. "No, Barack, this way," an aide told him, turning him in another direction, where four hundred people erupted in cheers. Soon the schedule went from ambitious to undoable, because so many voters were showing up at every stop, all wanting to meet the man who had given the speech in Boston. Events scheduled for forty-five minutes stretched to two and a half hours. The candidate had to split off from his wife and the girls, who were too young to last through ten rallies, luncheons, and meet-and-greets per day. Michelle, Malia, and Sasha took off in the RV, attending a few events a day, while Barack's bus traveled far above the speed limit in a fruitless attempt to stay on schedule.

During those frantic few days two things became clear to the Obamas: Barack was not going to be a typical U.S. senator like Paul Simon or Richard Durbin, riding the El or walking through O'Hare airport interrupted by nothing more than polite hellos. And the advisers had been right — the Obama family together was political gold. Even in the whitest parts of Illinois, the sight of two well-behaved little black girls, the older one solemn-eyed and the younger one mischievous, had an outsize effect on people. People wanted to touch the Obama children, play with them, ask them questions. "That was an eye-opener for Barack and Michelle," Thompson said, "a recognition that the girls were kind of celebrities."

Sasha had just turned three years old.

The Obama girls grew more popular at home, too. The teams in Malia's soccer league usually had about a dozen players each. When the new school year began that fall, thirty extra sets of parents asked for their kids to join Malia's team, according to one of the organizers.

TWO YEARS LATER, THE OBAMAS began the presidential contest determined to shield their daughters. Michelle Obama threw herself into research, conferring with Tipper Gore and having lunch with Maggie Daley, the Chicago mayor's wife, and Penny Pritzker, a businesswoman who had raised her children against the backdrop of a family fortune, to discuss how to keep Malia and Sasha grounded. Daley in particular warned her about what Pritzker called the "candy bar" problem: what to do when people offered your children things — favors, treats, opportunities — in an effort to become closer to you.

Their solution was to keep their daughters sheltered and their lives intact. Dad would be on the road, Mom would be home, and in their world of birthday parties, school projects, and ballet classes, not that much would change. Running while the girls were young was a big advantage, the president told others: his daughters, then eight and five, wouldn't be reading newspapers or have any real sense of what was happening.

"Our kids thrive on routine and stability and consistency," the candidate's wife said during the first summer of the campaign. "We're always checking," she said. "How are the girls, how are our kids doing? Every day we take a measure. We're measuring the pulse of our children. If your kid's not right, you can't function." She spoke to their teachers constantly, just popping in to make sure nothing was awry. Campaign trips were strictly optional for the girls, she added, who were mostly there to spend some time with their father. That summer they traveled to early primary states but stayed mostly behind the scenes, amusing themselves with a pink bag full of activities including a Nintendo DS, drawing paper, and Uno.

But she knew her children's appeal to voters. The other major Democratic contenders had family situations that were hard to identify with. The Edwardses had a happy-seeming marriage and adorable children, but they lived in a twenty-eight-thousand-square-foot mega-mansion, took their kids out of school for the campaign, and hired tutors for them. (On the trail the children often looked bored and worried aloud about what had become of their pet dog back at home.) The Clinton marriage was full of scar tissue. The Obamas lived a life a bit closer to voters' own. The night before their first New Hampshire trip, Sasha contracted a stomach bug, and Michelle stayed up all night doing laundry and wondering if they would be able to leave come morning. She told the story in an interview, stressing her regular-mom credentials. "We have a couple more weeks before school starts," she had told a crowd of Iowa voters that day, a few hours before the family's all-important visit to the state fair. "I have to get school shoes and spiral notebooks."

In photographs and videos, the ritual visits that presidential candidates make to the state fair look delightful. In person, they are sweaty, crowded, highly choreographed, and a little scary. Candidate and family pantomime a normal fairgoing experience while surrounded by staff, security, far more reporters than voters, and burly men hoisting camera equipment in their faces. On the broiling day the Obamas visited, most of the cameras belonged to the media, but some of them were from the Obama campaign, capturing the potential first family for direct mail and commercials. Both Barack and Michelle flinched at how their children were treated. "Come on! Give me a beautiful smile!" photographers called out to Malia and Sasha, as if they were starlets posing on a red carpet. Hearing the requests, the candidate's face tightened in anger so pronounced that staffers thought he might lash out. Instead he composed himself and beamed.

("This is not quality time," Michelle whispered a few minutes later as the cameras continued to click away.)

Not surprisingly, the Obama daughters both looked shy and skittish. At the pork producers tent—a monument to one of Iowa's most powerful industries—they sat silent and impassive as hundreds of people watched their parents chew their meat. When the Obamas stopped at the petting zoo, the baby pigs and goats drew little attention: Malia and Sasha were the adorable young creatures being fussed over. Only the rides afforded the Obama kids a bit of space. They climbed into bumper cars with their parents and happily smashed into each other. Here, at least, the press remained outside, on the periphery. Soon after, Michelle and the girls slipped off alone to try the other attractions.

A few hours later, with campaign staffers filming again, the candidate asked Malia if she had enjoyed herself. "I had more fun once the cameras left," Malia told him. "No offense," she said politely to the aide wielding the video recorder. "I don't like cameras."

AT THE END OF THE SUMMER, the Obama girls returned to school and normal life, but they handled their occasional campaign appearances with aplomb. In December of 2007, with just a few weeks to go until the Iowa caucus, they were drafted again, this time to shoot a Christmas commercial. The Secret Service, which had already been protecting the candidate for months, nixed the Obamas' using their own home, so Jacky Grimshaw, a neighbor, lent hers for the shoot. The set decorators had removed all her living room furniture, laid down tracks for a moving camera, and installed a fake propane blaze in the fireplace and a glittering tree. Where are we? Michelle asked when she walked in.

The setup was a little strange, allowed Peter Giangreco, the political consultant who supervised the shoot, but no one minded because the Obamas were just so happy to be in one place together. The girls did their parts perfectly, the family cracked up together, and the ad makers were delighted with how real and natural the Obamas seemed in their fake abode.

The Obama daughters had kept campaigning to a minimum during the school year, but by the spring of 2008, they were needed again on the trail, this time urgently. The primaries had dragged on far longer than anyone anticipated, and Obama could not seem to close the deal with Democratic voters. He still needed to get past the suspicions about his unusual background and his relationship with the Reverend Jeremiah Wright Jr.

Shortly before the Indiana and North Carolina primaries in May, Anita Dunn, then a campaign adviser, was reading a newspaper when she came across a voter's quote expressing surprise that Barack Obama was a good family man. On the trail, Obama had mostly been a solo act, telling the story of his life journey and his vision of the future. Dunn shared the quote with colleagues as yet more evidence he was a more appealing candidate when surrounded by his family. A few days later the entire Obama family was campaigning together in Indiana, with an itinerary very similar to their 2004 RV trip through southern Illinois. There were two picnics this time, plus a skating party. The candidate beat expectations in both Indiana and North Carolina, unofficially locking up the nomination, and political advisers were sure the family-man message had helped.

Every candidate with children deployed them in moments of pressure: it was an unspoken, unavoidable rule. Bill and Hillary Clinton were known as the most fiercely protective parents in the business, but at the 1992 Democratic convention, the Clinton campaign used Chelsea to recast her father after headlines about his relationship with Gennifer Flowers. At thirteen years old, she was his key character witness, relating how great a father he was in the "Man from Hope" video. A second later, the tape cut to Bill Clinton talking about Chelsea's forgiving reaction to his admission of marital transgressions. That was six years before the Monica Lewinsky scandal and the famous photograph of Chelsea walking between her parents, seemingly holding them together.

In the fevered final months of the 2008 contest, the girls appeared far more widely than they had at the start. On the Fourth of July, Malia's birthday, the family sat for an interview with *Access Hollywood*, a popular evening entertainment show. The Obama daughters had never spoken on the public stage before, and they were utterly charming, Malia answering the lighthearted questions thoughtfully and Sasha piping up. Their parents looked happy and proud, but after a few days of criticism for doing the interview, Obama called it a mistake. (That was the paradox of the Obama girls, David Axelrod said later: it was precisely because they were kept out of the public eye, because they were not scripted or performing, that they seemed so appealing.)

A few weeks later, however, Malia and Sasha made their biggest public appearance yet, at the Democratic National Convention during a prime-time broadcast. They emerged after their mother's speech, and together the three stood onstage and spoke by videoconference with the candidate, who was watching with voters in Kansas City, Missouri. Advisers had been divided on whether the moment would be too corny, but once again the girls were a hit. A few weeks later, on election night, an army of volunteers covered the critical state of Florida with get-out-the-vote literature featuring a glossy photo of the candidate embracing his younger daughter. Obama, who had begun the race vowing to protect his daughters, had relied on them to carry him to victory.

As soon as the campaign was over, the isolation of the presidency began to set in, not just for Barack Obama but for the family. Michelle narrowed the circle Malia and Sasha were allowed to play with, other parents noticed. The girls got together with their closest friends but not with casual ones. When Malia's class gave a fifth-grade band concert, the group performed the program twice: they played for parents and siblings in the usual venue, Mandel Hall, but because the president-elect could no longer attend school concerts without massive interruptions and distractions, the children played a separate concert for an audience of three—Barack, Michelle, and Sasha, who sat in a classroom.

When the family left for Washington, many of the extra soccer players who had signed up to play with Malia dropped the program.

IN THE WHITE HOUSE, the Obamas forged a kind of compromise solution to the problem of putting their children on display. The real Malia and Sasha, the actual human beings, were protected more tightly than ever before, but they also became abstract characters who played an important role in their father's political rhetoric.

Being a presidential child could be an extreme affair, dazzling one moment, frightening the next. Grover and Frances Cleveland were so horrified at the way tourists pawed at their two young children that they moved out of the White House, heading a few miles north on Connecticut Avenue and giving the neighborhood Cleveland Park its name. Caroline Kennedy attended her own nursery school in the upstairs solarium so that the family's privacy would not be compromised. (When the Kennedys integrated the school, enrolling children of some of the few black officials in the administration, the move was interpreted as an embrace of civil rights.) Chelsea Clinton was mocked on *Saturday Night Live* and by John McCain. Worst of all was the fear that an enemy or lunatic might try to harm the president's children. When American troops captured Saddam Hussein's sons in 2003, they found photographs of Jenna and Barbara Bush tacked up in their lairs.

For their part, the Obama girls were carefully protected by an elaborate protocol that gave them as much cover as possible. At the beginning of the administration, Robert Gibbs had spent weeks negotiating with network executives and other media figures over how and when Malia and Sasha could be photographed or filmed. When the girls were alone on their private schedules, giving a concert at Sidwell or getting ice cream with a friend's mom, they were off-limits. Shots of them at official White House events, like the Easter Egg Roll, were fine. If the Obama daughters were traveling with their parents, they could be filmed or photographed only if a parent was in the picture too. So a picture of the president and Malia browsing in a bookstore on Martha's Vineyard was okay with the White House; a photograph of her walking the dog with Sasha was not. The White House could not, of course, prevent pictures from being taken or disseminated, but there were quiet means of enforcement; for example, Washington gossip columnists or photographers who chronicled Sasha stopping for after-school excursions found themselves exiled by the White House. "You're done to us," as Robert Gibbs put it in an interview, describing the penalty.

The pool coverage system meant that if the president went to a soccer game of Malia's, the news would be beamed to reporters across the nation, in a report like this one by Kevin Diaz of the *Minneapolis Star Tribune:*

Saturday, April 17 [2010]
Pool Report # 1

Presidential Motorcade, about a dozen vehicles in all, leaves WH at 9:33 a.m. for drive to Rudolph Field in N.W. Washington, where daughter Malia is playing a league soccer game (unclear if connected to Sidwell Friends, her school).

Immediately pass a small group of protesters at 15th and Pennsylvania holding a banner proclaiming "March for Justice and Immigration Reform."

Traffic not blocked. Motorcade starts and stops with light Saturday morning D.C. traffic.

Motorcade mostly uneventful except for motorbike rider who slides into the last police vehicle after it turns west onto Gallatin from North Capitol St.

Biker dusts himself off, glares at police driver, who glares back, and biker then drives off without apparent injury.

Motorcade continues and pulls up to Rudolph Field at 3rd and Ingraham Sts. NW at 9:51 a.m.

POTUS steps out onto the field wearing a black baseball cap, black jacket, and jeans. Wearing sunglasses against glare of sunny cool morning. Takes his place alongside a small clutch of parents, watching girls in green jerseys kick a soccer ball around, apparently warming up for a game.

Pool then drives around the block to park. Awaiting next move.

Malia herself was closely guarded: the reporter could see or write no more without fear of exile.

The first daughters were also fiercely protected by Marian Robinson, who had precious powers no one else in the family did: she alone could slip out of the White House, nod to the agents standing at the iron gates, cross Pennsylvania Avenue, and pick up a vial of medication at CVS. She became her granddaughters' escort, riding with them to and from school and browsing in stores with them as agents tagged behind, doing everything with them that their confined parents could not. Marian refused to do anything that could compromise her freedom, because without her, Malia and Sasha would lead far narrower lives. She refused almost all interviews, and she even grumbled good-naturedly about attending public events. If a stranger stopped her on the street she would barely acknowledge who she was. "You look a lot like Mrs. Obama's mother," passersby would say. "I get that a lot," was her standard reply.

Inside the White House gates, the Obamas adhered to the hyper-involved, child-centric parenting style of their generation and class, conducting educational conversations at the dinner table, filling their weekends with enriching activities. During one of Jacqueline Kennedy's frequent vacations from the White House, she left her then infant son, John, with relatives; during the month she was gone, his father visited the child once. Barack Obama was the extreme opposite: he was determined not to let his job take him away from his children more than necessary. The first lady, meanwhile, built her schedule almost entirely around her daughters; any afternoon or evening event she agreed to attend had to be good enough to merit time away from them, she told her staff. It was hard to say who was protecting whom: were the Obama parents protecting their children from politics? Or were they using their children to protect themselves?

Worried that the privileges of the White House could spoil her children, Michelle tried to limit the staff's constant efforts to feed and polish and assist and perfect. The first time the Obamas traveled to Europe as president and first lady, they called home to chat with the girls. The White House operators could not locate Malia and Sasha, who were playing around somewhere on the lawn. Later, when the Obamas returned, the operators were so contrite about their failure to connect them that they made plans to issue Malia and Sasha their own cell phones. Michelle had to step in to say she wasn't ready for them to have their own phones.

Michelle had never been a lax mother: fellow parents from the soccer team in Chicago remember her standing on the sidelines, watching Malia's footwork and defense skills, not lingering in the stands with a latte like the other parents. In the White House, she pushed and watched her daughters relentlessly: if the girls went on a trip, they had to write their parents a report. The first lady watched what her girls were eating. "Before they get a second helping I'll ask them, 'Are you really hungry? Or is this something you want to do because you're bored?'" she said. The girls were not permitted to surf the Internet or watch TV during the week, their parents said. But they took swimming and tennis lessons, and played soccer, lacrosse, and basketball. In a telling tribute to the power of Michelle Obama's personality, she even managed to persuade Dan Dufford, the girls' piano instructor from Chicago, to relocate with his wife to Washington to continue teaching her children.

"I tell them sports are something I want them to engage in because it's good for them," Michelle said in an interview. "It's good to practice teamwork, to understand what it means to suffer a loss, to win with grace. Also, I have them do a sport that they like and a sport that I like. I want them to understand what it feels like to do something you don't like and to improve. Because in life you don't always get to do the things you want." When she chose tennis for them, Sasha was frustrated, "because she couldn't hit the ball. Malia didn't understand why I was making them play it. But now they're starting to get better and they actually like it. And I'm like, 'Mom was right!'

"Now, my kids are young, so we'll see if I've driven them crazy," she finished, seeming to suddenly realize that she sounded like the single most intense mother on earth.

AT THE SAME TIME, Malia and Sasha played a key role in an ongoing narrative told by their father, in which he pitted his daughters' sincerity, diligence, sense of responsibility, and purity of intention against what he called the cynicism and laziness of Washington.

In late May, at a press conference about the oil spill, the president added an impromptu bit to his prepared remarks. "I woke up this morning and I'm shaving, and Malia knocks on my bathroom door and she says, 'Did you plug the hole yet, Daddy?'" It was a striking word picture: the president caught by surprise, perhaps in his bathrobe, dealing with the expectations not just of the nation but of his own daughter. (Soon radio and television host Glenn Beck was crudely imitating Malia on his radio show, whining in a fake-high voice, "Daddy, did you plug the hole yet?" and, "Why, why, why, why, do you still let the polar bears die?")

Malia was not always wild about making cameo appearances in her father's interviews and speeches. Early in the administration, when she scored a 73 on a science test, he called her out not only at home but also to the nation. "Malia will tell you, my attitude was if she came home with a B, that's not good enough because there's no reason she can't get an A," he told *Essence* magazine. As soon as he finished the interview, he realized his mistake. "Oh my god, I don't know why I did that," he told Gibbs. In the end, he apologized privately to his daughter.

But he didn't stop mentioning her. As he hit the trail during the summer of 2010 for the midterm elections, he was searching for the right way to describe the utter frustration he felt with opponents, to rally the Democratic faithful to his side. At a July fund-raiser in Kansas City for Robin Carnahan, a candidate for U.S. Senate, the president wove Malia into an analogy he liked to use for the Republican response to the economic crisis. "Even though she's five foot nine now, she's still my baby," he said. "And she just got braces, which is good, because she looks like a kid and she was getting—she's starting to look too old for me." The audience laughed, and the president started to explain his central point. "In a couple years, Malia is going to be able to drive," he began. "If your teenager drives into a ditch, your car, bangs it up, you've got to pay a lot of money to get it out—what do you do?" he asked. "You take the keys away! These folks"—meaning Republicans—"drove the economy into a ditch, and they want the keys back." The audience applauded. "And you got to say the same thing to them that you say to your teenager: you can't have the keys back because you don't know how to drive yet."

He sounded sarcastic and cutting, nothing like the above-it-all, inspiring figure from 2008. And he wasn't done. "You can't have the keys. You can't have them. Maybe you take a remedial course," he continued. The crowd was clapping and he only seemed to get more excited. "I'll take you out to the parking lot and you can drive in circles. But we're not going to let you out on the open road. You can't drive."

It was quite a mash-up: Obama's fatherly love and his disdain for his political opponents. If he considered that it might sound condescending to compare the Republican leadership to a bunch of teenagers who needed remedial courses, he didn't show it.

White House advisers later dismissed any suggestion that the president was trading on the popularity of his children. But Obama knew what the polls said: his role as father was one of the most appealing things about him. Voters liked his sweet, poised daughters and the fact that in the age of disgraced politicians like Eliot Spitzer and Mark Sanford, there was not even a whiff of sleazy sexual scandal to him. Even voters who were unenthusiastic about his job performance and handling of the economy thought he was "an honest, loyal husband, a family man," as the Democratic pollster Celinda Lake put it.

In a way, it was no surprise that he continually turned to his daughters in speeches. He needed to finally make a connection with the public, and in politics as in life, his daughters *did* help connect him to other people. It also made sense that he tended to mention them in politically uncomfortable moments, from the oil spill to fund-raising for the ominous-looking midterm elections. In contrast to the disappointment, worry, and frustration of those events, his daughters clearly made him feel good. They *did* speak well of him. Once again, Obama was retreating to a comfortable place.

As the summer progressed and Malia-the-character continued to pop up in her father's speeches, Malia-the-human-being was far away from the political world. The Obamas had somehow managed to arrange for her to go to summer camp, and they talked about her getaway with joy and relief.

The details were closely held. The public did not know the state she was in or the name of the camp. She still had Secret Service protection, but she lived in a cabin, not an armored mansion; she played sports without a pool reporter nearby; her meals came from the camp mess; and there were no motorcades, camera phones, or famous parents on television. Campers were allowed no electronic devices and only one phone call home all summer.

"She's having the exact same camp experience as all those other kids," said Melissa Winter, the first lady's deputy chief of staff, responsible for many of the logistics behind the first family's life.

There was one little difference, though. Unlike regular parents, the first lady admitted to an adviser with a laugh, the Obamas did not have to wait for postcards to find out how their daughter was faring at summer camp: The Secret Service agents posted at the camp were feeding them quiet reports. Michelle, ever vigilant, had found a way to keep an eye on Malia from afar.

Chapter Eleven

HAPPY BIRTHDAY, MR. PRESIDENT

JUNE–SEPTEMBER 2010

The midterm elections arrived early to the White House. Everyone knew what was coming: the Democrats were going to lose the House, captured with blood, sweat, and tears four years before, and when the new Congress was sworn in, most of the president's legislative agenda would almost certainly be a lost cause. None of it would happen for months. But all summer the administration reeled from the blow even before it landed, going through all the postdefeat rituals—buckling relationships, accusatory blowups, who-gives-a-hell disregard—ahead of time.

There was little to look forward to, it seemed: The White House announced a "recovery summer," but the economy was not recovering. The economic team was still hamstrung on when to move forward on deficit reduction. The energy legislation was collapsing in the Senate. Asked to articulate the president's goals and aspirations for the rest of his first term, advisers gave flat answers. The president talked about execution, about implementing health care and financial regulatory reform, of systems and bureaucracies—hardly a rousing or energetic vision. "He's best when he's full of hope," one aide said—but hope was in short supply.

Obama's relationship with Emanuel had become a strange mix of dependence and resistance. The outside world, and even some of the West Wing, saw them as unified, but Obama was guided by a chief of staff who did not match him in temperament or philosophy. The approach of the midterms marked the natural, painful culmination of their year and a half of differences. Obama checked on polls, but he did not see himself at the center of the midterm efforts, aides said, an unusual position for the leader of his party. Emanuel was obsessed. He had commandeered the 2006 Democratic recapture of the House, handpicking and nurturing candidates himself, and now many of them were going to lose their seats on Obama's watch, voters speaking in proxy judgment of the president's actions. The clearer it became that a lot of the members Emanuel had mentored would not be reelected, the more difficult his White House job became. His colleagues knew what was coming, but Emanuel was convinced they didn't fully understand, "like everyone was in la-la land and he was Diogenes," one aide said. Several aides used the same phrase to describe Emanuel that summer: he was still acting as if he was chair of the DCCC, congressional Democrats' campaign organization.

It was the exact issue Chris Edley, the Berkeley Law dean, had tried to warn Obama about: Emanuel was invested in keeping the House in Democratic hands, which meant it was hard for him to separate lawmakers' needs from those of the presidency. Rahm didn't want the White House to do anything that could hurt vulnerable Democrats; the president was sticking closely to his own agenda.

Over the spring and early summer of 2010, the president and his chief of staff still talked constantly, and at the end of the day, they would often take lengthy walks outside together, looping the

South Lawn. ("Oh, the boys are on their walk," Michelle would comment.) Emanuel later denied he was ever on the ropes, but other aides said Obama was getting ready to move on. "The president always valued Rahm," one said. But he was more settled in his role and "less quick to excuse or overlook operating idiosyncrasies," he continued. Obama was already talking about a new chief of staff after midterms, "someone with the energy and drive of a Rahm but the organization skills of a Pete," meaning Pete Rouse, an obvious candidate himself. By summer's end, even David Axelrod, so close to Emanuel that he signed his wedding contract, told colleagues Emanuel needed to go.

The issue came to a head with a relatively little-noticed presidential speech on immigration in July. Obama badly wanted to overhaul the nation's poorly administered immigration system. Its capriciousness caused tremendous human suffering, Obama had pledged to fix it during the 2008 campaign, and he would need to answer to Latino voters in 2012. The idea had once enjoyed bipartisan support, including from his Republican predecessor, but in the past few years, the immigration debate had taken on an increasingly ugly, get-the-foreigners-out tone, and Republicans and some Democrats were abandoning the cause. On the campaign trail, Obama had proposed a two-step solution: increased crackdowns on illicit crossings and employment of undocumented workers to make sure people were playing by the rules, followed by a more welcoming step, the creation of pathways to citizenship for those already in the United States. By the summer of 2010, the president had already done much of the first part, to the consternation of Latino groups and many other supporters, but he did not have enough Republican votes to deliver the second. He had put the harshest part of his policy into effect but could not pass the more humane part, a situation that ate at Obama, advisers said. The solution was so obvious—the model for comprehensive reform had been on the table for years—and yet the political situation prevented any progress from being made. "There are certain things that nag at him. This is one of those things," Axelrod said.

A few weeks before the speech, when Michelle Obama visited a Maryland elementary school, a dark-haired second grader, legs neatly folded on a gym floor, asked her why the president was "taking everybody away that doesn't have papers."

"That's something that we have to work on, right?" Michelle Obama said. "Making sure that people can be here with the right kind of papers."

"But my mom doesn't have any papers," the girl said.

"*Everybody* in Congress needs to work together to make sure that happens," the first lady said pointedly.

The exchange was painful for the first lady, an aide said later. The cameras had been rolling and the second grader had unintentionally put her mother at risk—a reminder of how many innocent people, like that child, her husband could not help. There wasn't much the first lady felt that she could do about it, though; if she spoke up, it would almost surely backfire. Instead, all she could do was exhort Republicans to cooperate, though she said it so blandly it didn't sound as if she was saying much at all. The encounter in Maryland only undergirded the president's belief that he had to give immigration reform another push, to build a new coalition of supporters, advisers said. He had been saying for a long time that he wanted to give a speech on the issue that was as frank and stirring as the famous speech about race he had given during the campaign, and he decided that now was the time.

Emanuel had been trying to hold off the speech for months, according to aides: Once again he felt the president needed to be saved from causing political harm. He thought the timing was madness. Immigration legislation wasn't going anywhere; there were zero Republican votes for it in the Senate. Arizona had just passed a harsh new law—supported by a majority of Americans—cracking down on illegal immigrants. Stirring up such a charged issue before the midterms was asking for trouble, especially for vulnerable Democrats, and it could make the president look weak, by proposing something he could not deliver. At Obama's insistence, the speech was finally scheduled, but the text came to him late, and when he looked over the first draft during a trip to the Midwest, he found the language much too tepid—he wanted it to be bolder, more inspiring. He sent it back to Axelrod for revisions, but when the new draft arrived, he was so unhappy with the text that he stayed up most of the night rewriting it.

The result was the kind of oration he had given more often during the campaign than since taking office—historical, sweeping, attentive to all sides of the debate. He spoke about the proud but contentious history of immigration to the United States and cited success stories from Albert Einstein to Google's Sergey Brin. "Immigrants have always helped to build and defend this country," he said. "Being American is not a matter of blood or birth." He ended with the famous Emma Lazarus line about huddled masses yearning to breathe free.

His impassioned remarks faded almost as soon as he gave them. The media and others were puzzled—why this, why now? Without legislation pending, a speech didn't mean that much in the currency of Washington; a speech alone was not enough to move a debate. Obama became quietly furious at his team for not giving the address more support, for not delivering the one he had wanted in the first place or talking it up more in the press. The first lady fumed, too: she took it as more proof that her husband's advisers were poorly serving him. She knew how important immigration reform was to him—he had been working on it since his Senate days—and she wanted him to be the kind of leader who took on tough issues. Besides, if he was the president of the United States, why was he up all night writing his own speech? The speech incident confirmed her worst fears, and by that point, several aides said, Michelle was bluntly telling her husband that he needed a new team.

Very few people knew the president was angry, but word of the first lady's displeasure got around the West Wing. As was often the case, it was hard for advisers to determine where the president's feelings ended and the first lady's began. He was so reticent and she was so vocal. Was she encouraging his worst suspicions about his staff? Or was she just channeling her husband, taking her cues from his private reaction, expressing the outrage he was not?

Obama still had that special, nearly familial trust with Jarrett, a quality that Emanuel had never shared with him. Obama quietly told Jarrett that he wanted her to watch his back more closely, two other aides said, to take charge of making sure that his other advisers were delivering what he wanted.

It was an awkward solution to an awkward problem. She was not the chief of staff. It was another of the president's retreats into the familiar, and it was exactly why Emanuel had cautioned against Jarrett's working in the White House. West Wing staff had to have solidarity; they had to protect one another, to work together to carefully manage the president from below. As in the campaign, Jarrett's very presence could seem like a rebuke to other advisers: the president and first lady's best friend, there to watch and report back to the Obamas. The more she played enforcer, the more the others would resent her. Besides, she had her own strong feelings about what needed to change, and they were not far from the first lady's. Jarrett and Emanuel had never gotten along from the start, tolerating each other but never developing real trust, and she had also been increasingly critical of Robert Gibbs, telling others in the West Wing that the president needed a less abrasive press secretary.

In July, midterm fever got worse. Robert Gibbs was criticized by Democratic leaders on Capitol Hill for publicly saying they could lose the House, even though it was plainly true. Congressional leaders were demanding that the president campaign more. To counter the criticism, Patrick Gaspard, the political director, put together a memo for the leadership emphasizing everything the White House had done, and Bill Burton, the deputy press secretary, suggested they leak it to Jonathan Martin, a reporter at Politico.com. Gibbs signed off on the decision, according to several aides. The ploy backfired: Nancy Pelosi, the Speaker of the House, and Harry Reid, the Senate majority leader, grew angry that the White House had leaked and tried to spin the situation.

Emanuel was in a rage about the leak. He berated the staff, not once but twice, at his 7:30 a.m. meeting for top aides and at another close-of-business meeting. "Just because someone wants to put their dick on the table, we have to deal with this!" he yelled, eyeing Gaspard, who he clearly thought was the culprit. Gibbs, who had approved the leak, said nothing. Emanuel was still screaming at his morning meeting the next day, alternating between subjects: the Politico leak, all the races Democrats were going to lose. "We don't know what we're doing. We're not using resources well," he fumed.

In his slight Haitian accent, Gaspard talked back. "Respectfully, we're not the DCCC, there's but so much we can do," he said. "We don't want to own this." Rahm became volcanic again, screaming about the memo. Gaspard said he had written the memo but not leaked it; Emanuel told him he didn't believe him, and launched into another round of swearing. Again, Gibbs did not acknowledge his role.

Fraying relationships, squabbling advisers, the ire of congressional Democrats who wanted him to campaign more: Obama tried to flee it all, to get out of the White House. He still read his ten daily letters from the public, but now he craved more personal contact, not to mention a clearer demonstration of his caring than people could see from televised speeches. He told advisers he wanted to do a series of small events in family backyards and at businesses. "At least I can stand there with a group of people and interact with them in a genuine way," he said, according to Axelrod. "Even if it's not great for the enterprise, it's good for me."

So the president set off to places like Des Moines and Columbus, where his vast operation alighted on one ranch house or small shop at a time, the agents, vehicles, lights, and reporters making it look like the scene where authorities take over Elliot's home in *E.T.* The president talked with a family or small group of business owners, answering questions that were almost all about the economy, as reporters listened in. The setup was artificial, one aide conceded, but for Obama, anything was better than being in Washington.

Looking directly into voters' eyes, the president saw up close just how little people understood his initiatives. At a sandwich shop in New Jersey, one participant said he was surprised to hear that the health care legislation included tax credits to help small businesses cover employees. The president's face fell, a mix of disappointment and incredulity. A week later, at a fund-raiser, he told a story about an exchange between President Abraham Lincoln, one of his lodestars, and someone who came to the White House looking for a patronage job. "If it wasn't for me, you would not be here," the applicant said. And Lincoln said, "Is that true?" the president continued. Yes, the job seeker said, I helped get you elected. "Well, I forgive you," Lincoln-channeled-by-Obama said.

MICHELLE OBAMA ESCAPED IN A different way, one that made the tensions inside the White House even worse. Her four-day vacation in Spain in late July, which spurred negative news reports across the country and no small amount of consternation inside the White House, originated with the death of a seventy-six-year-old retired Chicago Transit Authority bus driver and his granddaughter's tenth birthday. The former bus driver was Ovelton W. Blanchard, Anita Blanchard's father and Marty Nesbitt's father-in-law. He grew up in segregation-era Mississippi, where the public schools for African Americans were so rudimentary that his parents sent him away to a modest boarding school founded by black parents who wanted something better for their children. There he met Barbara Jolly. Together they attended Mississippi Valley State University and moved to Chicago in search of opportunity. Jolly became a teacher, but even with a college education, the best job Ovelton Blanchard could get was as a bus driver. The Blanchards pushed their girls toward a better life, and Anita and her sister graduated first and second in their high school classes, attended Northwestern and Stanford for their undergraduate degrees, and graduated from Harvard and the University of Chicago medical schools. Back home their father was promoted from bus driver to supervisor. He was an oak tree, Nesbitt said: just like Fraser Robinson.

He died at the end of June 2010. The Obamas did not attend the funeral, due to their official schedules and the fuss they would cause. That same summer, Roxanne Nesbitt, Marty and Anita's daughter, was turning ten. According to family tradition, that meant she got to go on a trip with her mom anywhere she wanted. She chose Spain. Michelle and Sasha Obama wanted to go, too.

In the private sphere of friendship, the trip made sense. Like the Obamas, the Nesbitts had come a long way financially, and both families wanted to give their children opportunities like European trips. "I want my girls to see the world," the first lady told aides. Malia had escaped to camp, and the first lady wanted Sasha to have an adventure as well. Besides, Anita was asking her to come. "I think under any other circumstance Michelle would have said, 'Okay, maybe I shouldn't do this trip,'" Nesbitt explained. But "Michelle really wanted to be there for Anita and she didn't want to back out," he said. She was trying to take a slice of private life back, and she wanted to get out of Washington too.

In political terms, however, it made no sense at all. The rule in the White House was no foreign vacations: they looked terrible, potentially worse than sumptuous ball gowns or redecoration, against the background of unemployment. Couldn't the first lady vacation someplace in the United States? To make matters worse, she would be gone on the president's birthday, a fact the press would notice. To the exasperation of advisers, she still had not agreed to a campaign schedule, and with three months until midterms, she was sending exactly the wrong signal to voters. This was going to be the opposite of a campaign trip, they feared: she could *repel* votes instead of winning them.

Several aides said they were unwilling to confront the first lady outright, to tell her not to go—even the normally fearless Gibbs threw up his hands. Jarrett and Sher delicately laid out the risks for her, but the first lady was unmoved. The president, meanwhile, who felt perpetually guilty about what his wife had given up for him, just wanted her to be happy. "If she's gone through all those sacrifices, essentially for him, he's not real anxious to say, this thing that you really want to do, you can't do that for political reasons," one aide said. Together the three Obamas shared pie—his favorite dessert—in an early birthday celebration before the first lady and Sasha left.

Watching Michelle Obama depart was painful, White House aides said. They knew what was in store.

As soon as the first lady arrived for her four-day trip, European photographers set on her, sending images of her vacation around the world. She strode through the Spanish streets surrounded by security personnel, wearing a one-shouldered designer top, dark oversized sunglasses, and a joyless expression. Those images appeared on television along with shots of her hotel, a luxury beach resort where rooms started at five hundred dollars a night. (She had originally wanted to go to Madrid, to stroll and visit cafés, but the Secret Service had nixed the idea.) Rumors circulated that the first lady was traveling with forty friends. That was false, but the group commanded over thirty rooms because of security needs. Though she paid for her own room and food, and her friends flew commercial, the air force jet she flew on cost $11,351 an hour to operate. According to government rules, she only had to pay the cost of first-class tickets for herself and Sasha. The American economy had shed 131,000 more jobs that month. "A modern-day Marie Antoinette," a *Daily News* columnist wrote, back in New York. The trip was yet more fodder for those who believed her husband's spending was out of control.

In response to reporters' questions about the trip, Robert Gibbs asserted simply that the first lady "was a private citizen and is the mother of a daughter on a private trip." His logic was awkward. *Was* the first lady a truly private citizen? Then why were she and Sasha ending their trip with lunch with Spanish royalty?

As the group toured southern Spain, they knew the criticism at home was mounting far beyond what they had expected, but the first lady tuned out. "When she gets to a point when there's no point to reading it, she just stops," said an aide who was on the trip. "She had made a decision she felt she could live with," Sher said.

Within a week the first lady's approval ratings were in a double-digit plunge. It wasn't clear whether the trip to Spain, like the expensive clothing and shoes, hurt Democrats, or how much visual reinforcement it gave to Republican and Tea Party charges about out-of-control spending and an indifferent administration. But it was hard to argue it helped.

*　　*　　*

AT LEAST THE PRESIDENT HAD an enticing extracurricular project: choosing players and teams for the basketball tournament that Marty Nesbitt, Michael Strautmanis, and Reggie Love, the president's personal aide, had been planning for his birthday since spring.

Barack Obama loved casual pickup ball. In a life that carried him through wildly disparate settings, it was one of the few constants. As a teenager, he slipped away from his Hawaii prep school to university courts populated by "gym rats and has-beens" who taught him "that respect came from what you did and not who your daddy was," he wrote in *Dreams from My Father*. He continued to play at Occidental College, at a gym in Springfield, in Chicago health clubs but also on playground courts in city parks. At the court he liked to frequent at the University of Chicago, homeless players mixed with winners of the world's most prestigious academic prizes. "It's a great equalizer," said Arne Duncan, a teammate then and later the secretary of education. "No one cares who are you or what you do."

Once, at Harvard Law School, he and his friends played at a state prison against a team of inmates. The game had been the brainstorm of Hill Harper, later an actor on *CSI: NY*, who was working on outreach for the black law student group and had struck up a correspondence with an inmate. Harper planned the game to demonstrate that the law students cared about the prisoners. "Basketball could be a signal, we support you, we're not removed from everything going on," Harper said later. Obama immediately said yes to the plan, and the men played on a basement court with guards standing watch. The warden instructed the visitors that in case of a hostage situation, they were to scatter themselves to the corners of the room. The law students lost; as Harper pointed out, winning might have been unwise.

When Obama's life changed with his election to the U.S. Senate, his basketball game did, too. In 2006, as he played on an outdoor court in Hawaii with Nesbitt and other longtime friends, firefighters inter-rupted the game at a crucial point—they wanted pictures.

Two years later, on the morning of the Iowa caucus, Obama and his friends played in a freezing Iowa gym. They were short one player so they conscripted the guy who ran the place. After the Iowa victory, playing before a vote became a good-luck ritual. But on the morning of the North Carolina and Indiana votes, Alexi Giannoulias, a young Chicago politician Obama had mentored since meeting him on the courts back home, drove to the basket with the ball in his hand and unintentionally slammed into the defending candidate. Obama fell to the floor and lay there for several minutes, unable to catch his breath or get up. He eventually insisted on returning to the game, but text messages bounced around Obamaland: *Oh my god, did you hear?* Obama's rib was bruised, he discovered later, but there was no time to rest, and for weeks, his chest ached from the injury. Several regular teammates later said they made sure never to foul him again.

If Obama had known his friends were going easy on him, he would likely have been disappointed, even angry. The president and his friends, mostly middle-aged men who prided themselves on com-peting with much younger players, hated the idea of anyone conde-scending to them on the court. "I don't want someone out here who's letting up on us," Nesbitt said. "We only play with people who don't care" that they are playing with the president, he said. To create a suf-ficiently competitive game for the president in Washington, Reggie Love scouted local players, turning up guys—not important officials, just good players—he knew from his own college basketball days, or friends of friends. The group met at a court at an army base when the weather was bad, on the court behind the White House when it was nice.

Yet instead of feeling entirely like regular pickup ball, the games had a Ye Royal Basketball quality. Butlers in formal black-and-white uniforms inflated the balls, which were emblazoned with "Barack Obama" or the presidential seal. The seal also decorated the blue bumpers that wrapped the bases of the baskets.

On the court, the president captained his own team, sometimes choosing Reggie Love, a former captain of the Duke team and the best player of the bunch. "That's like saying I'll take LeBron first," Senator Bob Casey, a sometime participant, laughed. Other players noticed Love holding back, shooting from outside instead of driving the ball to the basket, because he didn't want to dominate the game entirely.

The celebration for Obama's forty-ninth birthday was the basketball competition to end all basketball competitions: a four-team tournament at a military base not far from the White House, consisting of the president's longtime friends, favorite NBA stars, and retired greats, played in front of wounded veterans and participants in the White House mentoring program. The event demonstrated a timeless truth of the White House: no matter how badly things were in the outside world, sometimes it was just fantastic to be the president of the United States.

Obama loved planning the event. "He was very personally engaged in picking the players and teams," Strautmanis said. "He wants fair teams" — a mix of pros, amateurs, and veterans. (Even LeBron James, the highest-paid player in the NBA, was on the third of four teams, which meant he was not on the court initially. "I didn't get picked?" other players heard James mutter. "I'm on team C? How'd I get on team C?") It was, essentially, a private all-star game, with the three or four pros on each of the teams doing most of the playing and the amateurs slipping in and out. But the president didn't hang back. "He's competing," John Rogers, who also flew in from Chicago, recalled later. "He's out there making shots and encouraging everyone else to be in there fighting."

Everyone wore specially made t-shirts that said "POTUS 49." The president was in a good mood—the best anyone had seen in a while. He loved the sight of Maya Moore, a University of Connecticut star and the only female player, outmaneuvering some of his old hoops buddies along with NBA stars like Dwyane Wade. (She was the second leading scorer in the tournament, according to Nesbitt.)

After a game or two, everyone started commenting on the president's performance on the court. Normally, he was a good player, with great endurance and a sneaky left-handed jumper, though not quite on the level of his friends who had played college and professional ball. Now he was playing better than he had in years.

It helped, of course, that the pros weren't playing that hard. "I think that people were kind of goofing off at first," Strautmanis said. "They were kind of letting up a little bit. No one was playing the hardest defense in the world on the president."

His team just happened to remain undefeated through each game. On the last one, Obama drained a three-point shot to win the tournament, just the way he had won at Camp David the year before. Walking off the court, he had a gigantic smile on his face. Finally, something had gone right.

A FEW DAYS LATER HIS mood sank again. The Obamas, minus Malia, were headed on a photo opportunity disguised as a vacation, a family trip to the Florida coast intended to generate news copy and images that would show Americans that the president was still attending to the Gulf and that its waters were safe for swimming.

The night before setting off, the president hosted a dinner for Muslim Americans to mark the start of Ramadan, just as an uproar was spreading against the establishment of a Muslim community center in downtown Manhattan. There was nothing radical about the proposed institution; it was modeled after a Jewish community center.

However, opponents, including many of the same conservative activists who resisted trying Khalid Sheikh Mohammed in civilian court in New York, were protesting that it would desecrate the memory of Ground Zero. The week before, Gibbs had stated that the White House would stay out of the fracas. (Emanuel felt strongly that the issue was a political loser with the public, an emotionally charged debate with mostly symbolic import and, like immigration, a dangerous topic to address right before midterms.)

In his remarks at the dinner, the president spoke out anyway. He felt strongly about the issue and wanted to weigh in. "Muslims have the same right to practice their religion as everyone else in this country," he said. "That includes the right to build a place of worship and a community center on private property in lower Manhattan, in accordance with local laws and ordinances."

The New York media took his comments and ran with them. "PREZ: BUILD THE MOSQUE," read the cover of the *Daily News* the following morning. "ALLAH RIGHT BY ME," the *New York Post* said. "Obama Strongly Backs Islam Center Near 9/11 Site," said the *New York Times* headline. Playbook, the widely read Washington morning newsletter published by Politico.com, devoted nearly the entirety of its space to reaction to the president's remarks and predicted they would be even more controversial than his excursion into Henry Louis Gates's conflict with the Cambridge police a year earlier.

On his way to Florida, the president privately fumed at the coverage. The headlines were inaccurate: he had not endorsed the construction of the Islamic center; he had said that Muslims had the right to build houses of worship. A few hours later, passing a cluster of pool reporters, he stopped and let it rip. "I was not commenting, and I will not comment, on the wisdom of making the decision to put a mosque there," he said. "I was commenting very specifically on the right people have that dates back to our founding. That's what our country is about."

Once he made those comments, the news spread fast: the president was softening his statement from the evening before, trying to take back some of his support for the Islamic center in light of the criticism. Obama grew even more infuriated. Was the press listening to him? Did they not understand that constitutional protections extended even to unpopular projects? He told aides he wanted to go to the back of the plane, where the press sat, to explain his position yet again—a move that would only make things worse, they convinced him. Instead, the White House issued its third statement in twenty-four hours, saying that the president was not in fact backing off the prior evening's statement. Back in Washington, Emanuel blew up over the president's comments and fumed for days. Obama's statement had come at the worst possible time, he complained to others: the leaking oil well in the Gulf was finally being capped, the White House was ready to move on, and the president had managed to stir up a new hornet's nest. Emanuel talked in surprisingly personal terms about the president's remarks, another aide recalled, about the friends of his in Congress who were going to get questions about mosques, about the Jewish voters who would accost him in synagogue.

Meanwhile, the Obamas seemed to have no problem taking Sasha on the Florida trip—indeed, she was possibly the only person who had enjoyed the journey, one aide surmised. The initial plan had been not to release any photographs of the family's dip in the Gulf waters, but the president surprised aides by asking them to distribute one of him and Sasha swimming together. Once again, an adorable Obama daughter provided a positive image at a key moment.

Between the Spain trip, the immigration speech, and the Islamic center statements, it was as if the Obamas were having a what-the-hell moment with regard to public opinion, the press, and the advice of their political advisers. They felt people just did not seem to understand their motivations or intentions: How could anyone think that

Michelle Obama, who had devoted much of her career to serving the underprivileged, was a Marie Antoinette figure? How could liberal supporters think that Barack Obama, whose own father came from abroad, was not serious about fixing the immigration system? The president and his wife were stubborn, separately and together, and when criticized they seemed to alternate between wanting to explain themselves and letting people believe whatever they wanted to believe.

A few days after they returned from the Gulf, a new poll showed that more Americans than ever, 18 percent of adults and 31 percent of Republicans, thought Barack Obama was Muslim. (The survey was taken before the president's comments on the Islamic Center.) Only a third said he was a Christian, down substantially from the prior year, and another 43 percent said they did not know his religion at all. It was astonishing—some of the same people who had criticized him as being in the thrall of Rev. Jeremiah Wright Jr., his former pastor, now believed him to be a devout follower of the prophet Muhammad.

Some Democrats cried malpractice at the White House for not countering the Muslim rumors with professions of Christian faith: Could aides please just stick a Bible in the president's hand once in a while? Get him to join a church already? Early in the presidential campaign, Obama had heavily marketed his own religiosity; he won his critical primary victory in South Carolina in part by speaking in churches and distributing literature showing his head bowed in prayer. But ever since the Wright scandal, the Obamas had tried to argue that their faith was a private matter, off-limits for public discussion. Inside the White House during the summer of 2010, as outsiders quietly begged for the president to showcase his Christianity again, there was virtually no serious discussion of the matter, said David Axelrod and others. Telling the president that his staff had been strategizing about his religiosity "wouldn't be taken well," Axelrod explained. Since the Obamas had arrived in the White House, they had attended church intermittently, they would continue to do so, and that was that. There was no creative brainstorming about ways to underscore the president's Christianity for the public, another aide said, because all discussions had to take place within the category of things Barack Obama might actually be willing to do.

At week's end the Obama family, including Malia, left for another vacation, a real one this time, to Martha's Vineyard, where they shared dinners and beach visits with some of their Chicago friends. The island had long been a summer gathering place for African Americans who had climbed to the top of American life; in a sense, there were many first families there, men and women who knew the excitement and anxiety of going where no one like them had ever gone before. For once, no news events interrupted their trip, and the president and first lady seemed to loosen up a little after the terrible summer, letting off steam about their annoyances, joking about the absurdities of their situation, laughing about the president being a Muslim and their various escape fantasies.

Michelle seemed to have a harder time brushing off criticism than the president, according to friends. She was annoyed by the response to the Spain trip, the idea that she didn't know what sort of suffering was going on in the country, that there was something wrong with a mother taking a trip with her daughter. Who cares, the president said, urging her to let it go. For the first lady, it wasn't so easy.

As they relaxed, friends noticed how certain perks of the presidency had become normal to the Obamas. At one point, the first couple invited their old friends Allison and Susan Davis to sit with them on an empty beach, entirely cordoned off for their use. Even the sky above them was clear of air traffic. After a few hours of lounging and talking, the group rose to leave, and Allison Davis started packing up, folding towels and such. "You don't have to do that," the Obamas told him. The staff took care of those things. "When I leave office there are only two things I want," the president added. "I want a plane and I want a valet."

While the Obamas were on vacation, the new rug, wall coverings, and furnishings that the president had ordered for the Oval Office were finally installed. The room would finally look the way he wanted, warmer and more approachable, more like a working office. Every president redecorated the Oval Office to his specifications, but advisers had postponed the changes again and again for fear of an uproar about federal funds and frivolity, and they were still nervous about the public reaction. By the end of the summer, the mood in the White House was so anxious, so taut, that even Thomas Donilon, the deputy national security adviser, whose work had more to do with Afghanistan strategy than fabric swatches, raised concerns at a morning meeting of aides. "I know this is out of my lane a little bit, but I really don't think you should be doing this," he said. "We know, we know" looks flashed across the faces of the political and press advisers. They had been through it about a thousand times.

When the White House publicly announced the changes, there was almost no criticism, though some people did feel the president had used too much taupe.

EARLY ON THE MORNING OF September 16, 2010, Robert Gibbs was scanning news clips on his BlackBerry when a story circulating in the British tabloids stopped him short. According to a new book being published in France, Michelle Obama had told Carla Bruni-Sarkozy, the French first lady, that living in the White House was hell.

It was a potential disaster—Michelle Obama's four-hundred-dollar haircut moment, he feared, with the worst possible timing, coming on the heels of the Spain trip and weeks before election day. She was going to look ungrateful and aggrieved, he worried, and he only had a few hours until the American media would start reporting the story as fact. He had to act before CNN and MSNBC put it in their story loop. "This is the only thing we're focusing on," he told colleagues.

The problem was that he could not find the first lady. He needed to make sure the story was untrue, to ask if she had said something else that had been misconstrued. But she was not around; she was playing tennis in Georgetown, because the White House courts were being resurfaced. Jarrett and Sher, the usual emissaries, were unreachable, attending a *Morning Joe* event. So he met with the first lady's press staff, directed the American Embassy in Paris to buy the book, produce PDFs of the relevant pages, and send them to the State Department for translation. He asked the national security staff to find his counterpart in France. He didn't want to issue a White House denial—that wouldn't be enough, he said in an interview. He wanted the statement to come straight from the Elysée Palace.

He finally found Sher, who located Michelle Obama, who said the statement was false. (If she was going to confide any of her White House frustrations, it was not going to be to the French first lady, she added.)

The French issued their denial around 11:00 a.m., Gibbs recalled later, and by noon the crisis had been averted. The U.S. media reported the story, with the French statement that it was false, and it did not catch fire. But at Emanuel's 7:30 a.m. meeting the next day, Jarrett announced that the first lady was dissatisfied with the White House's handling of the situation.

All eyes turned to Gibbs. Emanuel grew alarmed at the expression on the press secretary's face and reached out to take him by the hand. "Don't go there, Robert, don't do it," another aide later remembered him saying. Years of tension between Gibbs, Jarrett, and an absent Michelle Obama exploded, the other aides watching in shock or staring down at the table.

"Fuck this, that's not right, I've been killing myself on this, where's this coming from?" Gibbs yelled. He calmed down slightly and tried to probe, according to a half-dozen people who witnessed the exchange. "What is it she has concerns about?" he asked Jarrett. "What did she say to you?"

Jarrett did not give a specific answer.

"What the *fuck* do you mean? Did you ask her?" Gibbs shot back. Jarrett said something about the reply not being fast enough. It appeared to be the same problem that had dogged the relationship between the first lady and the press secretary for years: she felt neglected by him, he felt criticized by her.

Gibbs blew up again. "Why is she talking to you about it? If she has a problem she should talk to me!" David Axelrod was playing peacemaker, trying to soothe Gibbs.

"You shouldn't talk that way," Jarrett said, sounding unruffled.

It was Jarrett's tone, calm to the point of condescension, that finally undid Gibbs, others said later. He shook with rage, so frustrated one colleague thought he was going to cry. "You don't know what the fuck you're talking about," he hurled back.

"The first lady would not believe you're speaking this way."

"Then fuck her too!" He rose and stormed out. The rest of the group sat stunned.

Emanuel grew very still for once. "Everyone knows Robert has done a really good job on this," he said.

LATER, IN AN INTERVIEW, Gibbs admitted he had lost control. The complaint had just seemed so unfair, he said. He had successfully solved the problem and was *still* being taken to task. But he also said he had misdirected his rage. He said he emailed Sher after the meeting to ask what the first lady's complaint had been, cc-ing Jarrett, and Sher said there was no complaint. "Valerie made the story up," he charged. "Valerie went into the meeting to convey what Michelle was angry about when they actually hadn't talked about it."

After the Bruni incident he "stopped taking her at all seriously as an adviser to the president of the United States," he continued. "I didn't always think she was an effective messenger and I didn't think she was always playing the game fair." He even accused her of sabotaging other people to promote herself. "I think Valerie's belief is that there's one supreme adviser," meaning herself, and "her viewpoint in advising the president is that she has to be up and the rest of the White House has to be down." She saw anyone else close to Obama as a threat to her influence, he said.

Later, Jarrett refused to discuss the exchange, the accusations, or whether she had discussed Gibbs's work quashing the "hell" rumor with the first lady, but it appeared that she had been too trigger-happy with her criticism in the meeting: two East Wing aides said that Jarrett had indeed misspoken. The first lady had no issue with the White House response to the book about Bruni, one said; she was annoyed at Jarrett and Sher for not checking their BlackBerrys during the *Morning Joe* excursion.

Jarrett "does a remarkable job balancing her friendship with the president," said Pete Rouse, who remained on good terms with members of the various factions even amid the squabbling. "I would never be worried about saying something in confidence," that she would tell the president or first lady, he said. Though some other colleagues did think Jarrett's dual friend/adviser role was problematic, few thought she made things up out of whole cloth or undermined others to increase her power. But Gibbs's accusations were proof that the president, so confident of his ability to mediate among competing advisers and to be his own best manager, could not. It was yet another thing Obama thought he would be able to reconcile, another rule he had tried to ignore, and the result was breakdown: "like a bad reality show," an outside adviser said later. This was what the once famously cohesive Obama campaign team had turned into: people who could no longer work productively together and long streams of *fuck*s.

In fact, the president did not know quite how dysfunctional the relationships among his top advisers had become. There was one thing all the aides implicitly agreed on: no one was going to tell the president or the first lady about the Gibbs-Jarrett blowup. A few hours after the press secretary's outburst, Obama called Gibbs into the Oval Office to thank him for his fast, excellent work handling the Bruni book.

PART THREE

CHANGE

Chapter Twelve

HER GAIN

SEPTEMBER–NOVEMBER 2010

On September 23, 2010, the Obamas and Bill Clinton performed what amounted to a one-act play about partnership and power for a New York City audience whose members ranged from Barbra Streisand to Barbara Bush. The occasion was the Clinton Global Initiative, the former president's yearly gathering of stars, donors, CEOs, and do-gooders. Michelle Obama was on the program to talk about her new initiative to support military families. *She* would be introduced by her husband, unusually enough, who would be introduced, just as unusually, by their host.

The former president came out first and praised the current one to the skies: The stimulus! A new college loan program! America's bright future, the coming wave of high-tech jobs!

But Obama was not there to discuss his work; he was there to discuss his wife's. "Bill Clinton understands where I'm coming from," he said after taking the podium. The former president, perched on a stool a few feet away, nodded, smiling. "He knows what it's like to be married to somebody who's smarter, somebody who's better looking..." — the familiar Clinton smile grew a little tighter, as if he was not sure he appreciated the assessment of him or his wife by the younger man — "somebody who's just all around a little more impressive than you are." On "impressive," Obama let out an uncharacteristic high-pitched giggle. Clinton's eyes crinkled and he broke into a slow, exaggerated clap.

The two men had disliked each other for years. In 2000, Clinton had endorsed Bobby Rush, even though presidents rarely intervened in primary races, dooming Obama's already weak candidacy. During the presidential campaign, Obama sometimes seemed like he was running against Bill Clinton, not Hillary. He had high-minded objections to Clintonism, criticizing the former president's leadership style as a permanent campaign, his policy ideas as small-bore. The former president, who told aides Obama had no idea what he was in for if he won, was reduced to ranting about Obama's naïveté, sometimes on video cameras, sometimes while red in the face.

Since Obama had been sworn in, he had passed the health care legislation that Bill Clinton never could, and his discipline seemed a rebuke to Clinton's lack thereof. But Obama's strained relationship with Bill Clinton wasn't merely personal; it went to the heart of his struggle with politics. His differences with Clinton — for that matter, his and Michelle's differences with Rahm Emanuel, who had been groomed by Clinton — were about public opinion and political salesmanship. Obama was weak exactly where Bill Clinton was masterful: at luring working-class white voters back to the Democratic Party, at weaving a compelling story about the economy, at making Americans feel he understood their needs. Clinton spoke up about Obama's shortcomings every once in a while, most recently telling reporters that the president just wasn't making the best case for himself with the midterms approaching. Even his praise from a few moments before had sounded like criticism: *you passed a whole new college loan program and no one knows about it*...

Two decades of Democratic Party history, the electoral battle of 2008, closely matched policy aspirations yet nearly opposite governing styles, the maestro of persuasion and the paradox of a president who struggled with politics, the two lawyers who had sublimated their careers to those of their husbands: it was almost too much for one small podium. Forget Bill and Barack for a second—*any* way you combined either Clinton with either Obama was interesting. Match Michelle with Hillary, absent that day, and you got two first ladies searching to define their power in the White House, one clearly absorbing the painful lessons of the other. Match Barack with Hillary and you got former antagonists, now a president and secretary of state with a productive, professional, not terribly warm relationship: two people on their best behavior. (The Obamas, the secretary of state remarked quietly to friends, never invited the Clintons to dinner in the White House.) Spin the wheel to match the men once more, and you had one president who did what the other never could, which was give Hillary Clinton a real job in his administration.

The current president was still talking, piling flattery on his wife. "Since Michelle and I first started dating twenty-two years ago, pretty much everybody I know who's met her at some point comes up to me and says, 'You know, Barack, you're great and all, I like you, but your wife, now, she's really something.'" He made the old hustings joke about how lucky he was that his wife did not run against him. It was an odd choice, given the context: Michelle Obama would be able to beat him, even though Hillary Clinton could not?

Then Obama turned serious. "No matter what the issue, there's only one thing that she wants to know, and that's, 'Who are we helping?' That's what she asks. 'Who is this going to make a difference for? Whose life is this going to improve?'

"While I get plenty of good advice from a lot of people during the course of the day," he continued with conviction, "at the end of each day, it is Michelle—her moral voice, her moral center—that cuts through all the noise in Washington and reminds me of why I'm there in the first place."

On cue, Michelle emerged onto the stage. She sounded as if she wasn't sure she was falling for all the praise. "It's weird that my husband introduces me, so I don't even know what to say," she said after the applause died down. "Thank you, honey."

She spoke earnestly about the challenges military families faced, the second big cause she was taking up as first lady. "Veterans find themselves becoming underutilized, underemployed—settling for jobs that pay less than they deserve; jobs that don't fully harness their talents," Michelle said. "Or they find themselves out of work entirely for months on end." She was drawing on the classic Michelle Obama themes, from way back at Public Allies—more access and opportunity for people whose assets society did not recognize—mapped out onto fresh territory. She sounded tentative and a bit beaten down in moments, a bit more hopeful in others. Her tone was less confident motivator than sincere pupil. She smiled only once.

"It's hard to spend years serving your country, only to find that the value of that service isn't fully understood," she continued. "It's hard to give so much, for so long, for a cause greater than yourself, only to come home and find that there's nowhere you quite fit in." She sounded as if she might have been speaking about herself and her husband—especially her husband.

BILL CLINTON HAD STUMPED TIRELESSLY for midterm elections when he was president, headlining rally after rally, his stamina and appetite for human contact legendary. Obama's schedule was much lighter: again, a reflection of the two men's different attitudes toward making a public case. Then again, not every Democrat in Congress wanted him—that fall, Clinton was far more popular than the president in many districts.

A few days before election day, the president returned home to stump for Illinois candidates, speaking to thousands of people gathered on a grassy strip at the center of Hyde Park. The crowd could not have been more enthusiastic, but the venue itself was a marker. Two years earlier, he had barely campaigned in Chicago during the general election; there was no reason to. Now the Republicans had forced him back and back again, to the point where Obama was defending territory just a few blocks from his own home, in bluer-than-blue Chicago. The governorship of Illinois was probably going to fall into Republican hands, and Obama's friend Alexi Giannoulias, onstage that night, was probably going to lose a tight, brutal race for the president's old seat.

Standing on a giant platform across the street from his daughters' old school, his face bathed in light and projected on a giant screen, Obama sounded sheepish, even a little pleading, about the change in his fortunes. He recalled inauguration day nearly two years prior. "Beyoncé was singing and Bono was up there and everybody was feeling good," he said. "I know that good feeling starts slipping away. And you talk to your friends who are out of work, you see somebody lose their home, and it gets you discouraged. And then you see all these TV ads and all the talking heads on TV, and everything just feels negative. And maybe some of you, maybe you stop believing." Just as he was disappointed with the public, the public was disappointed in him. The relationship was reciprocal and both sides felt betrayed, misunderstood, let down.

The big news of the midterms was the Tea Party. A year and a half after its founding, it had become a genuine electoral force, with an energized if somewhat eccentric crop of challengers to Democratic-held seats. (One Senate candidate, Christine O'Donnell, made an ad claiming she was not a witch; another, Sharon Angle, had bizarrely claimed that the September 11 hijackers had entered the country through Canada.) "I don't see why people think that these people are any further out there than the people already here," the president laughed to aides. Obama was joking, but it was not clear if he understood the difference between the more conventional Republicans who were already in office and the renegades who were coming.

In the Chicago speech, he leaned hard on his credentials as a historic figure. He tried to make the loss of his support sound like the latest in a long line of lofty, inspiring American struggles. "I know things are hard sometimes, but you know what, this country was founded on hard," he said. He went through the story of the thirteen colonies, the Declaration of Independence, the abolition of slavery, women's voting rights, the end of the Great Depression, and victory over fascism. "At every stage we've made progress because someone stood up," he said. The implication was clear: forget about the polls, I'm part of a loftier story.

The following day, Halloween, the president flew back to Washington, stopping for one last rally in Cleveland on the way home. Two years before, right before he won Ohio, sixty thousand people had turned up to hear him speak there. Now Ohio Republicans were about to win the governorship. He spoke in a half-full arena to about eight thousand people.

In the late afternoon, Obama stepped off Marine One and walked toward a White House decorated with pumpkins and fake spiderwebs and bathed in orange light. The celebrations organized by the East Wing were far more modest than the prior year's. Costumed characters stood on the North Portico, handing out treats to kids from military families and local schools. As night fell, the first couple came out and joined everyone else on the front porch, the first lady in a festive orange sweater and glittery mascara. The president looked happy to be around kids, and he and Michelle had another reason to be pleased: earlier in the afternoon, Malia and Sasha had succeeded in trick-or-treating in an undisclosed location.

Robert Gibbs had tried to cancel the party that followed, worried the celebrations would look clueless occurring just a few days before an impending electoral disaster. Once again, a former aide said, Gibbs was using the "first, do no harm" rule. But Michelle told aides she felt strongly about celebrating the holiday, David Axelrod backed her, and the White House hauled out the orange lightbulbs and candy bags as planned. Like her husband's introduction of her at the Clinton event, it was a small sign of the newfound power she wielded inside the White House.

NO EVENT CAPTURED MICHELLE'S changed situation as dramatically as an early fall meeting inside the Oval Office. That was the president's domain, but the meeting was being held to satisfy and appease the first lady.

Michelle had finally agreed in theory to do some campaigning for midterms. But as she had said many times before, she had requirements. She wasn't going to get on an airplane or stand in front of a crowd until she knew the whole picture: the electoral strategy, where she could make a difference, how she fit in. She seemed to be looking out not only for herself but for the entire enterprise: withholding her participation was the only way she could make sure that there *was* a thought-out plan in the first place, and that the midterms were not going to be a repeat of the Massachusetts fumbles.

At the meeting, the first couple sat surrounded by the top members of the West Wing political team. The president kicked off the meeting, then handed things over to Emanuel, who was supposed to speak. "Um, Patrick has the plan," he said, handing things over to Gaspard. Rahm seemed too terrified to speak, others said.

One by one, they came before the first lady, laying out their offerings: arguments, details, statistics. The speechwriters sat poised with pads, ready to take notes that would help them craft the first lady's appeals to voters. Gaspard, the political director, began with an overview of the general election environment. David Axelrod did a PowerPoint presentation on the midterm strategy and how campaigning by both Obamas would fit into it. Everyone smiled in amazement: Axelrod on PowerPoint? He was a shambling figure, a by-the-seat-of-the-pants guy with food-splattered ties, and for years Michelle had worried that he was too improvisational. Now he was doing things on her terms, with planning and precision.

Axelrod ticked through polling data she had never seen before, including one point in particular: Michelle was powerful on her own, but the public absolutely loved seeing the Obamas together. It was basically the same idea the advisers had intuited during the presidential campaign, about how Barack Obama was more appealing when surrounded by his family. But now, with Michelle Obama a well-respected first lady and her husband a weakening president, the information took on a whole new meaning.

In an interview a year earlier, the Obamas had adamantly protested the idea that they were marketing their marriage for political gain; they had acted offended at the very thought. ("Most of the images that are out there are somebody else's images," the first lady had argued.) Now they listened attentively as advisers explained how, by appearing together, they could draw votes. It was yet another way the size of their union kept expanding; on top of everything else, it was supposed to help stem Democratic losses.

"This is a *great* presentation," the president said with an *I*-never-get-this-treatment grin. The location of the meeting, and his obvious approval, were lost on no one.

The first lady barely asked any questions. She was satisfied, aides said, and not just with the data. No longer was anyone asking her to fill in at the last minute, or emailing her dates in the expectation that she would say yes. She was getting what she had wanted for years: to be treated like a principal, a partner in the enterprise. The power dynamic between the Obamas, between the West and East wings, had finally changed, ironically in no small part because Michelle had played the role of not-very-political wife and mom so well. The less popular her husband became, the more powerful she became.

Though Michelle appreciated the presentation in the Oval Office, she had also agreed to campaign for another reason: because her husband had asked her, as Emanuel had urged. As always he was loath to suggest political responsibilities for his wife, vigilant about keeping her out of the fray. But he needed her help and made the request personally to her, according to an aide.

Still, Michelle's agreement was limited: eight events between Labor Day and election day. Numerous candidates had requested her on the stump, and her total number of events was a fraction of what the political team would have liked.

"She basically agreed to do nothing," one aide said, more bemused than frustrated.

AS MICHELLE OBAMA WAS RISING, Rahm Emanuel was leaving—or escaping. His departure reflected the great accomplishment and messy internal dynamics of his tenure. In September, Chicago mayor Richard M. Daley said he would not run for reelection, and Emanuel, who had long eyed the job, jumped at the chance to run. Obama immediately said on television that his chief of staff—who would make a great Chicago mayor, he stipulated—would remain on the job through the midterms. But that left Obama with a chief of staff who was simultaneously running the White House, hovering over midterm races, and planning a candidacy of his own. To further complicate matters, African American leaders in Chicago were recruiting Marty Nesbitt to run against him. Nesbitt was an appealing candidate: a successful businessman and civic leader with powerful connections, an inspiring story, and a good chance of winning the black voters key to securing the job. For the president, a Nesbitt candidacy would be bizarre: his best friend and his chief of staff vying for the same seat, potentially pressing on the deepest fault lines in Obamaworld: black versus white, Obamaniks versus Clintonites, Chicagoans versus Washingtonians, outsiders to the system versus professionals. Besides, the president had said many times that he cherished the way his relationship with Nesbitt stood outside politics; it was a refuge. If he ran, win or lose, that would change.

In the end, Nesbitt stood down—the timing wasn't right, he decided, and as an electoral novice and the president's best friend, he would be open to charges of nepotism. The former chief of staff was an extremely strong candidate—experienced, hard to intimidate, passionate about what he wanted. Nesbitt aligned himself with Emanuel, throwing a fund-raiser, and Obama's African American friends talked about establishing leverage over the man who seemed likely to be mayor: he would have to pledge to devote attention and resources to black neighborhoods if he wanted to win, and deliver if he wanted to be reelected. To court black voters, Emanuel shamelessly elided what had really happened in the White House: at one meeting, with an African American women's group called Harriet's Daughters, Emanuel was questioned about his record of diversity in hiring. "I hired Valerie," he said, conveniently forgetting that they had been bitter rivals in the White House and that he had tried to prevent her from coming in the first place, trying to send her to the Senate instead.

Emanuel hoped for a formal endorsement from the president, but Jarrett told colleagues she was against it. Despite her rivalry with Rahm, she framed it in impersonal terms: mayors all over the country asked for Obama endorsements, and if the president gave one, he would have to give others. Supporting his former chief of staff had risks: Emanuel was the strongest candidate in the race, but he wasn't a sure thing, as he had not lived in Illinois full-time for years. If he turned out to be ineligible, the administration could look sloppy or nepotistic. (Emanuel said that he had never asked for an endorsement, and Jarrett said she never spoke to the president about it.)

Even though he had been talking quietly about Emanuel's departure for months, Obama seemed to find the actual event difficult to accept. A president was dependent on his chief of staff. Aides pointed out that Emanuel saved the president from doing the parts of his job he liked least — dealing extensively with Congress, for example. With their work together done, their tensions past, their relationship grew warmer, colleagues said: the president gave Emanuel an enthusiastic send-off, including a press conference with a near endorsement and a rare reception for just a select number of guests upstairs in the residence. As a going-away gift, Obama gave Emanuel a framed copy of their to-do list for 2010. Most of the items were checked off. Both men were list-keepers, and in the end, that was what their relationship was really about: getting things done.

The party for Rahm was lovely but formal, said one person who attended. You didn't sink into the Obamas' couch and trade opinions and confidences late into the night, the way you did with the Clintons. You showed up on time and there was no mistaking when the party was over.

* * *

THE NIGHT BEFORE ELECTION DAY, the results of Michelle's Oval Office meeting were on display in Philadelphia. Volunteers papered downtown with glossy get-out-the-vote flyers showing a large color photograph of the first couple, each with one hand clasped around the other's waist and the other hand waving to a cheering crowd. (It had been taken a few weeks prior, at a joint campaign appearance in the crucial state of Ohio.) The president gazed off into the distance, but the first lady smiled into the camera's lens, making direct eye contact with whoever was reading the flyer. The flip side of the flyer named a few Philadelphia-area Democratic candidates and urged voters to turn out for them.

That evening, students milled around a stone-covered quadrangle on the University of Pennsylvania campus in Philadelphia, waiting for the first lady to speak. The music blaring from loudspeakers and the young crowd in jeans and hoodies gave a hint of festivity to the evening. (Even a campaign rally for losing candidates had more energy than many White House events.)

After a long wait and introductions upon introductions, the first lady came out in a black blazer, looking more than usual like the lawyer she used to be, and launched into the final version of a speech she had been laboring on for weeks. She had diligently worked on the address with David Axelrod and Sarah Hurwitz, the West Wing speechwriter who most often wrote for the first lady. The three went through many drafts, in part because it was a tough assignment — Michelle Obama did not even know some of the candidates, her husband wasn't running, she did not want to sound political, and yet she wanted to say something she meant. In private, she was so insistent about her husband's accomplishments that the tone of the speeches was hard to get right. "I think she has a very strong sense of advocacy for him and for what he's trying to do. The temptation is to get drawn into the fray a little bit more, and that's not a great role for her," Axelrod said. He wanted her speech to sail above that, he said; to talk about the meaning of her husband's time in office, but in a way that sounded universal themes, not political ones. "It was very important to her to own it," Susan Sher said. "A lot of really good speeches were not okay for her because they weren't her voice."

Standing at the podium, Michelle began by reminding the audience that she was the "mom in chief," that she was speaking out of hope for her children's future. She referred to her new life in the White House as "very interesting." Her tone was gentle, with no trace of vehemence. "I know change has not come fast enough," she said, casting herself on the audience's side. "It takes a lot longer than any of us would like." But together they had come too far to stop, she told the audience, shaking her head no, almost as if she were rejecting her own impulse to give up. She used the old, familiar Michelle Obama lines about expecting things to be hard, about being willing to expend effort.

She referenced her own unhappiness in the White House obliquely, reaching for the figure of her father, talking about how her sacrifices and struggles were so much less than his. She described Fraser sitting on his side of the bed, frustrated because his fingers, ridden with multiple sclerosis, could not button his shirt. He went to work "without complaint, without regret," she said. Her eyes were big and sincere. "I don't have time to be tired or frustrated or worried," she said, once again mingling her story and the audience's. They were frustrated with her husband's time in the White House? Well, so was she. She had the same concerns; she was on their side. But she was staying with it, her eyes told the audience, because her parents had struggled to give her a better life, and now the president was struggling to give the next generation the same.

My husband could not do it alone, she declared, speaking for herself and for them. Like her, the audience had no choice. "Yes, we must," she said, instead of the familiar "yes, we can."

"Get to work!" she called into the autumnal darkness by way of good-bye.

Chapter Thirteen

HIS LOSS

NOVEMBER–DECEMBER 2010

I love elections," a younger Obama practically sang on November 7, 2006, to documentary filmmakers whose cameras were trained upon him. It was one of the best nights of his career: an army of Democrats, commanded by Rahm Emanuel and assisted by David Axelrod and plenty of appearances by the new Illinois senator with the soaring career, were taking control of Congress. "It's even more fun when you're not on the ballot," he continued.

November 2, 2010, was its opposite, a near undoing of those gains. The House was gone for Democrats, and dozens of members of the Tea Party had won seats. The swing states of Ohio, Wisconsin, New Mexico, and Pennsylvania all put new Republican governors in place. Exit polls showed that the Democrats had lost the female vote for the first time in thirty-two years. The White House's strategy had been to contain the damage. The strategy had failed.

Michelle went to sleep early, as usual. (There was no point in staying up, she said later.) The president phoned Democrat after Democrat who had been defeated. Many had lost at least in part because of votes the president had asked them to cast. Few answered their cell phones that evening—they were thanking supporters or cuddling their kids—so he left messages. *This is Barack Obama. I'm so sorry. It was a tough night for Democrats. Thank you for your service to the country. Give me a call.* He told a few favorites to come for a visit so they could talk.

"Some election nights are more fun than others," the president said at the beginning of his press conference the next day. For months he had been tearing into Republicans. Now he recited a rote pledge of cooperation, a desiccated version of the original Obama ode to bipartisanship. "I am very eager to sit down with members of both parties," he said. "No party has a monopoly on wisdom." He defended his health care overhaul passionlessly. He had already explained it a thousand times before.

His first few answers to journalists did not have much animation either. But he turned his final reply, about whether he was out of touch with voters' economic struggles, into a soliloquy on the deterioration of his relationship with the public.

"Folks didn't have any complaints about my leadership style when I was running around Iowa for a year," he said. He referenced Republican charges that he was strange—too black or foreign—but obliquely. "They understood that my story was theirs. I might have a funny name, I might have lived in some different places, but the values of hard work and responsibility and honesty and looking out for one another that had been instilled in them by their parents, those were the same values that I took from my mom and my grandparents." He was reading hard-luck letters every day from the public, he said. "Nobody's filming me reading those letters," he protested. He was not admitting to being disconnected from the public—he just noted the *appearance* of disconnection.

Then he acknowledged something he had never said in public

before. "The relationship I've had with the American people is one that built slowly, peaked at this incredible high, and has gotten rockier," he said. With that, the lines on his face deepened, the corners of his mouth sank, and his gaze dropped downward. By Obama standards, it was an uncommon display of vulnerability, a frown so distinctive that it made the front page of newspapers the next day.

Inside the White House, aides debated whether he was actually contrite or whether the frown was an offering, a show of emotion for a press corps that clearly craved it. There was nothing spontaneous or vulnerable about the president, some pointed out. Beyond the volumes of his own memoirs, confession was a language he did not speak. The remarkable thing about the internal debate over the frown was how many high-level aides inside the White House still felt they could not fully read their boss.

Whether the frown was real or not, Obama didn't seem to regret any of his decisions at all, telling aides the same thing he had said in speeches before the midterms: the results were a reaction to economic anxiety, not to his policies. The House had turned over because the country wanted to see both parties working together instead of just Democrats in charge. "There are people in politics for whom losing is a deeply personal statement, and they measure their worth, their self-worth that way. He's not that way," Axelrod said. It seemed like yet another effort he was making to insulate and protect himself from politics; another instance of his not fully accepting what he had wrought.

"There's no question he believes he's doing exactly the right thing," said Tom Daschle. "He looks back with great satisfaction over the first two years." Obama's lack of regret infuriated some members of his own White House. "It has the feel of a husband struggling as he apologizes to his wife because he knows he is supposed to apologize," one top aide said. "In his heart, he thinks it is his wife's fault."

For the thousandth time, the Clinton veterans serving in the Obama administration marveled at the differences between their old boss and their new one. After Bill Clinton received his own scalding in the midterm elections of 1994, he examined and reexamined his choices, torturing himself over what he could have done differently, hiring the consultant Dick Morris to perform a political makeover. Clinton surrendered himself to public judgment; Obama was too inner-directed, too suspicious of what the common denominator thought, to give himself over that way. Besides, his White House had suffered through pre-midterm stress disorder all summer; now the event was past them, at long last. He wanted to move on.

In a senior staff meeting after the midterms, the president calmly propelled his staff forward, acknowledging defeat but quickly looking past it. The White House felt surprisingly like business as usual, aides said, with the president's signals the same as they had been a week, month, or year before. The old Congress had a lame-duck session of only a few weeks, and the president had a long list of items he wanted to push through. "I've got some ambitious goals," he said. It seemed absurd at the time, Axelrod said: weren't they supposed to be reeling?

THE MIDTERM ELECTIONS WERE ONLY the second loss of the president's political career, after his 2000 defeat by Bobby Rush. Back then, Obama invited Rush's media consultant, Eric Adelstein, out to lunch and asked for a ruthless critique of every single thing he had done wrong. He wanted to improve, to compete, and he was never going to make the same mistakes twice.

Now Obama did something similar. Unusually for a president, he did it without any staff, save his personal assistant. Bypassing his army of schedulers, and with little consultation from anyone else, Obama invited outsiders to one-on-one meetings and lunches. Even issuing the invitations was "a link to the outside world that he had been missing," Jarrett said. Tom Daschle got the call, along with the *New York Times*'s David Brooks, the president's favorite pundit. So did Clinton counselors such as David Gergen and Vernon Jordan, and a few Republicans, too: Matthew Dowd, who served in but soured on the Bush administration, and Ken Duberstein, a former Reagan chief of staff.

The meetings took place in the Oval Office, and the lunches took place in the private dining room just next door, decorated with a red carpet embroidered with gold stars and a portrait of Lincoln with his advisers. The meals all started pretty much the same way. The president and his guest sat at opposite ends of the polished wooden dining table, a small, tasteful flower arrangement between them. A waiter brought in lunch, always something healthy, maybe salad and then fish with vegetables, served in small portions. There was little of the gossip or storytelling that almost always accompanies a good political lunch. (Obama was finally reaching out, but that didn't mean he was actually going to *schmooze*.) He cut the small talk off after a moment or two, eager to get to his big question.

"Tell me everything you think we did wrong."

He meant everything: policy, political strategy, management, communications. He sat back and listened, saying little, usually finishing his food long before his guest.

The lunches lasted an hour or an hour and a half, a long stretch by presidential standards. The guests were very frank. His White House was factionalized and dysfunctional, several told him, with too many different power centers competing for access and influence—Biden, Emanuel, Jarrett, Axelrod, Gibbs. Things were getting stuck between them, and nobody knew where the true power was. He had surrounded himself with people who were too close to him, who had no outside view and little prior White House experience. He needed a more traditional structure, with a streamlined decision-making process flowing through a chief of staff who had true authority. The president had not invested heavily enough in bipartisanship, Democrats and Republicans alike told him; he had been too easily deterred by the obstructionist strategy. Midterm voters were not merely expressing frustration with the economy, they said: they were reacting to him as well. Some disagreed with his policies, too—he had taken on too much, some said, particularly with health care. His relations with business leaders were terrible, a disaster in a bad economy. But the president's communication with the public was awful, he had that right. (Two-thirds of Americans who voted in the midterms, Brooks wrote around the same time, told pollsters that the stimulus was harmful to the economy or made no difference, even though economists overwhelmingly agreed it had helped.) The president had acted without bringing the American people along with him, and his midterm campaign message had done little to address voters' real concerns about his policies.

One encounter was more bittersweet than the others. On a late fall morning, the president hosted a breakfast for a handful of members of Congress who had lost their seats: Kathy Dahlkemper, from Pennsylvania; John Spratt, the House budget chairman, from South Carolina; Jim Oberstar, the House Transportation Committee chairman, from Minnesota; and Melissa Bean, from Illinois. All were from moderate middle America districts. Over breakfast in the Roosevelt Room, they told Obama that unless he acted quickly, he was going to end up like them in 2012—out. The general message to him, said Dahlkemper, who lost her seat after only one term, was that he needed to step it up politically. The group tried to convey to him the worry they felt back in their home districts, the sheer anxiety that was driving voters. The Tea Party was a huge wave and he shouldn't underestimate its force, Spratt told him.

Dahlkemper told the president she had lost because of "horrible messaging" from his team. "No matter what I would do, there was this much larger message that needed to come from the White House," she said. The administration's failure to showcase what it had done, even on relatively narrow issues like water quality, had hurt them, the group agreed; if the administration had been highlighting its accomplishments, they would have had better tools for combating attacks.

This group, too, was struck by Obama's lack of regret. "In retrospect we can look back and say we could have done things differently, but I had a very ambitious agenda," Oberstar recalled Obama saying. "In the end, this is for the greater good of the country." He seemed entirely sure he knew what was best for the country; he seemed to think that he was a better judge than the public.

The first lady didn't attend the lunches, but she was excited about them: her husband was finally reaching out beyond his tiny circle, gathering fresh opinions. The midterms should have been a devastating loss for her — the Scott Brown loss multiplied. After the drubbing Bill Clinton took in 1994, then first lady Hillary Clinton felt lost, disoriented. Shortly after the election, she told Dick Morris, her husband's newly arrived political consultant, about how little she felt she understood. "I don't know which direction is up or down," she said. "Everything I thought was right was wrong." Hillary Clinton retreated to the East Wing, moved away from a policy role, and soon started working on an entertaining book.

Michelle Obama was in a very different situation. The midterms didn't only give her leverage with the political team; they provided massive outside confirmation of her view that the White House needed internal change. Now even more people were saying publicly what she had been saying privately for so long: the president had to make his circle bigger, improve his message, bring in new advisers, create a more organized West Wing.

Like her husband, she was still sure he was doing the right things for the country. "She does think there are worse things than losing an election," Susan Sher said. "Being true to yourself, for her, is definitely more important." She sometimes talked with Sher about what would happen if her husband lost in 2012. You've always got to have a Plan B, she believed, just as she had told the Public Allies all those years before. "I know we'll be fine," she told Sher.

What Obama himself thought of all the meetings and lunches was mostly a mystery. He was still the poker player, reacting serenely, with only occasional defensiveness, several of the outsiders who met with him said. He was more willing to admit failure in private than in public: he knew he had lost a sense of the "social presidency," as Dowd put it. (Three years earlier, Obama had insisted to Dowd, the former Bush adviser, that he would never become isolated in the White House; now he admitted he had.) He knew his relationship with the press, much better during the campaign, was in poor shape. The question of how he should have handled the Republican oppositional strategy was still up for grabs, he said; there was no really good response. He admitted he needed to reorganize his White House.

Some guests left wondering if he fully understood how much his White House needed to change. The president was naturally suspicious of traditional power structures; would he be able to create one, to run everything through his chief of staff? Rouse had been working on the reorganization plan since February 2010, an eternity in presidential time; when would something finally happen? Would Obama be able to reach out to opponents he loathed and who loathed him, and say good-bye to Axelrod, the message guru who had been unable to craft a successful message? Did he feel the urgency, the desperation, that everyone else did?

In other words, would Obama finally start acting—in the most necessary and overdue way—like a politician?

* * *

A FEW DAYS AFTER THE ELECTIONS, the Obamas lifted off for India and Indonesia. It was a classic rule of the presidency: if you were facing a defeat at home, change the subject, jet off, generate impressive photos with spectacular backdrops. Some Democrats groaned: India was drawing jobs from the United States, so did the president have to go there, of all places?

In Mumbai, while the president was in discussions on trade relations between the two countries, the first lady visited with a group of orphans and runaways, kicking off her shoes to play hopscotch with them, dancing and shimmying to the beat of a song from a Bollywood movie. The first lady's staff knew the formula by now: put Michelle Obama in a roomful of kids—especially kids who were outsiders in one way or another—just let them interact, and they were likely to end with a Moment that generated warm, positive images and video. "All we had to do was set the stage," Melissa Winter, her deputy chief of staff, said later. It was the original, defining visit to the London school refined, repeated, staged again and again by East Wing staff, turned into a reliable formula to convey what she wanted to stand for on the world stage: the idea that anyone could grow up to be anything. The images that beamed around the world, of the first lady elegantly defying convention and caste, were the opposite of the ones from her Spain trip. She looked joyful, accessible, down-to-earth—"value added," she approvingly told her team later. "Value-added" was a favorite Michelle-ism, one of the highest compliments she gave. It meant that the moments were beneficial to the administration; that they helped the president in some way.

While some fellow Democrats may have disapproved, the trip was perfect for the president, lifting him out of dreary postloss Washington and putting him back into a world he had left behind decades ago. Obama had been trying to visit Indonesia, one of his childhood homes and the world's most populous Muslim nation, ever since he arrived in office, postponing twice already. He and the first lady only had time to spend half a day there, but that was enough for him to eat his favorite childhood dishes, accept a medal on behalf of his mother, who had pioneered microcredit loans for poor Indonesians, and create another memorable image of Michelle.

He and the first lady visited the largest mosque in Jakarta, removing their shoes out of respect, huddling in conversation with the imam. The resulting photos were striking, mostly because of how different the familiar first lady looked: out of respect for Muslim tradition, she had donned a flowing yellow suit and printed headscarf for the mosque visit. Let people at home think they were Muslim, the Obamas seemed to be saying: in international and diplomatic terms, it was a profound gesture of respect, and pictures of it appeared in newspapers around the globe.

The president always pronounced foreign places and names with perfection, every vowel, consonant, and inflection in place. It was the Obama virtuosity again, letting no A go unplussed. But he was also challenging the stereotype of the parochial, blundering American — exactly how his predecessor had been perceived abroad. In Jakarta, he ended his speech with the extraordinary sight of a U.S. president speaking perfectly accented Bahasa. Once again, the farther he was from Washington, the more comfortable he seemed.

THERE WAS A REASON the president had such an aggressive agenda for the last few weeks of the Democratic-controlled Congress: he knew it would be his legislative swan song, the last time he could capitalize on the 2008 Democratic takeover of Washington before the new Republican Congress was sworn in. There was the lingering issue of the Bush tax cuts, which would soon expire; an extension of unemployment insurance; a new version of the Strategic Arms Reduction Treaty; the repeal of the military's Don't Ask, Don't Tell law; and the

DREAM Act, a miniature version of immigration reform that would allow high-achieving children of illegal immigrants a path to citizenship. Initially, though, everything looked stuck.

There was one more item on the list, too: an update of the federal laws on children's nutrition, which Michelle had championed as a part of her anti-obesity work. The old version of the bill, which had been on the books for decades, was almost a misnomer, because it offered no nutritional standards at all — no rules in place, for example, to guide what went into the food for the thirty-one million children a day who ate in public school cafeterias. The new version included revised standards for school meals, including requirements for more produce, and a bit more money — a few cents per meal — to help pay for them. The bill had passed the Senate, thanks in part to Michelle's personal appeals to legislators, but it still had to get through the House.

The entire process was a classic, torturous legislative stop-start: the bill looked like it wasn't going to progress, then it inched forward, then it looked dead, then it breathed again. The first lady pushed the House leaders hard, and the West Wing legislative team pushed with her. For the moment, she no longer cared whether anyone thought she was too Hillary Clinton–like, too involved in policy, said an adviser: she just wanted the bill to get through Congress and onto her husband's desk. Yet as the December days ticked by and the holiday recess approached, the House was still in deadlock.

Michelle was working in the East Wing when the news came in that the bill had the votes to pass. Everyone went running into her office to celebrate — the whole team, including the interns. Only months before, she had felt left out of her administration's business, and yet the legislation *she* had championed had now broken the congressional deadlock, creating some long-needed momentum for other bills to move.

She was so excited that she threw a party, a smaller counterpart to her husband's celebration after the passage of his health care bill —

not upstairs at home, but in the Diplomatic Reception Room, attended by everyone from the White House who had worked on the effort. A picture captured the first lady's glee: she faced the team, her fists clenched in triumph, everyone cheering back at her, their hands in the air.

Barack Obama signed the nutrition legislation his wife had championed at a ceremony held in a modest elementary school. He and Michelle walked onto the school stage holding hands. In front of everyone, he proceeded to needle her mercilessly. "Had I not been able to get this passed I'd be sleeping on the couch," he said, cracking himself up. He was momentarily lifting the curtain of her polished public image, hinting at the force of her disapproval, as if he wanted to let others know what he faced at home. He repeated the joke, to make sure everyone had heard. "We won't go into that," the first lady said, looking embarrassed.

BY CHRISTMAS, AN OVERJOYED PRESIDENT was signing bill after bill, including the repeal of the Don't Ask, Don't Tell law that had prohibited gay people from serving in the military. From the start, gay activists had worried whether he would come through on its repeal. "None of them believed he was committed," said Jarrett, who attended the meeting with the gay rights advocates. "He would walk in those meetings, many of them, and he would say—I'm going to get this done."

There was a look Barack Obama got in his eyes when he accomplished something others said he wouldn't be able to, a defiant told-you-so satisfaction. That was the look he wore when he signed the repeal in a room full of cheering, emotional supporters. After inscribing his name he slammed his pen down. "This is done!" he declared. It was one more campaign promise off the heavy list of responsibilities Barack Obama was carrying. He lingered to shake hands afterward, looking lighter and younger than he had in months.

The nuclear arms reduction treaty he had championed passed, too, and a food safety bill, and a bill providing health benefits to those who had responded to the September 11 attacks. In a way, it proved Obama's critique of politics perfectly: once members of Congress didn't have to worry about reelection, they could do so much more.

Not everything made it through. The DREAM Act failed, with Democrats five votes short in the Senate. But after negotiations over the expiration of the Bush tax cuts, the administration eked out a compromise: the tax cuts, even those for the richest Americans, would be extended until 2013. In exchange, the White House won several hundred billion dollars in tax credits that amounted to more stimulus for the economy. Many congressional Democrats and outsiders fumed that the president had allowed the tax cuts for those making over $250,000 to continue.

The tax cut discussion was only the first round of a debate about to dominate Washington: how to control the federal deficit without choking off the economy or hurting vulnerable citizens. Because of the collapse of a congressional spending bill, the federal government would only be funded through March, which meant a Republican-led House could try to force a shutdown in the spring to force Democrats into unpalatable cuts. Over the summer of 2011, the limit on how much the federal government could borrow would need to be raised, too, but that was usually a routine vote; presidents of both parties had raised the debt ceiling limit many times before.

All of the congressional activity meant the president had to delay his annual vacation to Hawaii by a few days, but this time, his wife and children went ahead of him, so they could start to relax. When he flew west, he was giddier than aides had ever seen him. He was actually *singing* on Air Force One: "Mele Kalikimaka," a Hawaiian Christmas song. "I've won, and I've lost, and I can tell you, winning is a lot better than losing," he told aides on the plane.

"He felt as though he really was providing what a still-fragile economy needed to right itself," Jarrett said. Economic signs were picking up again a little, and maybe with the new stimulus, the country would turn the corner. He could finally move forward on reorganizing his White House; he brought along with him a sheaf of memos with suggestions. Pete Rouse was in charge on an interim, possibly permanent, basis, and internally, things were calmer than they had ever been.

For one of the first times since his inauguration, he had made good on his central promise of bipartisan cooperation. On the airplane, he called Senator Mitch McConnell and incoming Speaker of the House John Boehner, savoring every word of those conversations, said an aide. He had finally won Republican votes, not just on the tax bill but on the Don't Ask, Don't Tell repeal, the arms treaty, and others. "Part of why he enjoyed the lame duck is not just because so much was accomplished but that it was accomplished in a bipartisan way, because that is really more of who he is," Jarrett said.

The president even thought the new era of Republican House control might be surprisingly favorable to him. "The ironic twist is that he may find it easier to get things done with them because they can't just say no the way they did to him in the beginning," Jarrett opined at the time. That was Obama, the self-described eternal optimist, convinced everything—even Republican control—would come out in his favor. The president said the same thing himself in a news conference: "Over the next two years, they're going to have to show me what it is that they think they can do." They would.

Chapter Fourteen

Everything Becomes Political

JANUARY–APRIL 2011

By the beginning of the year, Barack Obama's reaction to the midterm loss, so hard to discern back in November, was becoming clear: he had indeed decided to turn himself into more of an overt politician.

Obama was capable of remarkable self-transformations: from a child raised in Indonesia and Hawaii to a member of Chicago's black community; from an atheist to a Christian; from an Afro-wearing community organizer to the pride of Harvard Law School; from a wonkish academic to a presidential candidate who could mesmerize tens of thousands of people at a time, to the first black commander in chief of the biggest superpower on earth. Now he turned his formidable powers of self-improvement to skills like handshaking, strategizing, appeasing, wooing, negotiating, and connecting. It wasn't that Obama had never pumped hands, made a decision based on a poll result, or told an ethnic group what it wanted to hear. But now he threw himself into the political aspect of the presidency with vigor, with the same athletic determination with which he had improved his bowling score.

In fact, while the midterm defeat had appeared to wash right off him, it had actually jump-started Obama's natural competitiveness and multiplied it, aides observed. He no longer repeated his claims from a year or so earlier: that he and the first lady were fine with one term, that he was going to make the right decisions regardless of the political cost. Now his language shifted: there was *no way* he was letting a Republican win the 2012 race, he told advisers. He still stipulated that he would only do so much to position himself politically at the expense of what he believed in, but he wanted to go directly after the independent voters he had won over in 2008 and lost in 2009 and 2010. The weak economy really did look like it was finally improving, and his approval ratings were on the upswing. And he still had not given up on making health care reform popular, or at least neutralizing the issue.

After waiting so long to reorganize his White House, he instantly rebuilt it into a different place: more hierarchical, reconfigured to suit divided government and prepare for the 2012 race. Emanuel, Axelrod, Gibbs, and Summers were all leaving or would soon. (Axelrod had originally hinted he would stay longer, but his departure was announced by late January. Gibbs left the administration for an unspecified role outside. Both men insisted they had planned on leaving anyway.) Of the original top advisers, only Jarrett was still in place. She was never leaving; she had sold her apartment in Chicago, and she was family.

The old Obama White House had the squabbles and chaos but also the familiarity and bonds of a dysfunctional but tight-knit family. The new Obama White House felt more corporate, with a more organized planning process, hierarchy, and structure. Barack Obama's world was now run largely by two figures, Bill Daley and David

Plouffe, both former managers of presidential campaigns, both taciturn and methodical. Daley, the new chief of staff, both was and wasn't an Obamaite. He was a Chicagoan, of course, son and brother to mayors, and he had quietly advised the president for years, serving as a high-level outside fixer. His naturally thick skin had been toughened when he ran Al Gore's devastating, contested 2000 loss to George W. Bush. Daley was a banker, expected to smooth over the administration's difficult relations with business groups, and he was not guided by a sentimental attachment to the Obama cause. A few months earlier, he had bluntly declared that pursuing health care had been a mistake, telling Peter Baker of the *New York Times* that "the election of '08 sent a message that after 30 years of center-right governing, we had moved to center left—not left."

David Plouffe replaced his good friend David Axelrod. Axelrod, expressive and emotional by nature, was about words and feeling, about trying to capture the right language in a speech, about trying to tell a story of Obama—a narrative that had steadily lost coherence since January 2009. Plouffe, unassuming and reserved, was all about strategy. He had guided Obama to victory in 2008 in part on the strength of sheer analytical skills, by studying the electoral calendar and figuring out how to exploit even minor shifts in population and demographics to great advantage. Unlike Axelrod, he was a Washingtonian who had served as deputy chief of staff to House majority leader Dick Gephardt.

Of all Obama's tasks, none was more perplexing than how to form a better relationship with Republican congressional leaders. Paradoxically, for Obama to beat the Republicans he also needed to improve his relationship with them. He needed to convey optimism and forward motion to the public and to fulfill his promise of bipartisanship. Many Republicans, including but not only Tea Party members of Congress, personally despised Obama. Though Obama wasn't exactly wild about them either, venomous hatred was not in his emotional vocabulary. (Even during the bitterly fought 2008 primary, he had never been able to work up the hatred for Hillary Clinton that many of his advisers felt.) When he talked about Republicans, it was with exasperation and disdain, tending to believe that their charges against him were all an act to rile up voters, said one of the few Republicans with whom he regularly conferred. Like his distaste for pumping hands and giving overly impassioned speeches (he referred to applause lines as "red meat," as if the crowd were hungry animals), and like his failure to recognize the real anxiety that underlay the protests against his health care plans in the summer of 2009, his take on GOP animosity was part of his overall belief that politics was fake.

In January, at one of his periodic lunches with Tom Daschle in his private dining room, the two men discussed how the president might possibly form a relationship with House Republicans. Staring at the problem was like looking at a ladder with no rungs: it was hard to name more than a handful of GOP officials in all of Washington with whom Obama shared a personal bond or productive relationship, and the new Tea Party arrivals had won election by specifically promising to destroy Obama.

Still, the only way forward, Daschle told Obama yet again, was "inclusion, inclusion, inclusion." He would have to be relentless, especially with the Republican leadership and others with whom he might be able to find common ground: inviting them over on weekends, having them to Camp David, doing little things to build trust on the big things. If they refused the invitations, fine: Obama should just keep issuing them. "If you only have one lunch occasionally it's such a big deal," Daschle said later — the point was to establish a routine, which would help build a relationship. Obama should even consider going to the Capitol to break bread with congressional Republicans — the president of the United States, humbly knocking on the door of their House. In fact, the president should even go to their *districts.*

He had to find a way to bridge the gulf, Daschle said. He would have to somehow bond with his enemies. That's what Americans wanted. That was the only way things were going to get done. That was who he was elected to be.

ON THE EVENING OF JANUARY 8, the Obamas went to Valerie Jarrett's rented Georgetown apartment for a home-cooked dinner with Eric Holder, the attorney general, and Sharon Malone, his wife, who had become close with Michelle. Their mood was shocked and upset. That afternoon, a gunman had appeared at a meet-your-representative event at a Tucson shopping center for Gabrielle Giffords, an Arizona congresswoman, then shot her in the head at close range and killed six constituents who had come to hear her speak. No one knew if Giffords was going to live or die — in a brief statement the president had given that afternoon, he had referred to her in the past tense before subtly correcting himself.

Gabrielle Giffords wasn't just any politician to him; he had felt a kinship with her for years, ever since he campaigned for her in 2006. When the president talked about members of Congress he tended to divide them into two categories: the ones he considered overly self-interested, no better than aldermen in Chicago, and then the ones he considered smart, independent, and principled, like Giffords. Like Obama, she was an original who defied stereotypes: a Jewish woman in beat-up cowboy boots, she was a Democrat with support from some local Republicans; a workaholic who fell late in her thirties for Mark Kelly, a NASA astronaut; a solar energy and immigration reform advocate who also believed in gun rights and owned a 9 mm Glock. Giffords had voted for the health care overhaul despite political risk to herself and barely held on to her seat in the midterms. Before that

election, Sarah Palin had put her on a map of twenty House Democrats she wanted to unseat, showing Giffords's district in crosshairs.
("Don't Retreat, Instead — Reload!" Palin later wrote on Twitter.)
Giffords and Obama had that in common, too: they had both been
attacked with the ugliest possible rhetoric by Republicans.

That evening, as the Obamas sat around Jarrett's dining table, the
violence seemed like the direct result of incendiary right-wing rhetoric. That had been the first couple's precise worry for years, that
heated political rhetoric would result in physical harm. "We have
families," one aide remembered Michelle saying during the presidential campaign, after a run of menacing language at Republican rallies.
"We have *children*." After a gunman shot and killed a guard at Washington's Holocaust museum in the summer of 2009, authorities discovered evidence that he might have been plotting to harm David
Axelrod. Soon after, the president faced the grim task of signing executive orders giving his top advisers their own security details.

Now it was as if the Obamas' deepest worry about public life, the
terrible possibility that had loomed over them for years, had finally
come to pass, not over them but others: a favorite member of Congress; a little girl, Christina Taylor Green, close to their own youngest
daughter in age; and five other innocent victims. Who was going into
public service anymore with these kinds of risks?

The president and Holder had spent much of the afternoon conferring with law enforcement officials, and now they spent the evening
hours talking with Jarrett and their wives. We have to figure out a way
to change the discourse, they agreed.

Washington was in mourning the next week, with legislative business dropped; moments of silence, including one outside the White
House with the Obamas; and many conversations about whether members of Congress now needed full-time protection. It was becoming
clear that Jared Lee Loughner, the gunman, was mentally ill, his rav-

ings too scattered to reflect any clear ideology, but the capital was scared anyway.

In his presidency, Obama hadn't much played the traditional role of expressing the nation's grief. Now he prepared to speak at a memorial service for the victims four nights after the accident. It was hard to know what he might say: Would he call out Republicans for using incendiary rhetoric for political gain? What was there to *say* about nine-year-old Christina and her child-sized coffin? Was this going to be another deadening, disappointing Obama speech, like the one over the oil spill?

At 1:20 a.m. on January 12, he hit the Send button on an email to advisers with the text of his speech. By midday, he and the first lady were in Tucson, at Giffords's bedside, and at 6:45 that evening he stood on a platform at the University of Arizona. Though it was a memorial service, the crowd was clapping and screaming with enthusiasm, and the president nodded solemn thank-you's back.

With humble opening words, he took himself out of the presidency, placing himself with the thousands of mourners before him and the millions watching on TV. "I have come here tonight as an American who, like all Americans, kneels to pray with you today and will stand by you tomorrow," he said. In simple language, he painted a picture of the tragedy, starting with the "quintessentially American" scene of a congresswoman and her constituents chatting outside a supermarket. He described every victim in clear, affecting detail, from George Morris, who tried to shield his wife, Dorothy, from the bullets, to no avail, to Christina, the only girl on her Little League baseball team. Unusually for him, he used paper instead of a teleprompter.

Michelle sat at the front of the audience, next to Mark Kelly, and just a few places away from John and Cindy McCain. She was following every word, nodding a little, her eyes flickering with his words.

"Our hearts are broken," he said, shaking his head a little, his voice full of emotion. "Our hearts are broken."

Then he got to Giffords. He had just come from the hospital, he said, and gave a long pause. "I want to tell you—her husband, Mark, is here, and he allows me to share this with you..." The first lady clutched Kelly's hand in hers, her face knit in anticipation.

"Right after we went to visit...Gabby opened her eyes for the first time." Michelle closed her own eyes briefly, pantomiming her husband's speech a little, showing the relief her husband was expressing. She did that sometimes, acting out the words he was saying during his speeches, as if she could give them some of her animation and help propel his message across.

"Gabby opened her eyes for the first time," the president said again as the crowd roared its approval. "Gabby opened her eyes." It was a refrain, bringing unexpected joy and relief in the middle of great pain. "Gabby opened her eyes, so I can tell you she knows we are here." The first lady was still holding Kelly's arm, their fists pointing upward in a gesture of triumph. With her other hand, she wiped her nose; she was crying. Kelly stood to accept the applause of the roaring crowd and Michelle gave him one of her all-enveloping hugs.

The president warned against coming to simple conclusions about what Loughner had done and who was at fault. "Rather than pointing fingers or assigning blame, let's use this occasion to expand our moral imaginations, to listen to each other more carefully, to sharpen our instincts for empathy," he said.

At that moment, being African American seemed to make the presidency easier for Obama to figure out rather than harder. There was no place like the black church for sustenance in the face of unfair, sudden tragedy. With Obama's repetition and refrains, he was speaking the language of the church, translating it for a wider audience, deploying it for national uplift. Bill Clinton had done the same in his time, but Obama had the advantage of actually being black. He quoted Job, his command of Scripture rebuking those who said he was not a Christian. That told-you-so look flickered in his eyes—*I will mention Jesus on my terms, you jerks.*

He ended by returning to Christina Taylor Green. "Imagine for a moment, here was a young girl who was just becoming aware of our democracy," he said. "She saw all this through the eyes of a child, undimmed by the cynicism or vitriol that we adults all too often just take for granted."

It was the same way he had been speaking to crowds about Malia and Sasha for months, but now Christina was the little girl whose sincerity and hopefulness contrasted with the ugliness of politics. "I want to live up to her expectations," he said. "I want our democracy to be as good as Christina imagined it." The applause returned to a roar.

Twitter lit up with approving messages. "The president is back," one flashed. "Yes, ladies and gentlemen, we do have a president," said another. He had finally connected, not by faking it, but by finding something real to say at a time when no one knew what to say. He wasn't imposing his own agenda this time; he had correctly read, for once in a long while, what the country wanted and needed from him. The speech stood outside politics, but in a way that was good politics. Republicans congratulated him on his generous, reasonable, civil, unifying address.

The expression on Michelle's face was one of deep satisfaction. He had given the kind of speech she knew he could give. The look on her face said: *this is the president I wanted you to be.*

NOT ALL OF THE PRESIDENT'S ATTEMPTS early in 2011 to make more friends and stop alienating people were so graceful. His State of the Union address, a few weeks after the Tucson speech, was more pedestrian, an upbeat message about national competitiveness, about jobs, science education, and the industries of the future. His cadence felt a little artificial, like he was reciting lines instead of speaking them. Obama had never had a strong economic message, not even during the 2008 campaign, and he still did not. The joblessness rate had fallen a bit, but it was still 9 percent, and science education was no comfort to the unemployed.

Obama kept up his renewed commitment to politicking even as he managed a foreign policy crisis over the pro-democracy movements roiling the Middle East. He called top Wall Street bankers out of the blue, startling some of the richest men in New York at their desks: *this is Barack Obama calling, I just want to see how you're doing.* Along with Joe Biden and Daley, he hosted the Republican congressional leadership for lunch at the White House. He made an awkward but conciliatory speech to the U.S. Chamber of Commerce, the business lobby group that had fiercely opposed (and funded opposition to) much of his agenda. Biden was heavily deployed in the charm offensive; unlike his boss, he was a natural pol, disarming and funny. (In contrast to Obama, with his stiff refusal of photo requests, Biden sometimes walked into rooms full of strangers and told anyone who *didn't* want a picture with him to clear out.) The vice president even flew to Kentucky to speak at Senator Mitch McConnell's lecture series at the University of Louisville, a strong gesture of respect and goodwill.

At Super Bowl time, Obama retired his stubborn, long-held principles about continuing to root for his favorite sports teams. The Pittsburgh Steelers and the Green Bay Packers were playing each other, and even though he loved the Steelers, even though Chicago Bears fans *never* rooted for the archrival Packers, he stayed neutral, he announced in an interview. Pennsylvania and Wisconsin were both swing states. When the Chicago Bulls played the Charlotte Bobcats, he hosted a viewing party for Illinois and North Carolina Republicans and Democrats. Unlike at his first Super Bowl party, he kept only one eye on the game, schmoozing and working the room.

Just a few years after Obama derided the Clinton-style permanent campaign, the White House turned its attention to lists and outreach, with goals of one hundred different kinds of events across the country per major issue—a hundred on immigration, and on and on. More visitors than ever tramped through the Oval Office for visits, and this time, Obama posed for photos: handshake, smile, picture, handshake, smile, snap.

In March, a fascinatingly jolly president visited the U.S. Capitol for a bipartisan St. Patrick's Day luncheon, where he told a story about the warm bond between President Reagan and Tip O'Neill, the former Democratic Speaker of the House. "Before six o'clock, it was politics," he said. "After six o'clock, they could be friends," he said. Barack Obama and John Boehner, *friends?*

The most important sign of Obama's new approach was the way he handled his budget negotiations. Democrats and Republicans had to reach an agreement by April 8; otherwise the government would shut down.

Two years before, he had complained that the budget process was Kabuki; now he donned his mask and robe and took his place in the drama. He knew that in order to reduce the looming deficit, Americans at all levels were going to have to pay more and get less, a solution as necessary as it was sure to be unpopular with voters. Obama had said it plenty of times, as had the bipartisan fiscal commission he had put together the year before. But his budget put off the hard choices, skipping over the recommendations of his own commission. This set a trap for Republicans: they would have to make the first move on aggressive cuts to social safety net programs, and then Democrats would attack them for shredding the checks that the elderly and poor relied on. It was exactly the kind of political game Obama once professed to hate, and it seemed to work: Paul Ryan, the Republican budget chairman, proposed stark cuts, and on cue, the president responded by saying Ryan's cuts would leave many seniors unable to afford health care.

Obama's strategy, though, was immediately assailed by Republicans as irresponsible, and it worried some Democrats, because he was allowing Republicans to frame the debate on how to reduce the deficit. An hour before federal agencies were set to grind to a halt, the two sides settled on a $38 billion slash involving every broad category of government, save for the Departments of Defense and Veterans Affairs. White House officials thought it was a good sign: yes, the debt ceiling limit would need to be raised over the summer, but they had proven that they could work with the Republican leadership. It was the largest single cut ever made to the federal budget in one year, but it was not nearly enough for the Tea Party freshmen in Congress: "a raindrop in the ocean," one called it.

Obama told advisers that seeing the congressional Tea Partiers in action and living through the budget debate made him feel even more strongly about reelection than he had a few months earlier. He felt the Republicans were more extreme than ever, that they wanted to dismantle the entire social contract, the policies and programs that kept the elderly and poor afloat. If a Republican won the presidency, he told them, nothing would stand in their way. The man who had once resisted campaigning seemed surprisingly excited for the 2012 campaign. He told advisers that he couldn't wait to start talking to voters, that he wanted them to see him not in isolation but as a choice: Obama or a Republican leader? He had to win in 2012, he said; he saw himself as the only thing standing between the country and the abyss.

Chapter Fifteen

A BETTER PLACE

APRIL–MAY 2011

Barack and Michelle Obama first appeared together on Oprah Winfrey's talk show in October 2006, just as they were deciding whether he would pursue the presidency. He was already a celebrity on the rise back then, Michelle was still unknown to the public and new to television, and they showed few signs of the polished public teamwork they would develop later.

Barack, smooth and ingratiating, recounted a story about the time he was working on arms control legislation in Washington and Michelle called to ask for help with an insect infestation in their house. "Is John McCain stopping by Walgreens to grab ant traps on the way home?" he asked with mock incredulity. His comic timing was perfect, and Oprah and the audience roared. (The other politician he named just happened to be a Republican purported to be planning a 2008 run.)

Michelle, however, sat beside him with an uncertain expression. She was being cast as the scold, and Barack was offering a thorny issue in their marriage — his perennial absences and failure to share household chores—as comic fodder for viewers. She looked like she wanted to say something, but between Barack, Oprah, and the audience, it was hard to speak. "If he's not, he should be," she interjected hesitantly.

Nearly five years later, a completely different couple reappeared on Oprah's couch. It was the final month of her daytime talk show, and, like the host's other greatest-hit guests, the Obamas were coming to pay their respects. When they walked out onto the stage, Oprah practically yodeled with excitement.

Very gently, the host acknowledged everything that had gone wrong with the presidency, asking Obama about his disappointments, about whether he wished he had addressed the economy first instead of health care. (He *had* addressed the economy with the stimulus, he said.) Oprah more or less knew some of the answers beforehand. Over the years that she had first backed the president, she had become a friend to the Obamas; they had dinner together a few times a year. In the interview, she gently urged the couple to open up and share their true experiences and emotions about their time in the White House. Few knew more about the relationship between vulnerability, confession, empathy, and connection than Oprah Winfrey. For two years, the Obamas had exercised caution, worried their words would be held against them but becoming increasingly cut off; now, as friend and interviewer, Oprah seemed to be coaxing them and suggesting that, yes, people would understand.

"What do you know for sure about marriage?" she asked them, a classic Oprah question.

Michelle repeated, almost to the word, what the Obamas had said in their speeches on the Hawaii hilltop all those years ago at the president's sister's wedding: marriage was not easy; it was a struggle. "Melding two lives and trying to raise others—that's a recipe made for disaster. There are highs and lows. But at the end if you can look at each other and say I like you . . ."

In that first appearance all those years ago, she had been an awkward second fiddle to her husband. But in this interview, the spotlight was hers, at some moments because her husband gave it to her, at other moments because she stole it. When Oprah asked the president if he was disappointed in how difficult it was to get things done in Washington, Michelle broke in again. "It can be painful to watch." She had come a long way, not just in title, and now she seemed more assertive than he did.

When the topic of reelection came up, the president deferred to his wife. "Michelle has always had veto power over these kinds of decisions," he said.

"I should use it more," she interjected in a tone of dawning recognition, cracking the audience up, adding what an honor it was to serve and how much more the president had to get done.

For two years, Michelle had stopped speaking about her husband's agenda or vision in interviews; instead, she stuck closely to her script about her own work. But when Oprah asked her if she was surprised he had become president, she briefly answered the question and then veered in an entirely new direction: into a sharp defense of his tenure in office.

"I always told the voters: the question isn't whether Barack Obama is ready to be president. The question is whether *we're* ready. And that *continues* to be the question we have to ask ourselves," she said. She grew even more passionate, as if something was bursting out of her. "Are we ready for change? Are we ready for sacrifice and compromise, are we ready to really make the hard push? Because *he's* ready."

Knowingly or not, she was echoing the statements that got her in trouble during the campaign — the adoring view of her husband, a president the public was too lazy or ignorant to appreciate. It was the same view she had expressed again and again over the course of his political career: she believed he was special and good, and she worried about whether other people would understand and appreciate him.

The comfort and safety of Oprah's couch had drawn it out of her: she thought Barack Obama was a victim of their lack of public appreciation, not a president whose inexperience and mistakes had weakened him. Her standards were high, and he had met them. "He has performed as I would have expected him to perform," she finished, sounding a bit like an exacting teacher.

During her outburst, the president had sat still. He looked intensely at her, listened to her every word. He surely knew that his wife's argument—that a shallow, immature nation did not appreciate its extraordinary president—was not exactly going to rouse the masses to his side. But the expression on his face looked a lot like love and gratitude anyway. His most vigorous defender had been locked away from the public in the polite confines of first-lady land for two years. Now, for one moment, she was back out.

SINCE THAT FIRST JOINT *OPRAH* APPEARANCE, since the days after the election when Michelle hesitated about moving to Washington, the president and first lady's positions had to a large extent reversed themselves. In perhaps the most unexpected and ironic twist of the entire Obama union, the woman who had not really wanted her husband to run for president, who experienced serious unhappiness when she first arrived, now seemed more settled, more at peace in the White House and in Washington than her husband was. "To me, she seems more content than I've seen her throughout this process since he's been running for president, which is a very good thing," Axelrod said.

Once she had struggled with the traditional contours of first ladyhood; now those limits protected her. Little to none of her efforts involved the news cycle, a rule she and her staff policed strongly. (If little green aliens took over the U.S. Capitol, she probably would go ahead with her planned announcement of a new playground-building initiative the following day.) She did not give an interview or pose for a magazine cover unless her presence would allow her to make a specific point about her work and she mostly appeared in publications like *Better Homes and Gardens*, answering gentle questions. She saw where things were going in the presidency — she had seen it for some time — and so she did what she could to "add value," to counteract the often negative news from the other side of the building. With Barack Obama wrestling with matters like how to respond to the alarming debt crisis in Europe, she became the custodian of the original Obama virtues — the sense that they were excitingly different from their predecessors, that they were role models, that they stood for access and opportunity, that they spoke and thought differently from most politicians.

Her husband's new West Wing team had helped to effect this change. When Bill Daley arrived in the White House, one of the first calls he paid was to Michelle Obama, just to let her know that he was eager to take her needs and concerns into account. Susan Sher returned to Chicago — she had been commuting to see her husband on the weekends — and Tina Tchen, another Chicago lawyer, who succeeded Sher as East Wing chief of staff, was finally invited to the small daily West Wing senior staff meeting. The president's schedulers no longer planned anything that could affect the first lady or her daughters without consulting the East Wing first.

(David Axelrod still felt badly about how things had gone in the beginning of the administration. "I wanted to be more supportive of her, but secondly I also wanted her to be fully integrated," he said. "This is one of the single greatest disappointments I had in my own self in the White House," he said, skipping over the fact that he may have had larger ones.)

True to Barack Obama's nature, he had taken on so much, and true to Michelle Obama's, she very tightly controlled how much she took on, how much she exposed herself. Michelle's alternative world did not depend on Washington institutions—the legislative system, the political press corps—to function. Her girls came first, she still said; but in some ways she seemed less like a first lady and more like the busy executive of a nonprofit. Her schedule was thick with meetings: briefings with her staff on how various initiatives were going or strategy sessions driven by her almost comical penchant for planning, planning, and more planning. She spent time in the office each week, and she also worked from the residence, emailing and calling with ideas, reviewing her speeches and briefing books.

Reporters still sometimes referred to Let's Move! as Michelle's "pet project," but the condescension gave her cover: the last thing she wanted was controversy. Thanks in part to her, Walmart announced a plan early in the year to reduce fats, sugars, and salt in the foods it sold and to cut prices on fresh fruit and vegetables, one of the first of a series of corporate efforts she'd encouraged that could subtly affect Americans' health. She and her team kept close track of other metrics, like the number of schools that introduced salad bars to their cafeterias. In typical Michelle fashion, they planned their work as much as a year in advance, and in 2011 and 2012 they intended to focus on filling "food deserts," areas where fresh produce was not easily accessible, with new stores and green markets; and on Latino and African American communities, where the obesity problem was generally most severe.

Besides, it wasn't important if Washingtonians were dismissive of her work; she wanted to take her case directly to the public, preferably in creative ways, like convincing Hollywood screenwriters to incorporate more stories about issues she cared about into their sitcom and film plotlines. One day that spring in the East Wing, Michelle and her aides gathered in front of a desktop computer in a small corridor office to watch a new Beyoncé Knowles video. The pop star, inspired by the first lady but acting on her own initiative, had recorded a song, "Move Your Body," devoted to kids and exercise. The video showed Beyoncé, curls flying, leading a bunch of normal-looking kids in a bouncing, jumping dance in their school cafeteria. "Shuffle, shuffle to the right, to the left, let's move," she sang, as the cafeteria turned into a club with glowing pink and green lights. As the video ended, the first lady beamed. Within a few days, millions of people watched it on YouTube.

"A lot of what we do is frankly bullshit," David Axelrod said. "That's the nature of government, it's the nature of politics. What she's doing is very real." Michelle's work "may end up having more of an impact" than many of the West Wing's policy initiatives, he said, continuing his praise campaign but also making a serious point about the Obamas' respective approaches.

The internal parameters for how the Obama White House did things were clearer, and the fights over how the Obamas should exist on the public stage had been resolved. The first lady still supervised social events, but those were routine now. "There are certain things that we just know every year we will do — for example, the Governors' Ball," Melissa Winter said. The first year, they had questioned every detail. "Now, we understand that we do it, we know when we need to start working on it, we know how it's implemented, we know how it's executed, she knows she enjoys it, we have fabulous entertainment. None of us have the level of anxiety that we did for the first one." Michelle's rebellious streak was still there, those close to her said, but she had learned to play the game.

Michelle became more strategic about her clothing, wearing fewer avant-garde pieces and more approachable ones. She still wore plenty of expensive labels, including designer gowns to formal evening events, but during the day there were more dresses from chain stores. When she gave an interview on the *Today* show to discuss the one-year anniversary of Let's Move!, she wore a $34.95 dress from the cheap-chic retailer H&M. Stores instantly sold out of the item. David Yermack, a business school professor at New York University, found that each Michelle Obama public appearance created an average of $14 million in overall value as measured by the stock prices of the companies that made the clothing she wore.

The military family initiative the first lady announced that spring—the same one she had previewed at the Clinton conference the prior fall—was even more politically astute, though also more abstract, than Let's Move! Its origins went back to her image problems during the campaign; advisers saw it back then as a way to stress her warmth and motherly concern. Support for the military was typically an issue associated with middle America Republicans, not Democrats from big cities. Her project was also spousal diplomacy of the highest-level sort; like every other modern president, Barack Obama had a complicated relationship with his generals, and his wife's work appealed to them. She enlisted other wives—Deborah Mullen, wife of Admiral Mike Mullen, the chairman of the Joint Chiefs of Staff; and Jill Biden, whose stepson, Beau, was a member of the National Guard who had served in Iraq.

So she pushed publicly for military families to earn more recognition and support for the spouses and children of service members, who often struggled at home with frequent moves, low pay, few support services, and the heartbreak of absence or loss. She wanted to persuade businesses to create transportable jobs for them, so that moving to another base didn't mean starting anew. Her team also identified high schools around major bases and tried to increase access to advanced placement courses there to give strong students more challenges. She was most passionate about removing the stigma in military culture about mental health issues—depression, anxiety, post-traumatic stress disorder. The first lady wanted to speak at mental health conferences, to urge psychologists and social workers to volunteer their services, an aide said that spring, though by late summer, the plan had changed: they were focusing on the timelier, and more politically pressing, issue of employment for veterans instead.

The effort said something about her own ideas of duty and sacrifice. She had not grown up in a military family or even known many military families before 2008. Her husband had never served. But she strongly identified with the women—some men, but mostly women—who stayed at home, raised their children, and worried as their spouses fought abroad. She herself had spent years with a partner working far away. The military ethos of looking straight ahead, serving a greater cause, and not complaining gave her a model of how to navigate first ladyhood. "Like a military spouse, I feel I'm serving my country, too," she said in a television interview. "It makes me want to do my job even better . . . realizing what these positions offer and not wallowing in the minor inconveniences that come along with it." Her efforts seemed like an answer to her husband's most terrible duty: if he had to send young Americans, many of them poor or members of minority groups, to risk their lives abroad, she would try to make sure their families were cared for at home.

Besides, as one aide pointed out, Michelle Obama was a natural for military life—square, ordered, strict.

SEVEN YEARS AFTER BARACK OBAMA first became famous, four years after the start of the presidential campaign, and two years after moving into the White House, the Obamas' shock over the transition to their new lives finally seemed to be wearing off. Amazingly enough, living in the White House was something they could get used to, sort of.

They couldn't outsmart the entire system of restrictions, but there were small victories. Michelle slowly made a few new female friends in Washington. One day when she needed fresh supplies for Bo, she went to Petco, walked through the aisles like a civilian, and even swiped her own credit card, with her real name, to pay. The woman who had hesitated to move, who had started out a prisoner in the White House, was slowly rebuilding a life.

The president's confinement was far more severe, but he managed to become one of several parent coaches for Sasha's basketball team. He tended not to stand on the sidelines during games, because it created too much of a spectacle, but at practices, he and Reggie Love put the girls through drill after drill. True to character, the president took the job very seriously, even creating special clinics to work on particular skills. One day, a White House photographer caught a striking shot of Reggie running a drill, the president lined up with the grade schoolers, moving in unison with the little girls through the motions. The picture was never released to the public, but people in the White House loved it. Finally, he was what his own father had never been, what he had never been, what his wife had always wanted: the kind of dad who was around to coach basketball.

The White House itself started to look a bit different, too. Downstairs in the East Wing, in concert with her work on child nutrition, the first lady backed the installation of a pumping room, so new mothers would have a place to express breast milk in private. Upstairs in the residence, the yellow walls of the Bush era were mostly gone, replaced by taupes and other natural tones, chosen to be restful. The Obamas sent Admiral Stephen Rochon, the chief usher who ran the household staff, on to a new job, and months later they replaced him with Angella Reid, the general manager of a Ritz-Carlton hotel. They wanted to finally start to update things inside the house, to make the residence more modern and functional.

At a Take Your Child to Work Day event a few weeks after the military families launch, Michelle called on an eight-year-old boy named Gavin. "How surprised were you when you came into the White House?" he asked.

"Shocked," she said.

"I think I visited the White House once before I lived here, and I went on a tour just like everybody else did," she continued. "So I knew what to expect on this floor, but then you go upstairs where the president and the president's family lives, and it was a shock. But it's not a shock anymore. It's just kind of normal. But it took a little while to get used to, because what would you think if you woke up and you were living in the White House? Would you be shocked?"

Yes, Gavin nodded.

ON A HAZY MAY AFTERNOON, Michelle Obama flew up from Washington and over the cliffs of the Hudson to speak to the graduating class of West Point cadets. The military grandeur and formality of the campus—a series of gray turrets and green lawns, litterless despite thousands of guests—made the White House seem almost casual by comparison. The dining room, or cadet mess, where the first lady was to speak, was a vast, echoing stone space lined with portraits of generals past. The cadets were in crisp white uniforms with red sashes, their families in formal graduation finery.

It was not her usual venue, to say the least. She almost never spoke at elite institutions, usually preferring smallish events; and she often picked spots that were not usually visited by powerful people: a child care center here, an urban supermarket there. After everyone else was seated, she entered down a long aisle lined with graduates holding cameras. As she made her way, everyone else looking at her, no one speaking, she seemed a bit like a bride. A single loud whoop broke the silence and the room erupted in cacophonous cheers for her as she walked to the head table.

The meal began with the traditional West Point toasts: "Ladies and gentlemen, I propose a toast to the president of the United States," a cadet called out. "To the president," everyone called in response.

"To the army," he continued, his words echoed by the diners.

"To the United States Military Academy," went the next one.

"To the ladies," he said. The women cadets—there were fewer of them, since women were still not technically allowed in combat positions—repeated it, too.

During dinner, the personal aides who traveled with Michelle left her alone to eat and talk with the dignitaries at her table. She did not like them to hover, they said, and the Secret Service was nearby if she needed anything. After dinner, she rose to the podium to speak, video projectors beaming her image to the corners of the room that were too far to see. She wore a red dress and pearls: classic first lady clothing.

No prior first lady had ever addressed the West Point graduating class, and the invitation had been greeted with some trepidation by the graduates and, especially, their parents. Military families were heavily Republican, and there were quiet questions about whether she belonged at the dinner and whether she was going to deliver a political message.

She did not. Her speech was formal, respectful, and a little restrained, with none of the instant synchronicity of, say, the Anacostia graduation. She spoke about the terrible bugle call that sounded periodically over campus, signaling that an academy graduate had been struck down on the battlefield. Many of the young people she was addressing would be in Afghanistan by the following year, and as she spoke of duty and sacrifice, her voice was soft. She predicted the family-related challenges they would face from the battlefield: the young officers-to-be would have to help their troops deal with the joy of having a new child and the disappointment of not being there for the birth. Soldiers would have faraway family crises, concerns about their spouses and children at home. "And just as our troops need your leadership and support, their families do as well," she said, "because they sacrifice and serve this nation right alongside anyone who wears our uniform." There was no separating the story of battle and the private family story: they were joined.

At the close of the speech, the Michelle Obama of May 2011 did something the Michelle Obama of January 2009 might have found surprising: she placed herself in a long line of American first ladies, going all the way back to the nation's founding. The first lady who had never identified with other first ladies told a story about Martha Washington.

When George Washington bade her farewell as he left to lead the Continental army in 1775, he was about to "chart the course of freedom for our country and our world," Michelle said, and yet all he wanted to hear was that his wife was all right on her own at home on their farm. "He asks her to be strong," she said, quoting from one of his letters: "'Nothing will give me so much sincere satisfaction as to hear this, and to hear it from your own Pen.'"

It was little wonder she identified with the story. Her husband was fighting his own war, he was not winning, and the fact that she had finally found a kind of equilibrium as first lady, that she was going to survive and maybe even thrive in some unexpected ways, was a mostly invisible but key advance in the Obama story.

Afterward, even parents who had been skeptical of the invitation said they approved. The speech was "classy," agreed one cluster of parents as they walked up the hills back to their cars. They sounded a little surprised, as if they had expected something else. If only for that night, the first lady had won them over.

Chapter Sixteen

WHAT WE CAME HERE TO DO

APRIL–AUGUST 2011

O n the last evening of June 2011, Barack Obama confronted the question that would haunt him all summer.

He was standing under a tent in Philadelphia, surrounded by tables where several dozen top donors were seated. The setting was lush, a manicured backyard behind a huge home, and the contributors were sympathetic to the president: they knew what he had been up against. Still, they were worried about his performance and his prospects for reelection. They wanted Obama to be more forceful, as Steve Cozen, one of the donors, said later: to "step up and tell the American people what he thinks, what his basic principles are that he won't compromise on."

The president had been taking questions for almost an hour. He had apologetically told the mostly liberal crowd that he had been forced to take a centrist point of view in his presidency because of divided government. (Never mind that Obama had told conservative Democrats in Congress that he was one of them, too: "I'm a Blue Dog at heart," he had said in more than one meeting.) He answered several questions from Jewish donors worried that the U.S. relationship with Israel had gone awry under his watch. Someone asked about the use of shale gas as an energy source, and Obama launched into a long, virtuosic explanation of the scientific and policy issues. The attendees were duly impressed, but some of them wondered why he was giving ten-minute lectures on the intricacies of energy policy when the moment clearly called for something more. He seemed to be displaying a kind of smartest-guy-in-the-room brand of insecurity, retreating into wonkery. Opinion columnists who met with the president a few weeks later suspected as much: Obama was using his command of policy to try to avoid answering broader questions, to run out the clock and effectively stonewall.

When Obama told the group he would take one more question, Judee von Seldeneck, the owner of an executive search firm, put her hand in the air. Something was bothering her; amid all the talk about Israel's security and shale gas, the real issue had gotten lost. She didn't plan what she was going to say, she said later. The words just tumbled out.

"When you ran for president, you awakened something in this country I haven't seen since President Kennedy," she said, looking directly at the president. "Why don't you provide the leadership we all expected from you and desperately need?" It was the elephant in the room: what had happened to the Barack Obama of 2008?

The other donors applauded.

His answer was weak, von Seldeneck said later. Looking irritated, the president used a line he deployed a lot that summer, about being wiser, grayer, and battle-tested. He blamed some of his ills on Congress, and said he needed to see the upcoming debt ceiling negotiations through. "I can't come untethered yet," he said, and von Seldeneck wondered what he meant. He acknowledged the way his former success hung around his neck. "I'm running against the Barack

Obama of 2008," he said, but also made what sounded like an unrealistic promise. "If you thought the last campaign was something, you just wait for the next one. It's going to be better," he finished.

Back at the White House, Obama told his advisers that the question had stung him. He understood how people felt: he felt trapped deep inside Washington trying to get things done, and his actions didn't look very appealing to people on the outside. "I wish I could do more," he told an adviser. The worst part of the exchange, he added, had been the applause.

By the end of that summer, Barack Obama was hitting a previously unimaginable low. His Democratic support was slipping, his poll numbers eroding, and members of his own party were exhorting him to fire his advisers and openly worrying about his reelection prospects. The president was finally pushing a modest jobs bill, but he knew it had virtually no chance of passing intact. His very first phone calls as president had been to Israeli and Palestinian leaders, pledging to work toward peace; those efforts had gone so badly that his administration was going to the United Nations prepared to veto a vote on Palestinian statehood, a measure he had endorsed not that long before. A double-dip recession looked increasingly likely.

His confrontation with Republicans over raising the federal debt limit that summer, which roiled financial markets and left him wondering how they could so get the better of him, seemed like a metaphor for much of what seemed wrong with the Obama presidency at the time: an ailing economy he could not cure, Republican opponents he could not work with or best, and the triumph of the Tea Party, the movement born to vanquish him.

The ceiling on government borrowing was finally raised on August 2, two days before Obama turned fifty. It was a reminder of how much he had tried to do—become president, change the very nature of Washington, pass transformational legislation—and how quickly. The calendar finalized it: Obama was no longer a young man, not by years and not by the weight of his disappointments.

THE STRANGE THING WAS, the spring before had been one of Obama's most satisfying few months in office, a time of feeling gratifyingly understood by the public and gratifyingly successful behind closed doors. Even the debt limit talks initially seemed auspicious.

In April, against the advice of many of his aides, Obama marched into the White House press room to address a wacky but persistent rumor that he had been born outside the United States. The rumor had been discredited again and again, to little avail: by spring, nearly 50 percent of those who planned to vote in the 2012 Republican presidential primaries agreed with it, the independent voters key to victory in 2012 were beginning to buy it, and Donald Trump, who rather dubiously claimed he was going to run for president, was darkly suggesting on television that it was true, and that Obama was in no way who he claimed to be.

Obama's arrival at the briefing podium seemed to mark a new and more advanced stage of Oval Office outrage. The gap between the way he saw the world—as a series of urgent crises and issues that he and his administration grappled with rationally, tirelessly—and the hoopla over tired rumors had become just too exasperating. "Normally I would not comment on this," he started. He didn't exactly look confident or forceful. But there was a budget crisis looming— "difficult decisions about how we invest in our future," Obama called it—and the media was allowing itself to be distracted by "sideshows and carnival barkers" like Trump, the president claimed. He was stopping just short of telling the reporters whose work helped shape his reputation that they were shallow and stupid. In fact, the charges about his birth had not dominated the news as much as he claimed, and many reporters were covering the rumors in a responsible attempt to discredit them. Obama was so fed up that he was a little irrational in his pursuit of the rational.

His outburst worked, though: the rumor quickly quieted, not only because he released a longer, more detailed version of his birth certificate than the one he had before but because something else happened that proved his point about how little the public sometimes knew about him and his job. A few days after his briefing room appearance, a team of U.S. Navy SEALs acting on secret presidential orders found and killed Osama bin Laden.

Obama had told barely any of his aides and none of his family of the top-secret plans, months in the making. In the three days after he ordered the raid but before it was carried out, he traveled with his wife and daughters to Cape Canaveral to watch a space shuttle launch that was canceled, played golf, and attended the annual White House Correspondents' Dinner. Later, he said that the worst-case scenario—the failure of the mission, the loss of the SEALs—weighed on him during those days, but he never showed it. This time his introversion suited the job perfectly.

That year, Donald Trump was a guest at the dinner, a gathering of D.C. media and a handful of celebrity guests, where tradition dictates that reporters and the White House each do a comic spoof. When his turn came, Obama targeted Trump, mocking him with a long riff on Trump's deliberations as "boss" on his television show *Celebrity Apprentice*. ("These are the kinds of decisions that would keep me up at night," Obama said, clearly finding the difference between Trump's decision and the one he had just made hilarious.) The jokes earned loud laughter throughout the room, but like the briefing room appearance, they were also surreal: the man who hoped to transform American politics was now denying conspiracy-theorist rumors and pummeling a reality-show clown.

A different Obama, the solemn commander in chief, stepped

back in front of cameras twenty-four hours later to announce that bin Laden was dead, the defiant told-you-so look back in his eyes. Suddenly *his* version of the presidency, the one he experienced each day but outsiders almost never did, was public. Describing his planning and decision making to correspondent Steve Kroft of *60 Minutes* a few days later, his expression was cool, hard, and satisfied: he had eliminated the country's top enemy, accomplished what George W. Bush could not, and finally shown the country the utterly serious matters he had been dealing with.

He had been involved in secret planning for the mission all spring, personally making the call to raid instead of bomb the compound so evidence of bin Laden's death would be conclusive. As usual, he had made the final decision to go ahead alone at night and informed his team the next morning. How involved was he with the overall planning? "About as active as any project I've been involved with," Obama told Kroft. Translation: he was not shy about taking credit. "The presidency requires you to do more than one thing at a time," he said gravely, in response to a question about the other things he had done that weekend, sounding like a man in need of recognition, trying to assert his authority.

The interview was one of the few times Obama himself allowed outsiders into the fascinating work of the presidency. He was such a gifted storyteller; he saw incredible things every day. Yet this was one of the few occasions he publicly shared a compelling tale about what he had been doing.

Though the decision to order the bin Laden raid had been a risky one—a fifty-five/forty-five call, Obama said later—it was not even close to the most personally trying exercise of the presidency for him, he told aides. In comparison to the raucous noise of domestic politics, there was something disciplined and satisfying about secretive national-security work. There was no messy Congress to deal with, no stroking and horse trading with legislators, and certainly no Tea Party resistance. Unlike politicians, who Obama so often complained were self-interested and unwilling to take risks, he could not say enough about his admiration for the SEALs: their bravery, skill, selfless risk taking and discretion (in accordance with military practice, their names were never released; they received no public recognition for their service or triumph; even the SEAL who shot the fatal bullet into bin Laden remained anonymous). For Obama, they were like Gabrielle Giffords, or his own children: figures whose virtue contrasted with what he saw as the venality of Washington.

After bin Laden's death, aides noticed that Obama was walking the way he did when he was happiest: on the balls of his feet, with a little bounce in each step. He was increasingly confident about reelection and dismissive of the Republican field: too dismissive, worried some of his election advisers, who wondered if he was yet again underestimating difficulty.

On a May trip he and Michelle took to Ireland and the United Kingdom, he drew on foreign crowds for the affection and approval Americans would not give him. At the first stop, he gave a delighted answer to the critics who thought he was too exotic or Kenyan or whatever: several years before, a genealogist had discovered he had roots in a small Irish town, just like many white Americans. "My name is Barack Obama, of the Moneygall Obamas," he told an overjoyed crowd of twenty-five thousand in Dublin. "And I've come home to find the apostrophe that we lost somewhere along the way." Loose and funny, he downright flirted with the crowd, in a way he no longer could or would at home.

The reception in London was just as warm but even grander, with British fans rising before dawn to line up to greet the couple. The English had not experienced the waning of the Obama presidency since the inauguration; to many of them, he was still the Obama of

2008, a figure of hope. It was like the Oslo trip all over again: the president had once again escaped to a place where people presumed the best about him and treated him as the historic figure he yearned to be. He addressed the British Parliament in nine-hundred-year-old Westminster Hall, an honor previously bestowed only on Charles de Gaulle, Nelson Mandela, and Pope Benedict XVI. The Obamas slept at Buckingham Palace, and the queen honored them with a state dinner that made American ones look like cookouts: there were gold candelabras, Beefeater guards in red costumes and white ruffs, and the queen herself in a glittering crown and blue sash toasting the president. The images from the trip were the last triumphant ones Americans would see of Obama for a long time.

THE SITUATION HE FACED AT HOME was dead simple. A contingent of congressional Republicans were saying that if Obama did not agree to slash spending by trillions of dollars, they would allow the United States to default.

After the near shutdown in April, Obama saw the danger but also an opening. He needed a deal and Republicans needed an escape from the politically dangerous charges that they were going to dismantle support for the elderly by slashing Medicare spending. He dispatched Biden and his economic team to begin talks with lawmakers, asking for one of two outcomes, according to an adviser: a "grand bargain," meaning a bipartisan deal that would take on seemingly intractable problems like higher taxes for the rich and entitlement reform, or the smallest compromise necessary. What he wanted to avoid, at all costs, was a deal whose burdens fell largely on the poor, a muddy compromise that satisfied no one, or a short-term plan that would require revisiting the issue before the 2012 election and would thus spur instability. ("It's hard work designing something that makes everyone mad, but that's kind of our sweet spot," he joked at a fund-raiser that spring, describing deals like the April budget compromise that generated no backing from opponents *or* supporters.)

Obama was heartened by the reports from the talks: the Republicans wanted a deal, and the two sides were discussing a far-reaching plan to overhaul the entire tax code, shrink federal spending by around $4 trillion over a decade, raise taxes on the wealthy, and finally make long-delayed but seemingly inevitable changes to Medicare and Social Security. His understanding of Washington had come a long way, and his overtures to the Republican leadership seemed to be paying off. He could once again be a bipartisan figure, rising above politics to do what was best for the country.

His aspirations collapsed the second weekend in July. Republican House Speaker John Boehner could not convince the Tea Partiers and some other House Republicans to vote for the deal: they were opposed to any tax increase. The Obama administration had made the mistake of thinking that the Republican leadership could deliver the membership; that enough lawmakers would compromise. In order not to hurt negotiations, the president had not made much of a case to the public and had not attacked Republicans. He had been willing to look weak in order to get something done. The strategy had backfired.

The talks struggled on and off for three weeks, the deadline looming, panic stirring over the potential combination of the worsening debt crisis in Europe, faltering economic signs in the United States, and a default on top of it all. The president continued to pursue a large deal to no avail as his own party members questioned why he had not foreseen the problem and pressured Congress to settle it during the 2010 lame-duck session. The days ticked by with a miserable *Groundhog Day* quality: someone would outline a possible deal, a flurry of hope would ensue, and by that evening or next, any agreement would be dead.

The decision to launch the bin Laden raid had been difficult, but he had been comfortable making it, Obama told an aide. It was all about rational calculation, and fights with Republicans often felt irrational to him. "I don't mind making tough decisions, and I'll live with the consequences," he said. He was more at ease with the exercise of power than the exercise of politics. Now he felt trapped, aides said. Default could mean an economic catastrophe, which meant he had to agree to a deal. In the strangely powerless experience of the presidency, this was the most powerless experience of all. "He feels this is not what he came here to do," a former adviser said.

Part of the art of being president was fighting without seeming like you were fighting—rinsing yourself of all defensiveness. Obama had trouble doing that even in his better moments. In public statements during those final weeks, he lectured and hectored his opponents. He told them to rip the Band-Aid off, eat their peas, do their jobs. "They're saying, 'Obama has got to step in.' *You* need to be here. I've *been* here. I've been doing Afghanistan and bin Laden and the Greek crisis." This time, instead of boasting about the seriousness of his job versus everyone else's, he seemed to resent it.

Once again he deployed Malia and Sasha in rhetorical battle. In contrast to dawdling Republicans, Obama said, his girls did their homework a day ahead of time. "It is impressive," he said. "They don't wait until the night before."

Doing homework on time was one thing, but what kids in the world, except Michelle Obama's, did it a day *ahead* of time? To get where he and his wife did, to break the barriers they had broken, they had worked so hard, always doing extra, always striving to be the best. But now they were at the pinnacle, and the president's comparisons made him look insufferable. The journalist Mark Halperin called the president a "dick" on television—an unfortunate word, but one that captured some of the prevailing Washington sentiment—and lawmakers seethed at being compared to children.

Despite Obama's enormous achievements, despite his successful lifelong effort never to become like his irresponsible father, his own public demeanor in those bizarre weeks faintly recalled the way people described the long-dead Barack Obama Sr.'s: embittered, disdainful of others, resentful that others did not see him the way he saw himself.

Obama was not known for second-guessing himself or admitting mistakes. But after a last-minute deal was reached—$2.4 trillion in spending cuts over ten years, with no new taxes on the wealthy, even though Obama had insisted upon them—he and Jarrett had long, searching conversations about the failure. "What do you think we did wrong?" he asked some of his other advisers. Some believed their mistake had been to try too hard to get the grand bargain; that allowed Republicans to run out the clock and maximized GOP leverage. "The president is a rational man who wants to think the best of people," an adviser said. Obama's main mistake in the negotiations, he said, was that he was "too willing to suspend his disbelief" about Republicans, too eager to think they would cooperate.

It was the same problem his wife had worried about for years: her husband was a believer and a conciliator; he seemed to have a kind of optimistic bias, trusting things would work out. Now, almost seven years to the day since he won an instant following with a speech declaring that the differences between red and blue America were false, he was faced with the consequences of his overconfidence. Because his promises had been grandiose, because so many had believed in him so ardently, the loss of faith by his supporters only seemed deeper.

In private, advisers were struck by Obama's sadness and anger. In his mind's eye, they said, he could still see the faces of his supporters in 2008, the crowds gathered in parks and on riverbanks, sometimes a hundred thousand people strong. He didn't understand how his own version of the presidency had come to depart so completely from the one the public believed, and he hated that the public thought he was weak, unsuccessful. "He remembers the aspirational excitement, he knows what's in his core and what he set out to do," Patrick Gaspard said. Marty Nesbitt and Eric Whitaker huddled close to him during those weeks, spending even more time in Washington than usual. "I just tried to be there, to be supportive," Nesbitt said.

Obama's rationale for another term still sounded mainly defensive: he had to run to save the country from Republicans, or he wanted four more years to validate the work he had already done as president. "I wouldn't underestimate how much it is about the last four," Robert Gibbs said. The health care overhaul was still a giant question mark, in danger of being rolled back through insufficient funding or struck down by the Supreme Court (which could rule on the constitutionality of requiring everyone to have insurance); or maybe it just wouldn't work the way it had been intended to. Premiums were still on the rise. The health care legislation had been the biggest bet of his presidency, and no one had any idea how it would turn out.

Even at his lowest moment, advisers said, Obama was eager to fight hard for reelection. The question no one could answer was whether he had the capacity to reboot, to accept his failures and formulate a new, affirmative vision of why he should be granted another term. The original premises of his candidacy—that he could unify Washington, that he could bring sweeping change to the country— were gone, and there was no way to bring them back. But the Barack Obama of 2011 was also a vastly more experienced candidate than he had been in 2008. Could he find a new story and new goals to share with a pessimistic, deflated country, or was he going to remain cut off, locked up, so convinced he was misunderstood that he could no longer make himself understood? With the Republican field still weak, it sometimes seemed as if the 2012 race would be won or lost in no small part inside his own head.

Michelle Obama alternated between avoiding and trying to compensate for the mess her husband was in. The debt limit crisis epitomized her worst feelings about Congress; she couldn't believe that other presidents of both parties had raised the debt limit numerous times without objection but that Republicans were blocking her husband. In public, she stuck to her strategy of staying far from the Washington debate and trying to counter the bad West Wing updates with better reports and images of her own. In June, she made an official trip to South Africa and Botswana with her mother and daughters, meeting with a frail Nelson Mandela and delivering a heartfelt speech about the connections between apartheid and African American history. The trip wasn't part of any larger presidential strategy, an aide said; she chose the destination because she thought it would be meaningful. It showed how far she had come in the year since her Spain vacation: instead of rebelling against her confinements, she was taking advantage of the opportunities that came with her position.

All the while, advisers were starting to make plans for the 2012 presidential race; mindful of past tensions over her campaign involvement, they briefed her regularly. They didn't have to worry. Michelle had been playing it safe, storing up political capital, and now she wanted to spend it all on her husband's reelection. In the fall of 2011, it suddenly seemed like she was everywhere: announcing a new hiring program for veterans, raising campaign funds. Campaigning and fund-raising was the one way she could finally fight back against the Republicans who she felt had blocked and humiliated her husband. After all, she was the more confrontational of the Obamas, the one who tended to slip into what one friend called "mama bear" mode when her husband was threatened. This would be the last race he would ever run, and his wife intended for him to win.

WHAT OBAMA REALLY LOOKED FORWARD TO, said his friends, was the period following the presidency, whenever it arrived. "He has this notion that he could go back to walk[ing] in the streets and go in book-stores, which is totally unrealistic," Whitaker said. He yearned for a different kind of freedom, too: once he was done with the presidency, Obama told Marty Nesbitt, he would be able to accomplish a lot, because he would finally be free of politics.

But the years following a presidency came with compromises, too. Former first couples generally were in the business of making money and ensuring that their years in the White House were remembered well. Both Obamas were planning to write books about their experiences. (One reason the first lady gave so few interviews, an adviser said, was that she was hoarding her memories and experiences for her own memoirs; she knew that sharing her own impressions could mean a less successful or lucrative book.) The memoirist president who had ridden to fame in part by revealing his struggles would face the choice of writing a true reckoning of a memoir or a more self-flattering one. Modern ex-presidents almost invariably chose the latter version; to do otherwise would mean writing negative things about people who had served loyally, and admitting more than a few strategically chosen mistakes that could tarnish a legacy. The same question went for Michelle's memoirs. Years before, she had said real change came from making people uncomfortable. Looking back on a life of good fortune and proximity to power, how uncomfortable would she be willing to get?

Still, Obama's comment to Nesbitt about looking forward to the years after his presidency made deep sense. It was the same thing Obama had always believed: after the next race, at the next level, he would finally be unencumbered by politics and free to create real, lasting change.

ON THURSDAY, AUGUST 4, the Obamas and a hundred and fifty of their favorite family members, friends, aides, donors, and celebrities gathered in the Rose Garden in the late afternoon to celebrate the president's fiftieth birthday. The debt limit crisis had ended a few days before.

There had been so many parties celebrating Obama's ascent: the 2006 book release party for *The Audacity of Hope,* where he had broken down talking about his debt to Michelle; celebrations at the 2008 Democratic convention and on election night; the late-night party that first night at the White House. But this one was different, an event to distract and cheer a struggling president. Obama's previous two birthday parties, the Camp David weekend in 2009 and the basketball tournament in 2010, had also been attempts at escape and reassurance, but now the mission was far more critical. It was a spectacular evening, a great success, guests said later. But it had an undercurrent of forced happiness, of the first lady trying with all her might to counter, just for one evening, the gloom that surrounded her husband. As always, she was masterful at infecting everyone around her with her own mood, for better or worse, and now she threw the entire force of her personality into dispelling the misery of the previous weeks.

The president had worked hard on the guest list. The kinds of people he invited to his parties had changed, with more bigwigs and celebrities. His attempts to separate his political and private worlds had yielded to the inevitable. The Nesbitts and the Whitakers were there, of course; and David Axelrod, Susan Sher, Robert Gibbs, and Rahm Emanuel came back for the occasion. Hillary Clinton came— their relationship had warmed a bit—along with cabinet members and key political allies, such as Reverend Al Sharpton, all of whom mingled with Chris Rock, Jay-Z, Tom Hanks, and assorted sports stars.

The first lady told guests they *had* to stay late, that they better have arranged babysitting at home. The president looked relieved to be at a birthday party and not a negotiating table, guests said. As afternoon turned to dusk and the U.S. Marine Band played jazz, the group helped themselves to a buffet of summer picnic food and settled in at the tables scattered around the garden and South Lawn.

Only one person gave a toast. When dinner was finished, the first lady climbed onto the podium where the band had played, pulled her husband and daughters with her, and delivered a stem-winder of a speech. She began by describing the Michelle's-eye view of the presidency: the tale of a tireless leader who drove himself relentlessly, who cared deeply about doing the right thing, who rose above Washington games, successfully passed the health care overhaul, appointed women to the Supreme Court, and killed Osama bin Laden. *She* was glad he was *her* president, she said.

Her husband, looking embarrassed, tried to cut her off. Maybe it was difficult to be called a great president in front of so many people on a week he could not have felt like one. "No, you're just going to stand there and listen," she instructed. "I know it makes you uncomfortable, but you only turn fifty once, so you're just going to have to take it."

Her description of the presidency in the birthday toast was similar to the one she had been using at fund-raisers that summer: another measure of how the Obamas' private and public lives, once so separate, had met. In both versions, she offered an upbeat, highly edited version of her husband's work, the most hopeful and sympathetic version of him at a time he wasn't particularly hopeful or sympathetic. It was almost as if she was restating his halting answer to the Philadelphia donor in more confident, forceful terms. At that fund-raiser, he had excused his own performance, but at the birthday party, she was praising it, arguing that everyone else had it wrong. As the president had said all those years ago in Hawaii, his wife was the one who saw his potential, who carried a vision of the person he wanted to be: a transformational leader. He couldn't always live up to that vision, and sometimes it even hurt him: Michelle had often encouraged his disdain for Washington, she wasn't always savvy about or sensitive to political realities, and her advocacy for her husband was so fierce it sometimes backfired. But he relied on it anyway: at a moment when even allies seemed to be doubting Obama, she was protecting him, fighting back.

Next she spoke about Barack Obama the father, the one who cared for his daughters amid the pressures of the presidency, read with them at night, took a huge interest in their sports activities. "Mostly mine," Sasha piped up. Malia had come home from camp for the day, and as Obama draped his arms around his daughters, he seemed to be relaxing into the toast. She thanked him for all their dinners together in the White House, for his stubborn commitment to almost always eating with his family.

"But that's not everything I want you to know about what he's doing," Michelle said. "Now I'm going to toast him as a husband."

The crowd went wild. It was the briefest part of her toast but also the most direct. In addition to everything else, he was taking care of her, giving her support and sustenance, the first lady said. She had been tough on him and he had put up with her, she said. Aides glanced at one another, amazed she was being so direct.

As darkness fell, the party moved inside, into the East Room, where Herbie Hancock, Wayne Shorter, and Ledisi performed, plus Stevie Wonder, whose music had been played at the first couple's wedding. The Obamas sat at a small table in front, holding hands, and the president allowed himself a few drinks. After the concert, the tables were pushed back, a DJ took over, and the dance floor filled. Sasha, a natural dancer like her mother, drew everyone's attention with her twirls. Soon a few conga lines snaked around the room.

In their nearly three years in the White House, the Obamas had changed positions with one another. After all of Michelle's protests about politics, all the suspense during those first few months in the White House about whether she would find her way, she was going to emerge from the presidency stronger and more at peace, aides predicted. For the rest of his term, for the rest of his life, the president was going to have to live with what he accomplished and what he did not. She had entered with her expectations low and then exceeded them; he had entered on top of the world, and had been descending to earth ever since.

Their debates with each other were probably never going to end; that was the nature of their relationship, a friction-filled marriage that had proved strong nonetheless. But the presidency had united the Obamas as never before. Their own bond seemed not only intact but strengthened, their points of view closer together than ever before. The same had happened to many of their predecessors: the White House tended to isolate couples but also draw them together, to force them to rely on one another far more than was necessary in the outside world.

The next day, one of the major rating agencies would downgrade the United States, a drastic show of lack of confidence in the country's economy and government. As the Obamas relaxed at Camp David on Saturday, twenty-two U.S. Navy SEALs would die after their helicopter was shot down by insurgents in Afghanistan. They were from the same unit that had killed bin Laden, their deaths the worst one-day casualty in the ten-year war. On Monday, the financial markets would start spinning wildly in response to the downgrade. It was probably the single worst week of the presidency to date.

But that Thursday night, the first couple stayed on the dance floor late. Even at state dinners, they usually swayed together for one number and then called it quits. But on the night of the birthday party they stayed out on the floor for song after song, as if they did not want to return to reality, as if they were willing the moment to last.

ACKNOWLEDGMENTS

My first thanks are to the hundreds of people I interviewed, the ones who are named in the text and the unnameable ones, who shared the experiences at the heart of this book. I'm also grateful to the assistants who scheduled (and re-rescheduled) interviews.

Though this book is an independent project, it grew out of years of reporting at the *New York Times*. Jill Abramson made me a political reporter, assigned me my first Obama story, and repeatedly blasted through the boundaries of what I thought I was capable of doing. Dean Baquet welcomed me into his Washington bureau, and when I told him why I needed to back out of this project he set me straight. Bill Keller may grouse publicly about reporters who write books, but in private he reveals his true, encouraging self.

I'm also grateful to Richard Stevenson, Alison Mitchell, and Rick Berke for lessons in political reporting, Gerry Marzorati and Alex Star for editing my work at the magazine, and Frank Rich, Steve Erlanger, and Jonathan Landman for bringing me to the paper and getting me started there. I owe perma-thanks to the current and former journalists from Slate.com who rescued me from law school, particularly Michael Kinsley, Jacob Weisberg, Judith Shulevitz, and David Plotz.

For wisdom on reporting methods, book writing, and covering

the White House, particular thanks to: Jonathan Alter, Charles Duhigg, Andrea Elliott, Sarah Ellison, Bruce Feiler, Charles Fishman, Jonathan Safran Foer, Tim Golden, Alexandra Jacobs, Ariel Kaminer, David Kirkpatrick, Mark Leibovich, Kati Marton, Joe Nocera, Jeff Posternak, David Remnick, Sally Bedell Smith, Michael Waldman, Daniel Zalewski, and Jeff Zeleny.

Alicia Bassuk, a friend and ace executive coach, counseled me on how to manage the project, an amazing act of generosity that supplied lessons I will rely on for a long time to come. Kevin Arnovitz, Christine Bader, Amanda, Colin, and Joan Hall, Noa Heyman, Eric Klinenberg, Vivien Labaton and Nicholas Arons, Alana Newhouse, Emily Nussbaum, Felicia Patinkin and Bill Piersol, Erika Meitner, Jen Sale and Lucas Miller, Rebecca Starr, Susan Robertson, Sarah Fulford, Stephen Marche, and Nick and Lynn Zerbib contributed outsized measures of food, faith, and shelter.

In Washington, Frank Foer and Abby Greensfelder, Shira Stutman and Russell Shaw, and Jennifer Daskal and Geof Koss fed and hosted me and talked through the story with me. (Shira insisted that Michelle Obama was *perfect* and that if I told her otherwise her world would collapse.) Frank has been my all-around partner, co-conspirator, and adored friend since we met in a college dorm in 1994, but I've never benefited from his insight, encouragement, and generosity more than I did with this book. We formed the vision of this project together and he read the manuscript twice, seeing it more clearly than I could.

In Chicago, Charlene Lieber fed, housed, and dressed me, Stephanie Lieber took me to Jimmy's Body Pump class, and both asked penetrating questions about what I saw unfolding. In New York, Wendy Kantor always had my back and often took Talia, my daughter. My career would not be possible without her generosity. Thanks to Stefanie Braverman, Talia thinks New Jersey is a magical land of art projects and basement playrooms. I am also grateful to the other eleven

Kantliebs, to Adele Ensle

Donna Mitchell, who ca

To the ever-growi

ask if you should drop

for Elyse Cheney's s

yes. She is brilliant

she would have m

assistant-diplom

Jessica Nash of

Penguin UK, my sing

Lindsay Crouse somehow ma

working at another job and running the odd

Jessica Weisberg checked the book with unflagging precisi

cacy, and insight. Cynthia Colonna transcribed interviews, and the

few times I picked up the special red phone to Kitty Bennett, master

Times researcher, she found the unfindable.

I could not have reported or written this book without Rebecca Cor-

bett, who also edited my coverage of the presidential campaign and the

Obama administration for the *Times*. Our relationship has been a five-year

conversation about ambition, power, gender, and public life, along with

source relationships and writing technique. If I said I've learned more from

her than from anyone I've ever worked with, she would warn me for the

hundredth time to avoid overstatement in my writing. She would be wrong.

Geoff Shandler, my editor and friend, backed and guarded this

project and calmly pushed me to put on paper what I saw in my head.

Geoff epitomizes what I've come to think of as the Little, Brown way:

genuine niceness coupled with quiet, fierce determination. Those

qualities are shared by his colleagues Janet Byrne, Heather Fain,

Peggy Freudenthal, Michael Pietsch, Mario Pulice, Mary Tondorf-

Dick, and many others. Liese Mayer helped every step of the way,

particularly by gathering the photographs, and I wish I could have the

counsel of Nicole Dewey in v

Thank you for sharing this

This book is dedica

Poland, did not atten

caust as a teenager

the United Stat

kalookiin Fl

help write

the pro

Wh

rious life areas beyond book publicity.

story and helping me share it with others.

ted to Hana Kantor, who grew up poor in

school beyond fifth grade, survived the Holo-

osing nearly everyone and everything, built a life in

s, and is still selecting the best tomatoes and playing

rida and the Catskills. As her granddaughter, I've tried to

the happiest possible ending to her story, to make good on

mise of America. I never once walked up the driveway of the

te House without thinking of her.

I became a political reporter at the same time I became a mother. Between watching Talia grow and covering the Obama story, the past five years have been the richest and most frantic of my life. One day when Talia was two, an Obama aide called and screamed at me, and Talia grabbed the phone and warbled the Barney song into the mouthpiece: "I love you, you love me." The day she whooshed down her first roller coaster, I wrote the first draft of what is now chapter 4 in a hotel room with Mickey Mouse–shaped soap.

Talia asked many times if I would write about her in these pages. Here are a few sentences for her, ones she can read by herself now: *I am putting away the computer now. Let's go to the playground. I can't believe how lucky I am to have you.*

The book is also dedicated to Ron Lieber, my truest and deepest partner, the one who told me what I most needed to hear: stop worrying; I am standing with you; yes, I will take Talia so you can work on Sunday. Ron sees stories, crusades, humor, and adventures everywhere, which makes him a great journalist but an even better husband.

NOTE ON REPORTING

The Obamas is the result of hundreds of hours of interviews with over two hundred people: thirty-three current and former White House officials and aides and cabinet members, but also the Obamas' friends and relatives, former neighbors, employees and colleagues, members of Congress, and finally the Obamas themselves. Several top advisers and close friends, including David Axelrod, Valerie Jarrett, Robert Gibbs, Susan Sher, Eric Whitaker, and Marty Nesbitt, gave me many hours of interview time each. I drew on my own interviews with the Obamas, including a forty-minute conversation with both of them in the Oval Office in fall 2009. I attended many of the public events described in this book myself, but I also relied on documents like White House transcripts, pool reports, videos, and work by other reporters, cited in the Notes.

Many of my interview subjects spoke on the record, but some would speak only on background, meaning that I could use the material but without their names attached. They were worried about discussing sensitive subjects without authorization or speaking at all. To counter the dangers of using anonymous reporting, I checked my material and then cross-checked it, taking a story I heard from adviser A and asking advisers B and C and friend D: is this a fair way of describing it? How do you remember this? Because of the factionalized nature of the early Obama White House, I made sure to speak to members of the various camps. I used quotation marks only when sources recalled statements clearly; otherwise, I used the source's closest approximation without quotation marks.

Though I gathered most of the material between April of 2010 and October of 2011, when I was on hiatus from the *New York Times* to work on this book, I benefited from having covered the Obamas for the newspaper since 2007, and I occasionally reached back to information I learned for earlier stories when it became newly relevant.

Notes

43 the festive air: Remnick, *The Bridge*, 573.

44 he had no idea: Alter, *The Promise*, 109.

46 Three of the other dead: Oppel, "Drone Airstrikes in Pakistan."

46 Thousands of tourists: Bush, *Spoken from the Heart*, 255.

47 picking up his dirty socks: Langley, "Michelle Obama Solidifies."

49 Michelle attended Princeton: Robinson, *A Game of Character*, 16, 122.

50 Until the Kennedy years: Lusane, *Black History of the White House*, 105, 231, 283.

50 Even by 2009: Chozick, "The White House Borrows."

Chapter Three: Ladies and Gentlemen, the President of the United States

56 he yelled: Argetsinger, "The Reliable Source."

59 Together they could deny: Hulse, "Senate G.O.P. Leader Finds Weapon in Unity."

61 "I wish I had the luxury": Cooper and Stolberg, "Obama Ponders Outreach."

66 "It's hard to give up control": Plouffe, *The Audacity to Win*, 8.

66 "I'm gonna think": Lizza, "The Gatekeeper."

68 Jarrett gave an interview to: Remnick, *The Bridge*, 274.

72 "Clinton invited the historian": Branch, *The Clinton Tapes*, 104.

72 "I'm going home": Swarns, "An In-Law Is Finding."

Chapter Four: The Lady Who Did Not Lunch

78 Michelle stood out: Scherer, "A Dip in Michelle Obama's Pool."

83 Her outfits and parties were perfect: Bedell-Smith, *Grace and Power*, 112.

83 Lady Bird Johnson: Marton, *Hidden Power*, 161.

94 English as a second language: Scherer, "A Dip in Michelle Obama's Pool."

94 children of refugees: Cadwalladr, "Of All the Schools in London."

97 trashed the ritual: Bush, *Spoken From the Heart*, 288.

Chapter Five: Campaign Promises

106 He urged his visitors: Isikoff, "Friendly Fire."

Chapter Six: The Walls Close In

129 the chair of Florida's Republican Party: McKinley, "Some Parents Oppose."

130 Alma Thomas: Cotter, "White House Art."

136 wrote a column deeming the shorts: Givhan, "In Her Choice of Shorts."

137 the administration would guarantee: Kirkpatrick, "White House Affirms."

Chapter Seven: Twenty-Six Hours in Wonderland

146 Jarrett was calling: Leibovich, "Man's World at the White House?"

152 his team was badly divided: Kornblut, "During Marathon Review."

153 on a yellow legal pad: Baker, "How Obama Came to Plan."

153 the federal deficit was a stunning: Montgomery, "Record-High Deficit."

157 Obama grew animated: Alter, *The Promise*.

159 When subordinates congratulated: Ibid., 357.

159 knew the jeers: Fouche, "Nobel Peace Prize."

162 It was the kind of irritant: Doonan, "Tinselgate."

166 The group settled into: Lee, "For Obama Vacation."

166 The group was belting out: Baker, "The Education of a President."

167 As news outlets related: Baker, "Obama Seeks to Reassure."

168 pounded out the rest himself: Baker, "The Education of a President."

Chapter Eight: The Biggest Marriage on Earth

171 Before the group departed: "Michelle Obama Greets White House Visitors."

183 praising the chief of staff for resisting: Milbank, "Why Obama Needs Rahm at the Top."

185 "Please, America, watch": Kornblut, "Michelle Obama Weighs In."

185 Now he finally gave his wife: The Reliable Source, "In Other News."

186 Originally the first couple: Sweet, "Michelle Obama, Malia, Sasha, New York."

187 For many staffers: Parker, "All the Obama 20-Somethings."

187 Michelle whispered: Kantor, "Michelle Obama Adds New Role."

Chapter Nine: The Bubble within the Bubble

196 Cheryl Whitaker: Williams, "Creating a Vision."

198 "They said my achievement": Saulny, "Michelle Obama Takes to the Trail."

199 elite business schools: Robinson, *A Game of Character*, 146.

201 Soon she had four or five thousand: Marton, *Hidden Power*, 283.

202 "I hate diversity workshops": Powell, "After Attacks."

204 Department of Justice: Kantor, "After 9/11 Trial Plan."

210 it was converted to a charter school: Givhan, "First Lady Michelle Obama Gives Anacostia."

Chapter Ten: Malia's Great Escape

222 plus a skating party: Tumulty, "Obama Gets Intimate."

224 When the Kennedys: Bedell-Smith, *Grace and Power*, 303.

224 Jenna and Barbara Bush: Bush, *Spoken from the Heart*, 285.

226 During one of Jacqueline Kennedy's: *Grace and Power*, 294.

227 'Are you really hungry?': Lee, "Michelle Obama's New Mission."

229 he called her out: Burt-Murray, "The Obama Interviews."

Chapter Eleven: Happy Birthday, Mr. President

242 That was false: Baker, "First Lady's Spain."

244 regular pickup ball: Djang, "President Obama Talks Basketball."

249 Only a third: "Growing Number."

250 There was no creative brainstorming: Kantor, "Obama's Christian Campaign."

Chapter Twelve: Her Gain

264 a half-full arena: Henderson, "As Obama Stumps."

Chapter Thirteen: His Loss

273 "I love elections": *By the People*.

279 "I don't know which direction is up or down": Harris, "Why Obama Loses."

282 microcredit loans: Stolberg, "Obama Pledges."

Chapter Fourteen: Everything Becomes Political

289 telling Peter Baker: Baker, "The Education of a President."

291 owned a 9 mm Glock: Stolberg, "For Giffords."

293 At 1:20 a.m. on January 12: Heilemann, "The West Wing."

298 "a raindrop in the ocean": Dennis, "Origins of the Debt Showdown."

Chapter Fifteen: A Better Place

304 a series of corporate efforts: Stolberg, "Wal-Mart Shifts."
306 cheap-chic retailer: Boyle, "First Lady Wears."
306 in overall value: David Yermack infographic.
308 walked through the aisles: Romano, "White House Rebel."

Chapter Sixteen: What We Came Here to Do

315 nearly 50 percent: Jensen, "Romney and the Birthers."
315 as much as he claimed: Tapper, "President Obama Tells."

BIBLIOGRAPHY

Alter, Jonathan. "The Audacity of Hope." *Newsweek*, December 27, 2004.

———. *The Promise: President Obama, Year One*. New York: Simon & Schuster, 2010.

Argetsinger, Amy, and Roxanne Roberts. "The Reliable Source." *Washington Post*, February 3, 2009.

Baker, Peter. "How Obama Came to Plan for 'Surge' in Afghanistan." *New York Times*, December 5, 2009.

———. "The Education of a President." *New York Times*, October 12, 2010.

Baker, Peter, and Raphael Minder. "First Lady's Spain Vacation Draws Criticism." *New York Times*, August 6, 2010.

Baker, Peter, and Scott Shane. "Obama Seeks to Reassure U.S. after Bombing Attempt." *New York Times*, December 28, 2009.

Bedell-Smith, Sally. *Grace and Power*. New York: Random House, 2004.

Boyle, Katherine. "First Lady Wears $34.95 Dress on *Today* Show." *Washington Post*, February 9, 2011.

Branch, Taylor. *The Clinton Tapes*. New York: Simon & Schuster, 2009.

Burt-Murray, Angela. "The Obama Interview." *Essence*, March 2010.

Bush, Laura. *Spoken from the Heart*. New York: Scribner, 2010.

By the People: The Election of Barack Obama. DVD. Directed by Alicia Sams and Amy Rice. Sony Pictures Home Entertainment, 2010.

Cadwalladr, Carole. "Of All the Schools in London, Michelle Obama Chose Us. That Makes Us Feel Pretty Special, I Tell You." *Guardian*, April 5, 2009.

Chozick, Amy. "The White House Borrows Some Notable Art." *Washington Post,* October 9, 2009, http://blogs.wsj.com/washwire/2009/10/06/the-white-house-borrows-some-notable-art/ (accessed July 25, 2011).

Cook, Marina. "A Couple in Chicago." *The New Yorker,* January 19, 2009.

Cooper, Helene and Sheryl Stolberg. "Obama Ponders Outreach to Elements of Taliban," *New York Times,* March 7, 2009.

Cotter, Holland. "White House Art: Colors from a World of Black and White." *New York Times,* October 10, 2009.

David Yermack infographic, http://hbr.org/hb/article_assets/hbr/1011/F1011Z_A_lg.gif (accessed September 21, 2011).

Dennis, Brady, et al. "Origins of the Debt Showdown," *Washington Post,* August 6, 2011.

De Zutter, Hank. "What Makes Obama Run?" *Chicago Reader,* December 7, 1995.

Djang, Jason. "President Obama Talks Basketball with Marv Albert," *The White House Blog,* http://www.whitehouse.gov/blog/2010/05/25/president-obama-talks-basketball-with-marv-albert (accessed July 22, 2011).

Doonan, Simon. "Tinselgate: My Side of the Story." *New York Observer,* January 5, 2010.

Fouche, Gwladys, and Ewen MacAskill. "Nobel Peace Prize: Norwegians Incensed over Barack Obama's Snubs." *Guardian,* December 9, 2009.

Givhan, Robin. "First Lady Michelle Obama Gives Anacostia." *Washington Post,* June 12, 2010.

———. "In Her Choice of Shorts, Michelle Obama Goes to Unusual Lengths." *Washington Post,* August 23, 2009.

"Growing Number of Americans Say Obama Is a Muslim." *The Pew Forum on Religion & Public Life Poll,* August 18, 2010.

Harris, John F., and Jim VandeHei. "Why Obama Loses By Winning." *Politico,* July 15, 2010.

Heilemann, John. *"The West Wing,* Season II." *New York,* January 23, 2011.

Henderson, Nia-Malika. "As Obama Stumps in Cleveland, Democrats' Enthusiasm Gap on Full Display." *Washington Post,* November 1, 2010.

Hulse, Carl, and Adam Nagourney. "Senate G.O.P. Leader Finds Weapon in Unity." *New York Times,* March 16, 2010.

Isikoff, Michael. "Friendly Fire at the White House." *Newsweek,* May 21, 2009.

Jensen, Tom. "Romney and the Birthers." Public Policy Polling, http://publicpolicypolling.blogspot.com/2011/02/romney-and-birthers.html (accessed September 21, 2011).

Kantor, Jodi. "Obama's Christian Campaign." *New York Times,* http://thecaucus.blogs.nytimes.com/2008/01/25/obama-and-faith-on-the-stump/?scp=1&sq=kantor+obama+christian+south+carolina&st=nyt (accessed July 22, 2011).

———. "First Marriage." *New York Times Magazine,* October 26, 2009.

Kantor, Jodi, and Charlie Savage. "After 9/11 Trial Plan, Holder Hones Political Ear." *New York Times,* February 14, 2010.

Kantor, Jodi, and Jeff Zeleny. "Michelle Obama Adds New Role to Balancing Act." *New York Times,* May 18, 2007.

Kirkpatrick, David. "White House Affirms Deal on Drug Cost." *New York Times,* August 5, 2009.

Kornblut, Anne E. "Michelle Obama Weighs In on Husband's Smoking." *Washington Post,* February 11, 2007.

Kornblut, Anne E., Scott Wilson, and Karen DeYoung. "During Marathon Review of Afghanistan Strategy, Obama Held Out for Faster Troop Surge." *Washington Post,* December 6, 2009.

Langley, Monica. "Michelle Obama Solidifies Her Role in the Election." *Wall Street Journal,* February 11, 2008.

Lee, Carol E. "For Obama Vacation, Comfort Is Key." *Politico,* December 22, 2010.

Lee, Sally. "Michelle Obama's New Mission." *Ladies' Home Journal,* September 2010.

Leibovich, Mark. "Man's World at the White House? No Harm, No Foul, Aides Say." *New York Times,* October 24, 2009.

Lusane, Clarence. *The Black History of the White House.* New York: City Lights Publishers, 2011.

Martin, Jonathan. "W. H. Pushes Back on House Dems." *Politico,* July 15, 2010.

Marton, Kati. *Hidden Power: Presidential Marriages That Shaped Our Recent History*. New York: Pantheon, 2001.

"Michelle Obama Greets White House Visitors." Video, *Conde Nast Traveler*, http://www.concierge.com/video/conde-nast-traveler/ condeacute-nast-traveler/condeacute-nast-travelerdestinations/ 15202147001/michelle-obama-greets-white-house-visitors/ 76418408001 (accessed July 21, 2011).

Milbank, Dana. "Why Obama Needs Rahm at the Top." *Washington Post*, February 21, 2010.

Montgomery, Lori, and Neil Irwin. "Record-High Deficit May Dash Big Plans." *Washington Post*, October 17, 2009.

Newsweek editors. "How He Did It." *Newsweek*, November 5, 2008.

Obama, Barack. *Why Organize? Problems and Promise in the Inner City*. Springfield: Illinois Issues, 1990.

Oppel, Richard, Jr. "Drone Airstrikes in Pakistan Continue into Obama's Term." *New York Times*, January 24, 2009.

Parker, Ashley. "All the Obama 20-Somethings." *New York Times*, April 29, 2010.

Plouffe, David. *Audacity to Win*. New York: Viking, 2009.

Powell, Michael, and Jodi Kantor. "After Attacks, Michelle Obama Looks for New Introduction." *New York Times*, June 18, 2008.

The Reliable Source. "In Other News, Barack Obama Has Quit Smoking, Says First Lady." *Washington Post*, February 8, 2011.

Remnick, David. *The Bridge: The Life and Rise of Barack Obama*. New York: Knopf, 2010.

Robinson, Craig Malcolm. *A Game of Character: A Family's Journey from Chicago's Southside to the Ivy League and Beyond*. New York: Gotham, 2010.

Romano, Lois. "White House Rebel." *Newsweek*, June 5, 2011.

Saulny, Susan. "Michelle Obama Takes to the Trail." *New York Times*, February 14, 2008.

Scherer, Michael. "A Dip in Michelle Obama's Pool." *Time*, April 2, 2009.

Stolberg, Sheryl Gay. "Obama Pledges Expanded Ties with Muslim Nations." *New York Times*, November 9, 2010.

———. "Wal-Mart Shifts Strategy to Promote Healthy Foods." *New York Times*, January 20, 2011.

Stolberg, Sheryl Gay, and William Yardley. "For Giffords, Tucson Roots Shaped Views." *New York Times,* January 14, 2011.

Swarns, Rachel. "An In-Law Is Finding Washington to Her Liking." *New York Times,* May 4, 2009.

Sweet, Lynn. "Michelle Obama, Malia, Sasha, New York Spring Break Visit: Broadway, Harlem, Brooklyn." *Sun Times,* March 25, 2010.

Tapper, Jake. "President Obama Tells Untruth in Birth Certificate Briefing." ABC News, http://abcnews.go.com/blogs/politics/2011/04/president-obama-tells-untruth-in-birth-certificate-press-briefing/ (accessed September 21, 2011).

Thomas, Evan. *A Long Time Coming: The Inspiring, Combative 2008 Campaign and the Historic Election of Barack Obama.* New York: PublicAffairs, 2009. Kindle Edition.

Tumulty, Karen. "Obama Gets Intimate in Indiana." *Time,* May 4, 2008.

West, Cassandra. "Her Plan Went Awry, but Michelle Obama Doesn't Mind." *Chicago Tribune,* September 1, 2004.

Williams, Diane Duke. "Creating a Vision of a Healthy Life." *Washington University in St. Louis Magazine,* Summer 2009.

Winfrey, Oprah. "Oprah Talks to Michelle Obama." *O: The Oprah Magazine,* April 2009.

INDEX